Unraveled

Unraveled

A WEAVER'S TALE
OF LIFE GONE MODERN

Elizabeth L. Krause

UNIVERSITY OF CALIFORNIA PRESS
Berkeley   Los Angeles   London

University of California Press, one of the most distinguished university presses in the United States, enriches lives around the world by advancing scholarship in the humanities, social sciences, and natural sciences. Its activities are supported by the UC Press Foundation and by philanthropic contributions from individuals and institutions. For more information, visit www.ucpress.edu.

University of California Press
Berkeley and Los Angeles, California

University of California Press, Ltd.
London, England

Library of Congress Cataloging-in-Publication Data

Krause, Elizabeth L.
  Unraveled : a weaver's tale of life gone modern / Elizabeth L. Krause.
    p.   cm.
  Includes bibliographical references and index.
  ISBN 978-0-520-25848-8 (cloth : alk. paper)
  ISBN 978-0-520-25849-5 (pbk. : alk. paper)
    1. Raugei, Emilia, 1920–2004.   2. Women weavers—Italy—
Carmignano—Biography.   3. Ethnology—Italy—Carmignano.
4. Fascism—Italy—Carmignano.   5. Italy—Politics and government—
1922–1945.   6. Italy—History—German occupation, 1943–1945.
7. Demographic anthropology—Italy—Carmignano.   8. Carmignano
(Italy)—History.   9. Carmignano (Italy)—Social life and customs.
I. Title.
DG737.58.R38K73   2009
677—dc22   2009006139

Manufactured in the United States of America
18   17   16   15   14   13   12   11   10   09
10   9   8   7   6   5   4   3   2   1

This book is printed on Cascades Enviro 100, a 100% post consumer waste, recycled, de-inked fiber. FSC recycled certified and processed chlorine free. It is acid free, Ecologo certified, and manufactured by BioGas energy.

For Hollis and Luca,
Inspirational forces of patience, courage, and love

Life is not what one lived, but what one remembers and how one remembers it in order to recount it.

Gabriel García Márquez, *Living to Tell the Tale*

Contents

13.   Neighbors   139

14.   A Weaver's Tale   151

15.   Progress   162

16.   Singles' Sexuality   169

17.   Amazing Grace   182

18.   A Burning Question   192

19.   Generation Gap   196

20.   "Wet" and Hidden Economies   204

        Epilogue   231

        Notes   241
        References   263
        Index   275

Illustrations

Cast of Characters

The characters appearing in this story are listed alphabetically by first name. Principal characters' names are real. The names of minor figures have been changed for unavoidable reasons, both legal and ethical. Pseudonyms reflect actual usage from northwestern Tuscany from 1931 as documented in household census records, which I consulted in the historic archive of the Commune of Carmignano. Dates of birth are actual when days and months are included and estimated when only years appear. The commune was part of the Province of Florence until it became incorporated into the new Province of Prato in 1992. Italian women kept their maiden names throughout their lifetime. Children carried the father's surname.

PART I

Aldobrando Manetti   Aldo, hatter and uncle of Germena
Amaretto Peruzzi   hatter, Parigi's brother (b. 1915)

Asia Grassi	straw weaver (b. 1915)
Beatrice Benveniste	professor of piano, Emilia's great-aunt
Carlo Raugei	Emilia's brother (b. May 17, 1925)
Delfina Cappelli	girl weaver (b. 1921)
Dora Cappelli	girl weaver (b. 1922)
Emilia Raugei	straw weaver (b. July 15, 1920)
Emilio Raugei	Babbo, Emilia's father (b. May 15, 1875)
Enza Chelli	Natalina's mother, newcomer (b. 1889, Vicchio)
Germena Santini	straw weaver, Aldobrando's niece and Silvano Santini's daughter (b. 1917)
Giorgio Gentile	stonemason, Parigi's distant cousin
Giovanbattista Raugei	peasant, Emilia's great-uncle (b. 1869)
Giovanna Paolieri	Mamma, Emilia's mother (b. October 19, 1891, Signa)
Hamidie Raugei	Emilia's half-sister (b. March 21, 1912)
Ida Innocenti	Parigi's mother
Lirua Lippi	straw weaver, Emilia's best friend (b. 1920)
Loretta Lunghi	Emilia's sister-in-law, Urbano's wife
Luigi Martelli	one of Emilia's neighbors
Magdalena Manetti	Germena's mother
Maria Raugei	Emilia's half-sister (b. July 17, 1917)
Matilde Raugei	Emilia's half-sister (b. July 23, 1913)
Milena Rossi	Natalina's sister (b. 1922, Vicchio)
Natalina Rossi	straw weaver, newcomer (b. 1917, Vicchio)
Nello Peruzzi	peasant, Parigi's great-uncle
Osvaldo Raugei	Emilia's half-brother (b. 1914)
Parigi Peruzzi	Parigi, Emilia's husband and peasant (b. October 1920)
Raffaella Cintolesi	Lirua's mother
Sergio Raugei	Emilia's half-brother, World War II veteran (b. September 1, 1915)
Silvano Santini	Germena's father
Tosca Petracchi	Asia's mother, politically engaged
Urbano Peruzzi	Parigi's brother

Vera Nunziati	weaver and Emilia's friend (b. 1920)
Vittorio	a boy in Emilia's neighborhood

PART II

Asia	Stefano's mother
Daniela	former sweater maker, Lorenzo's wife
Enza	Natalina's mother
Fabiana	seamstress, Natalina's daughter-in-law and Riccardo's wife
Fog	Natalina's father
Gabriella	psychologist
Giovanni	bachelor
Giulia	Marika and Stefano's daughter
Guido	Patrizia's husband, Emilia and Parigi's son-in-law
Lorenzo	former sweater maker, Daniela's husband
Marco	doctor
Marika	my neighbor, Hungarian immigrant, a nurse
Matilde	my research assistant
Nello	Matilde's father
Paola	a single woman
Patrizia	Emilia and Parigi's daughter
Riccardo	appliance repairman, Natalina's son
Roberta	neighbor woman
Stefano	my neighbor, Marika's husband, a railroad man
Telsa	Matilde's mother

Acknowledgments

The journey that culminates in this book has led me to rack up countless debts. I could not have seen this project through to its conclusion without the support, guidance, and encouragement of friends, family members, and colleagues.

My acquaintance with Emilia Raugei was as much luck as method, and her storytelling purely a gift. As with any gift, reciprocity was implicit. Telling the story of *Unraveled* pushed me to find a resonant voice uncommon in academic venues. The challenge brought aches to my heart some days and made it race on others. Ultimately, I am responsible for this story's effectiveness, but to the extent that this experiment proves a success, the credit deserves to be shared.

Throughout the many years of this project's evolution, numerous Italians offered me their friendship, hospitality, and perspectives: Adolfo Agostini, Massimo Bressan, Sergio Citerni, Giovanni Contini, Antonella del Conte, Gemma de Ninno, Francesco de Ninno, Elisabetta Gironi, Rita Liberti, Stefania Martini, Stellina Migaldi, and Giovanna Ugo. At the

Archivio Fotografico Toscano, Oriana Goti and Sauro Lusini have been gracious over the years. Countless others have helped me along the way in ways small and large.

Inspiration finds its source waters in many springs. My thanks to Peter Elbow, professor emeritus of rhetoric, for his inspiring workshops on writing and to Mary Deane Sorcinelli, then director of the Center for Teaching at the University of Massachusetts Amherst, for sponsoring annual faculty writing retreats. Elbow encouraged voice in writing through his techniques of free writing, and the center provided the mental and physical space so rare in our chaotic, modern working lives.

I am grateful to my colleagues in the "Beyond Reproduction" group of the Interdisciplinary Seminar in the Humanities and Fine Arts, at the University of Massachusetts Amherst for specific feedback on the introduction at a critical time in its development. Their encouragement to break away from the use of the academic voice as well as their ongoing nurturance has been invaluable: Mari Castañeda, Laetitia LaFollette, Marla Miller, Alice Nash, Monika Schmitter, Nina Scott, Amanda Seaman, and Pat Warner.

Deep gratitude is due to the Wenner-Gren Foundation for Anthropological Research for awarding me a Richard Carley Hunt Fellowship, which provided me the luxury of twelve months of full-time writing during 2005 to elaborate research I had conducted thanks to a U.S. Fulbright Grant and renewal during 1995–97, as well as a University of Massachusetts Amherst Faculty Research Grant for trips in 2002 and 2004. During the writing period, I produced several straight academic articles in addition to writing the first full draft of this crooked manuscript. The focused writing stint would not have been possible without the support of Ralph Faulkingham, former chair of the Department of Anthropology, and Janet Rifkin, dean of the College of Social and Behavioral Sciences at the University of Massachusetts Amherst. I am also obliged to my mentors at the University of Arizona—Ana Alonso, Jane Hill, Mark Nichter, Susan Philips, and Hermann Rebel—for their lasting influence, and to Anthropology Department head John Olsen for granting me visiting status.

While I was in Tucson writing the manuscript in 2005, through leads from the Society of Southwest Authors, I met Mary Bellin, whose honesty, insight, and encouragement to move beyond rough early drafts and surrender to storytelling were essential to the project. I soon joined a nascent writers' group, which we named Cereus Writers (pronounced "serious"), after a night-blooming cactus of the Sonoran Desert. I am grateful for the careful readings and thoughtful feedback, particularly on the chapters in Part I, from Geoffrey Notkin, Dennis Hull, Lynn Rae Lowe, and Deborah Mayaan. My interest in literary voice was also rekindled through participation in a book group, during 2005 as well as during my sabbatical in 2007–08, with a set of smart, engaging women in Tucson, including carpooling friends Lori Jones, Telsa Mittelmeier, Dana Pitt, and Robin Shambach. Writing "field trips" with Ann-Eve Pedersen were golden, as was her belief in the power of the story; inspiration for political will from Robin Hiller was priceless.

In April 2005, I participated in the workshop "Writing the Story of Oral History," organized by Mary Palevsky and Joseph Granados as part of the Southwest Oral History Association and the Society for Applied Anthropology meetings in Santa Fe, New Mexico. Palevsky graciously read and commented on chapter 20. From her oral historian's perspective, she encouraged me to see myself as a co-creator of a new narrative, inspiring my desire to reveal what was hidden.

Later that year, in December, at the annual meeting of the American Anthropological Association in Washington, D.C., I participated in an ethnographic writing workshop led by Ruth Behar. Her call to anthropologists to be "vulnerable observers" has carved out a space for unconventional approaches to representing social life, approaches that can and do morph into literary genres. Behar instilled in me confidence to write with honesty, and our conversation that began somewhat awkwardly that day evolved into a dialogue that produced a panel for which I served as organizer and she as chair, in December 2007 in Washington, D.C., again at the American Anthropological Association meeting: "Blurred Genres and the Search for Justice." This was a crucial moment for me, as I presented a paper titled "Manifesto for Voice," not knowing whether my manuscript would ever be published. I took courage from the successful writing experiments of many of my fellow panelists: Renato Rosaldo, Kirin Naryan, Paul Stoller, Russell Sharman, and Sasha Welland.

During spring 2007, graduate students in my Ethnographic Writing Seminar read the full manuscript and offered invaluable observations: Elizabeth Braun, Mary Hannah Henderson, Han Lee, Elizabeth Markham, Sinead Ruane, Boone Sheer, and Brion von Over. In addition, I am indebted to Milena Marchesi for her close reading of the work, engaging conversations, and careful attention to my Italian translations. Colleagues Julie Hemment and Alan Swedlund gave intellectual support and friendship throughout the adventure of seeing the manuscript through to its finish. Throughout the revision process, Marni Sandweiss offered encouragement as well as direction, especially on the introduction.

This manuscript's development also benefited from the eloquent, helpful, and rigorous responses of two reviewers, Lynn Morgan and Douglas Holmes, for the University of California Press. As I consider this book one of the progeny of *Europe and the People without History*, it has been a treat to share with the late Eric Wolf the same editor, Stan Holwitz, who has been a great advocate and sincere supporter. At the press, my thanks to Emily Park for overseeing production and Elisabeth Magnus for her keen attention to detail.

Finally, Marian Krause was among the first readers of the full manuscript, and her enthusiasm kept me going. Robert Fraker's feedback revealed genuine excitement for my efforts. Chris Brashear, as ever reliable, nurtured me with meals, companionship, and perspective, and he delivered a thoughtful and provocative reading just when I most needed it. And of course, profound gratitude goes out to all those whose names, real and fictive, appear in this book.

Introduction

History is hard to know, because of all the hired bullshit, but
even without being sure of "history" it seems entirely reasonable to think that every now and then the energy of a whole
generation comes to a head in a long fine flash, for reasons
that nobody really understands at the time—and which never
explain, in retrospect, what actually happened.

Hunter S. Thompson, *Fear and Loathing in Las Vegas*

This book tells the story of a person without history. Emilia Raugei was an
agile girl in the 1920s who grew up weaving Florentine straw hats in a hidden peasant economy. She worked under a cantankerous sister-in-law
whose communist father had abandoned her for the New World. She came
of age in the shadows of a fascist regime that wanted babies. She and people like her might be considered protagonists of a quiet revolution. Yet such
people have rarely been the sources or subjects of the stories told about the
past. Emilia is not a hero in the conventional sense. Her story does not
carry authority. It did not leave volumes in state archives. The only official
trace of it appears in a household census. That one sheet of paper, n. 156,
appears in the Foglio di Famiglia, the family registry, from the 1931 census
for the local hamlet, province, and municipality: Provincia di Firenze, Comune di Carmignano, Frazione di Comeana. In regal handwritten script,

with loopy "Rs" beginning each of the same surnames, the sheet provides entries for eleven people. It includes categories for paternal and maternal descent, civil status, sex, and relation to the *capo famiglia*, or head of household: in this case, Emilio Raugei, her father. It also has categories for profession, place and date of birth, entry into and exit from the commune, and date of death. Diagonal lines cross through the numbers beside two names. One person moved. The other died. Next to his name appears a cross with a hatch mark on each arm.

The registry uses the standard categories for counting populations: births, deaths, migrations. These are the cornerstones of demographic science. They are the minutiae that get counted, then lumped into an aggregate and managed. From these seemingly careful entries, data managers of nation-states, with increasing sophistication, tell us who we are. They turn people into categories. They create norms, from which emerge the deviants. Enumerators have been advising those in power what to do about populations regardless of whether the politics of the time were colonial, liberal, fascist, communist, or capitalist.[1]

Yet when I look at this single household sheet several things contradict the reality that I know existed in Emilio Raugei's household. The kinship is incorrect. "Ersilia" is listed as the mother of all seven children. In fact, she, Emilio's first wife, died from influenza several years before Emilia was born in 1920. Emilia's mother was Giovanna Paolieri, and her relation to the head of household is listed merely as *convivente*—cohabitant. Perhaps the couple never married, but why was she not recorded as the mother of her own children? Another error appears in the listing of professions. Emilio is noted as a *colono*, or sharecropper, which matches what Emilia told me. The two oldest males, one an uncle and the other a son, are similarly listed. Giovanna appears as a *trecciaiola*, or straw weaver. One daughter and one daughter-in-law are recorded as A.C. for *atta casa*, or housewife. But the spaces are blank for the three remaining females, including Emilia, who would have been eleven years old in 1931 and would have had at least six years' experience weaving for a global economy. I expect several of the other women in the household worked as weavers, too. The blanks speak volumes about the systematic cover-up of hidden labor.

In effect, these blanks are my inspiration. They are the empty spaces of history. They need filling in. They hold clues to the cultural roots of declining fertility, which has been constructed as a menacing conundrum.

As it happened, a core of international journalists in the early 1990s began reporting on declining birthrates in Europe. Seismic changes by 1992 earned Italians and Spaniards the distinction of having the world's lowest fertility rates, which have since hovered between 1.2 and 1.3 children on average over a woman's lifetime.[2]

Demographers have developed sophisticated technologies to count populations, and, largely as a result of their rigorous work, policy makers and politicians regard Italian and other European countries' birthrates as dangerously low. Colorful language lends strength to this valuation, as when the demographer Antonio Golini, popular on Italian TV talk shows, labels the trend as a "profound malaise" or when the prominent demographer-turned-politician Massimo Livi-Bacci describes young Italian adults who delay marriage and parenting as suffering from "a syndrome of lateness."[3] A majority of Europeans share the opinion that something is amiss in their societies. A survey published in 2005 found that 75 percent of Europeans considered low fertility a negative development. In Italy, 82 percent of respondents viewed the declining rate of births as "somewhat negative" or "very negative."[4] The simultaneous fear of global overpopulation with one of population "implosion" in Europe in the last two decades has led various governments to embrace pronatalist policies. Such policies can mean welcome relief for financially strapped families in need of welfare assistance or tax breaks. They can also be used to promote notions of the ideal family or to fuel discrimination by denying benefits to certain parents, such as couples in same-sex relationships or immigrants who are not citizens. The Berlusconi government in 2003 passed a baby bonus law that offered 1,000 euros to Italian or European citizens who gave birth to or adopted a second child. The law met with controversy when checks were mistakenly mailed to immigrant families, who soon received letters from the government requesting that the money be returned. Another controversial law limiting fertility treatment sent the message that the Italian state wanted babies but not at any cost. Due in no small degree to the pope's influence, the 2004 law on medically assisted reproduction codified dominant definitions of the family as consisting of a man, woman, and child from the same genetic material; it forbids infertile couples to resort to using donor genetic material that is not their own. The Church's position has also fortified the status of the unborn fetus elsewhere. In Russia, in 2006, former president Vladimir Putin offered incentives to nudge up the birthrate there, including nearly $10,000 in vouchers to parents giving birth to a second child. France, a country well known for its early demographic transition to smaller families, has a long history of policies with family-friendly incentives. A cover story of the *Nation*, "Missing the 'Right' Babies," in March 2008 reported that the U.S. Christian Right has hopped on the alarmist European bandwagon, amplifying forecasts of a looming "demographic winter" across the Atlantic. In June 2008, the cover story of the *New York Times Magazine* was titled "Childless Europe" and posed the exaggerated question, "What happens to a continent when it stops making babies?"[5]

Unraveled exposes the cultural roots of the profound yet quiet revolution from large to small families. My description of Emilia Raugei as someone without history is intended only in the most ironic sense. It echoes the intention of the anthropologist Eric Wolf's classic *Europe and the People without History* (1982) to demonstrate the historical connections between humble peasants and far greater economic and political forces that extend well beyond their not-so-small worlds. The chapters in *Unraveled* amplify silenced memories and link local and global forces that caused people to embrace a momentous shift in family making.

To bring the topic to life, I push ethnography beyond its conventional limits and blend genres of historical fiction with narrative nonfiction in two separate parts. Part I, "History Imagined," is written in the form of a novel that follows the life of the protagonist. Each chapter centers on a core experience from Emilia's life as told to me in numerous interviews and conversations. From those stories and additional ethnographic as well as archival and library research, I imagined how history happened, developing characters and plot to bring her story to life. Part II, "Memory Encountered," follows my stay in Carmignano during 1996–97 and subsequent visits to the area in 1999, 2002, 2004, and 2006. The people, places, and events are what I witnessed directly. The stories are selected but not invented. This part consists of straight narrative nonfiction with a twist: it seeks to unravel what was behind one memory that set me on a journey of sensual encounters with the past, with informal economies, and with the modern condition.

Ethnography, as a literary genre practically unknown beyond its social science practitioners, is celebrated for its thick descriptions based on painstaking, systematic, and often spontaneous observation. In many ways, not much has changed since Clifford Geertz suggested in *The Interpretation of Cultures,* more than three decades ago, that the point of cultural anthropology was to grasp the webs of signification that humans spin and respin. Arguments have ensued about the place of history and power in representations of cultural others. Exceptional ethnographies, such as Lila Abu-Lughod's classic and poetic *Veiled Sentiments: Honor and Poetry in a Bedouin Society* or her contemporary *Dramas of Nationhood: The Politics of Television in Egypt,* have managed to strike a respectable balance between symbolic and material influences. Empathetic understanding has remained a primary objective. In their millennial article "Manifesto for Ethnography," Paul Willis and Mats Trondman pointed to revelatory "ah-ha" moments as the redeeming quality of scholarship that takes seriously the nitty-gritty of social life. Ordinary life I did take seriously. To convey what it was like to live through this transformation, however, I became tempted to bend the rules of ethnography. Undoubtedly, others who have done so have experienced doubt and shame on the one hand and hope and elation on the other. While conducting fieldwork in Haiti, Zora Neale Hurston wrote *Their Eyes Were Watching God,* acclaimed for its vernacular voice, which was most likely shaped by her study of oral performances. Paul Stoller wrote the ethnographic novel *Jaguar* to bring to life the experiences of transnational African vendors who migrate to the United States. More recently, Tobias Hecht blurred fact with fiction in his book *After Life: An Ethnographic Novel,* begun as a straight research project on a street child in Brazil who grew up to be a transvestite prostitute, but finished as a collaborative work of compassion aiming to get across the inner lives of his characters.[6]

Some circumstances call the writer to stretch the limits of convention. In his review of an ambitious two-volume collection, *The Novel*, the literary critic William Deresiewicz observes that the novel itself appears to thrive "during periods of social and intellectual upheaval, when long-standing literary conventions and metaphysical beliefs can no longer carry the weight of lived experience." As the collection's editor, the Italian literary theorist Franco Moretti offers insight into the uneasy history of the genre. Fiction itself has puzzled many during its centuries of existence. (Scholars debate its origins, with views ranging from the Roman Empire, to the Middle Ages, to the sixteenth to eighteenth centuries in Europe and China.) Even within anthropology, the historian James Clifford rocked some boats with his assertion that "ethnographic writings can properly be called fictions in the sense of 'something made or fashioned,' the principal burden of the word's Latin root *fingere*." His point was not that anthropologists simply make things up ad hoc but that creative interpretation is inevitable in any attempt to represent social life. Similarly, the novel is strange because it relies on fictionality, which lies somewhere between truth and invention. "The novel isn't true, like history, nor is it manifestly false, like legend or fable, so what is it?" asks Deresiewicz. "The establishment of fictionality as an epistemological possibility midway between truth and falsehood is an enormous cultural achievement." Here, he defines fictionality as "persuasively representative."[7] Ultimately, good fiction persuades readers to identify with the feelings of someone else, even to imagine that they are that person.

How a woman with a fifth-grade education became the protagonist of this book deserves some explanation.[8] I met Emilia Raugei on Via La Volta, the last lane of a Tuscan hill town where she was born and where I lived as a cultural anthropologist conducting the second year of my fieldwork, from October 1996 to August 1997. The street was deceptively remote. A row of two-story white houses with red tile roofs looked out on a vineyard that sloped down into an expansive valley, where the hamlet's last herd of sheep grazed. The bucolic setting was right out of Frances Mayes's *Under the Tuscan Sun,* a book that delights aficionados of Tuscany with its bountiful offerings of mouth-watering dishes and beautiful landscapes. In the tourist mentality, if history exists at all, it concerns the likes of the Medici, Michelangelo, and maybe, on a rare gray day, Mussolini. The awestruck casual observer, taking in Tuscany while sipping a Chianti and eating a fine bowl of penne with a robust *sugo di cinghiale*, or wild boar sauce, could easily be seduced into assuming that serious history never found its way to the countryside.

Emilia's recollections proved an antidote to such fantasy. She had a habit of responding to my direct questions with elaborate stories pregnant with characters entangled in a shifting world. I became intrigued about how people from her generation and social station began forging a new way of life and how family making figured into the experience of becoming modern. Admittedly, her stories did not directly answer my questions about how men and women from large families would come to marry and have very few children. Drawing selectively on the past, as we all do, she shared memories about growing up as a Little Italian under Mussolini, about intimate and tense relationships among the villagers, about working as a straw weaver alongside girls and women connected to relatives overseas and beholden to counts in the village, about coming of age between the country and the city, about living with Nazis in her backyard, and about eventually entering adulthood as the last generation that would live under the roof of a patriarch.

Emilia's stories provided a portal to another time. The details spoke to the traumas and dislocations of the twentieth century. I sensed a person who had suffered so much more than I, who had lived through such tremendous changes, who had worked as a child when nobody thought that child labor was wrong. I was not nostalgic. I was convinced that this story of a "person without history" needed to be told to shed light on some of the complex forces and intimate experiences that led to fertility decline.

My demographer colleagues were not easily convinced. How could a woman from "quaint" Carmignano possibly explain anything, let alone the birthrate? Collaborations between demographers and anthropologists were born of necessity after a major conundrum emerged from one of the biggest undertakings in historical demography. The Princeton European Fertility Project, launched in 1963, sought a universal explanation for why women in virtually every European province from the late eighteenth to the mid–twentieth century had reduced by 50 percent the average number of children they bore. Might there be some universal reason why so many women began to limit births before reaching menopause? Modernization was believed to be the driver of the momentous change. But when researchers mapped and surveyed some six hundred provinces in Europe, the data disproved their hypothesis. It turns out that families began to shrink under a range of social, economic, and mortality conditions. The modernization model of economic development, based on a northern European notion of industrialization and urbanization, did not predict much. In their book *The Decline of Fertility in Europe*, John Knodel and Etienne van de Walle concluded that "cultural setting influenced the onset and spread of fertility decline independently of socioeconomic conditions." Unfortunately, this approach has often viewed culture as static traits rather than as dynamic practices and has not ended up clarifying much.[9]

A workshop at the University of Padua on September 19, 2003, explored the cultural aspects of the recent demographic trend. Bearing the no-frills title of "The Contribution of Qualitative Studies for Understanding Family and Reproductive Behaviors," the event brought together about two dozen participants, among them number-crunching demographers along with colleagues who had recently tried their hand at qualitative analysis. They had ventured into this unfamiliar terrain—moving away from examining numerical data to analyzing talk from focus groups—in an effort to try to get to the bottom of Italy's *bassissima fecondità*, or superlow fertility, which in the 1990s had taken population experts by surprise.

Invited to attend, I brought Emilia with me in the form of her voice burned onto a CD. I played a section from one of her narratives during a session convened in the Antique Archive of the Bò Palace, a breathtaking building with its impressive Anatomical Theater and Galileo's lectern, marble staircases, walls of leather-bound books, and portraits of forty great European scholar-alumni.[10] My decision to present the narrative of a former peasant felt risky, to say the least. But something crucial happened that day that gave me the courage to write this book.

The meeting was intriguing for several reasons. First, of the twenty-two scholars on the two-page program, all were Italian except for me. I was the only American. Second, I was the only anthropologist in a roomful of demographers, and my work was the most qualitative in the group. My paper, predictably controversial given the venue, offered an interpretation of how women in the early days of globalization had negotiated their roles as biological and social reproducers situated among various patriarchs: husbands, counts, capitalists, and the Duce.

As the demographers discussed the problem of low fertility, the anthropologist questioned whether the demographic trend needed to be framed as a problem. As the demographers focused on the current moment, the anthropologist brought history into the conversation by raising the specter of the fascist demographic campaign that had coerced women and men to increase the birthrate, yet failed.[11] As the demographers sought to figure out why Italians were having so few babies so as to change their behavior, the anthropologist aimed to understand what reproductive and social change means to people and how it connects to cultural practices and systems of power.

Discussion turned to my session. Massimo Livi-Bacci, a prominent demographer whose influential work I have both admired and critiqued, took the microphone to ask, *"Che cosa ci serve a noi demografi?"* (What use is this to us demographers?) I explained that such work seeks to show how people become conditioned as social beings. My goal was to remind scholars that when people like Emilia started to drag up recollections about the past—when large families were the norm, and when the fascist state valued the national collectivity above all else—their memories quickly turned to poverty, trauma, and unending work within a very rigid, hierarchical system. Debate ensued. The historical demographer Carlo Corsini, renowned for his work on infant mortality, offered an old Italian saying:

DAUGHTER: What does it mean to get married?
MOTHER: To bring a child into the world, to work, and to cry.

He then commented, "That's not a proverb, that's a disaster!" Was the disaster that the proverb spoke the truth about women's historic roles as mothers, workers, and wives? Or was it that many Italians, especially women, continue to have such negative associations with marriage and motherhood that they delay having children, have very few, or don't have any at all?

These lively happenings aside, the highlight for me was a report from the Focus City project, which consisted of research teams in five Italian cities who brought together married Italians, mostly in their forties, to learn what had led them to *decide* to have a child. Parents in the study emphasized that the costs of having a child far outweighed the benefits, and they associated more children with more chaos. The researchers came to a rather startling conclusion: What made parents decide to have their first child was a course of *nondecision;* the conceptions of most first children resulted from parents' "suspension of rationality."[12] The irony delighted me to no end. Here was a country with one of the world's most acclaimed low fertility rates, and the very discipline used to push population control in many corners of the globe had just discovered that even where women are having very few children, a good many of those children were conceived as a result not of planning but of pure old-fashioned passion.[13]

I left the conference with deepened understandings of our divergent opinions and purposes. In the months ahead, I looked to others who had written "history from below," including several socially minded historians, anthropologists, and journalists working in the 1960s.[14] Still, how could Emilia's story stand up to aggregate numbers and erudite arguments? I found inspiration in the French philosopher Michel Foucault's "genealogical method," which called for merging erudite with subjugated knowledge. Foucault recognized that knowledge was hierarchically ordered. Some knowledge counted a lot; other knowledge hardly counted at all. Valuable criticism could merge the two by drawing upon local, regional, popular, or other discounted forms of knowledge to perform emancipatory work.[15] The method, I thought, could make it possible for me to face the legacy of those forty illustrious men whose portraits lined the walls of the Bò Palace. It bolstered my courage to answer that prominent demographer whose "*A che cosa ci serve?*" reverberated in my thoughts. Why not take local stories seriously, even if they seemed to have no place in the grand plots of science that foretold population implosion?

Emancipating histories, however, turned out to be no easy task. With the help of an Italian research assistant, I converted my interviews from cassette tapes to transcripts, printed them out, and secured them into a three-ring binder. I pored over Emilia's memories, trying to make sense of her references to unfamiliar places and idiosyncratic experiences that were often unlike anything I had ever imagined, let alone experienced. What struck me, however, was how numerous dimensions of her life story connected in strange yet profound ways with the major tremors of the twentieth century. Her experiences lent form and gave life to the ways that people adjusted to major transformations. Her story demanded telling. The challenge was how to tell the story of a person who was a "nobody" and at the same time an "everybody"—though hardly a typical representative of anybody.

The memory around which much of the book revolves elbowed its way into an interview during my initial fieldwork. I sat across the table from Emilia in her small, dark kitchen. Her humble house was two doors down from the restored farmhouse where I was living in 1996 and where she had been born in 1920. I had barely formulated my question about how she and her husband had come to have an only child when Emilia launched into a tale of a communist uncle-by-marriage who, fearing fascist repercussions, stowed away in a crate of hats on a ship bound for Argentina and created unforeseen repercussions of his own.

That memory was initially only one chapter. Having finished a draft, I searched for feedback and located a writers' group open to members. As a newcomer, I had to "apply" by submitting a manuscript, so Emilia's story found its way into the U.S. mail. One afternoon a few weeks later, the phone rang. A confident woman's voice on the other end offered criticism. My idea had merit, she assured me, but the chapter as written was "too episodic." On the page, Emilia's words were like so many leaden weights on a fishing line, sinking quickly into the obscurity of an unforgiving sea separating two starkly different times and places. Wanting the reader to identify with Emilia's feelings and a world turned on its head was not enough.[16] The narratives did not speak for themselves. Bringing the narratives from there to here required not only translation but animation of the world in which her life had unfolded and of the relationships that made life what it was. I began to experiment with ways of bringing Emilia's memories to life. She was a skilled narrator. She had a gift for telling stories with vivid detail. She quoted people with regularity. As I transcribed her stories, images stood out.

I stole away to the Georgia O'Keeffe Museum in April 2005 while attending an anthropology conference in Santa Fe. Living in the Southwest for the year, I had been writing for four months with limited satisfaction and hardly any contact with anyone other than family and close friends. The busy conference hotel was just a few blocks from the museum. It was time for a break. *Black Mesa Landscape* with its undulating rust and blue mountains, *Untitled* with its splendid red and yellow cliffs, and *From the Plains* with its close-up of a billowing cloud in motion were some of many evocative canvases. Quotations from O'Keeffe were stenciled here and there on the walls. One caught my eye. I penciled it down in my notebook: "Nothing is less real than realism. . . . Details are confusing. It is only by selection, by elimination, by emphasis, that we get at the real meaning of things." O'Keeffe's insight seemed a call to emphasize the stories Emilia had told me.

Emilia's fragmented and episodic memories became my starting point. I wanted to do justice to the richness of the oral material. The narratives needed context. They needed life. The challenge was to find a way to negotiate the tension between life as it is lived and life as it is typed onto a page. Could there be a strategy that might be truer to her experiences and resonate with the reader more than her unembellished memories? I began to select and emphasize. Staying as true to her life story as possible became a guiding principle. I grappled with the fact that the act of turning life into text is both an act of violence and an act of creation. Through acts of recording, documenting, analyzing, and writing, the researcher does not simply "give voice" to a particular version of the truth but may serve as a co-creator of a new narrative, a new version of history even if it is always partial. I drew on archival work, on ethnographic and historical scholarship, on photographs, and on memories to write in a way that might prompt empathetic understanding. Blurring of genres was not merely an act of creation but also an act of love.[17]

The result is this book. In collaboration with those whose little-considered memories say much more than first impressions would suggest,

I hope to have created a meaningful and compassionate representation of life at a crucial moment in contemporary Europe. The project speaks to transformations related to sex and society. People I spoke with, including Emilia, often had trouble expressing the reasons that motivated them to have or not have children during an era when conscious control over one's fertility did not seem such an available, everyday matter as it is today.

Feminist movements aimed at empowering women through reproductive choice were not part of this story. I suspect that couples limited births as they adjusted to changing conditions and new imbalances. Ultimately, their decisions to limit the number of babies they had were embedded in these transforming social contexts and entangled with new struggles, ideologies, and desires. The process of trying to make sense of the memories eventually opened me to the upended social world that people were negotiating. I hope the stories in these pages illuminate something about the human condition and the ambivalent embrace of a modern way of life.

PART ONE History Imagined

ONE Postcards

Italy, 1927

Emilia Raugei was a young girl who wove plaits of straw in a hill town above Florence, and that foggy March day she had her heart set on winning a weaving game of the girls' invention. Only seven years old, she willed her fingers to maneuver straw strands for hours as she sat on a straight-backed chair in a circle with a group of girls, her head bent over her work and her arms immobile.[1] Some six meters of woven plaits, five centimeters wide, formed rings at her feet. The coils rested against a stone stairway that butted against the street where the girls had placed their chairs, a marginal space between the threshold of one of the girls' houses and the lightly traveled rural road in the Commune of Carmignano.

Emilia was the only one still wearing her school uniform: a white shirt, black tie and skirt, white socks, and black shoes. Her black beret tipped at an angle atop her head. Her dark brown hair framed her green eyes, fine nose, and full cheeks. She exemplified the perfect "Little Italian," the name given to children who attended the government-run, fascist school. Her teachers taught order and discipline, and she applied those lessons to her work.

After school, Emilia worked as a weaver, as she had since she was five. The labor came easily to her. She held the straw comfortably between her fingers and thumbs as she wove. Her slender fingers relied on the memory ingrained deep in her muscles to work the straw. Only one other girl, Asia Grassi, was faster, but she was also five years older.

The most skilled girls worked on a refined weave, a braid with five strands. Called *cappelli di punta,* these finely braided plaits were sent to Florence and fashioned into the most stylish and expensive hats of all. Fine ladies and gentlemen wore them thousands of miles away, in America. When Aldobrando Manetti came to pick up the finished plaits, he would leave a few lire and add a few postcards to the pile. Emilia handed the money over to Mamma without a second thought. Mamma in return gave Emilia any postcards that she had received from neighbors or her own kinsfolk who had left the village some years ago to start their lives anew in the New World. Of those who had emigrated, some were sorely missed, others were passionately resented, and a few all but forgotten. Mamma felt little sentiment to keep greeting cards once they'd been read. Her generation knew no clutter, and farmwomen like her swiftly passed along or disposed of the rare paper object that entered their sparsely furnished homes.

The girls broke at 4:30 p.m. for a snack of *schiacciata,* a flat bread seasoned with olive oil and salt. They rubbed the drippings of olive oil into the backs of their hands, dry from the straw dust and the spring wind. It was almost time to play their game in which the girl who made a knot the fastest won first pick of a postcard. They set the postcards on "the throne," a chair placed in the middle of their circle.

Emilia so badly wanted the postcard of the "mile of merriment" from the Canadian National Exhibition Midway. She loved the picture of all the people crowded into the Toronto street, the men with their spiffy straw hats, the women with their fashionable dresses, strolling past the vendors' stands and heading toward the roller coaster whose silhouette rose like a white mountain into the skyline. After school, Emilia had not gone home to change her uniform but had run directly to her friend Lirua Lippi's house just so she could hold the picture of the people at the fair before all the other girls took their places. She had fallen deep into a daydream when Asia's piercing voice jolted her out of it.

"Who wants to play our game?" asked Asia, ever a force to be reckoned with. A robust twelve-year-old, she had curly chestnut hair that framed her plump, round cheeks, which held their rosy color regardless of the season.

The girls stopped weaving, their hands in their laps, and said in unison, "I do! One, two, three, no one can make a knot faster than me. Go!"

The small hands blurred as the girls braided. Emilia's fingers swiftly twisted the straw, and she again imagined the noise of the hawkers at the fair. Her lips puckered as she tasted the pink fluffy-looking candy on a stick—sweet as sugar. She tilted her head back ever so slightly, closed her eyes, and imagined a strong breeze against her face as she cruised up and down the white hills of the giant roller coaster. She wanted to go to such a fabulous festival, but for now she would be satisfied just to have the postcard in her possession.

"Done!" Asia said as she jumped up from her seat and ran to the table with the cards.

Emilia looked up and nearly cried. Why hadn't she paid attention? *"Mannaggia!* Darn it!"

Asia gathered all the cards. Emilia held her breath. She hid her feelings. If another girl knew the card she wanted, she might take it. They were as envious of her skill as she was proud. Asia flipped through the stack and held up the picture of the fair for everyone to see. *No, please, not that one. I promise I'll concentrate harder next time if only I can win that card. It's mine.*

Asia twirled as if she were one of the ladies wearing a long dress with her hair blowing in the breeze. Emilia prepared herself to settle for the card with the pretty couple in a deep tango dip.

"Ma che?" Asia said. "Oh-la-la, how fake is this?" And she tossed it onto the table, making the other girls laugh.

Asia then showed everyone a postcard of a muscular farmer holding the biggest tomato she'd ever seen. "Imagine, a tomato as big as your head!" she said, passing it by. Another showed a pair of desperate-looking Patagonian Indians. The figures reminded her of the day laborers who came around searching for farmwork because they were without *signori*. The landed nobility demanded that the families deliver eggs, prosciutto, and brooms as tribute, but at least in hard times the counts looked after the *coloni*, or tenant farmers. The fair ones, anyway.

"I'll take this one," Asia said boldly, grabbing the one of the Indians. "It brings good luck."

"Let's play again. There are stacks of cards," Emilia said.

Asia skipped about in the center of the circle. "I'll watch and be the judge, since I'm much faster than all of you."

"You're also the oldest," complained Natalina Rossi, who despite being the newest to the group showed no fear of speaking her mind. Her family had moved from the mountains in Vicchio, and her blond hair, fair complexion, high cheekbones, and thin lips marked her as from more northern stock than the other girls, whose hair colors formed a brown-black spectrum ranging from chestnut to coal.

"I can't help it if my fingers are still small but fast," Asia replied. "Soon I will move up to be with the women. So who wants to play?"

"I do," all the girls said in unison. They gathered their strands, each with five in their hands. "One two three, no one can make a knot faster than me. Go!"

Emilia's nimble fingers flew over the straw as she twisted the ends. She tightened the knot and sprang out of her chair.

"*Belle e finite!*" shouted Emilia. "I'm done!" She picked up the postcard of the fair and held it tight to her chest. She wiped her watery right eye with the side of her finger, pressing her tears back, working hard to hide her joy. The last thing she wanted was to provoke envy in the other girls. Her effort to disguise her delight was aided by the clatter of an approaching horse and buggy. Distracted, the girls turned. Aldobrando was pulling up the lane with Germena Santini, his niece, sitting at his side. Emilia cringed, not because he was coming to check on the girls and deliver more straw for the week's consignment, but because Germena, just three years her senior, seemed to take pleasure in making mean comments to the girls and pushing them to tears.

Aldobrando found his niece's demeanor troublesome, although, Emilia suspected, it also served him well. As a hatter, he was as serious about his hats as her teacher was about penmanship. He expected high-quality product from the weavers, regardless of their age. He rarely lost his temper. Indeed, Emilia had heard him raise his voice only once when he was provoked, and it wasn't pleasant. He had a soft-spoken way of talking that mesmerized the girls, and they didn't give him any trouble. In conversation, they referred to him as *lo zio,* a term of endearment meaning "uncle." To his face, they called him Uncle Aldo. He doled out the work as systematically as it came to him.

Germena, on the other hand, mixed work with emotion. She suffered from a deep sense of insecurity. Jealousies haunted her like recurring childhood nightmares. Once Uncle Aldo had walked up just as Germena was laying into the girls because, she asserted, several of them were not focusing on their work. They had been talking among themselves, and she snapped at them. Several of the girls were so upset that they had stopped their weaving. Uncle Aldo sent Germena home early that day.

"From her mother she got her hard edge, and from her father she got the emotions," he had told the girls. "That's the mix we have to work with, and you know I understand how things are." Once again he had won over their loyalties.

This particular Monday afternoon there was an important order to be filled, and Uncle Aldo warned the girls about the *furia,* the urgency, of their work. It was a rush job with a quick turnaround. The order would have to be consigned to the buyers in Florence on Friday.

"I'll be back for these on Thursday evening," he instructed. "Can you handle it?"

"Of course, we can handle it, especially if you leave us a few postcards," Lirua said, flashing him a mischievous smile.

Aldo reached into a small bag in the front seat of his buggy and pulled out a few cards, then handed them to Asia.

"We won't be needing these," he said firmly.

A card with the image of a trolley car sat on top, and Lirua turned it over to glimpse a postage stamp with the word *Argentina* written vertically along its side and a postmark dated January 12, 1927. Her eyes went straight to the message, words penned in large script. She read it aloud:

> Dearest Germena,
> We think of you often and know you are a big help to Uncle Aldo. Your three sisters and new baby brother are all fine . . .

Germena reached over and grabbed the card from Lirua. "That's mine," Germena objected, shoving it into her pocket. She scowled for a moment, then went to fetch a chair, sat at the edge of the girls' circle, and began to weave, her eyes fast on her work. Aldo pulled away, glancing back to wave.

A heavy silence fell over the group, broken only when several of the younger girls, unfazed by Germena's foul mood, complained that they did not have postcards from this round of play.

"It's not fair," cried six-year-old Delfina Cappelli. "We didn't even get a single one."

"Oh get over it," Germena said. "Besides, it's a stupid game."

"No one said you have to play," Asia countered.

The girls ignored Germena and agreed to play the game four more times until everyone got to pick a card, with the older girls who had already won sitting out.

Lirua, who had already won a card, glanced back to see if Germena was looking, then leaned over and whispered to Emilia, "I bet they're not coming back. Otherwise they would have said something about it, don't you think?"

Germena stood up abruptly and threw her plaits to the ground. "It's not true!" she protested, and took off up the street, her arms swaying at her sides like oars pushing against an upstream current.

"Lirua, you shouldn't have whispered that so loudly," Emilia scolded.

"Do you really think she heard me?"

"She knew you were talking about her."

"Well, what do I care?" Lirua asked. "She doesn't like me anyhow."

"Lirua, we all have to work with her."

The sun filtered through a fog bank, producing faint shadows that lengthened the girls to twice their seated height, stretching well beyond the strands that amounted to meters, meters, and meters of plaits draped over their laps and cascading onto the floor.

"Let's go," sighed Dora Cappelli, the youngest girl and the last to take a postcard. She stood up, and Delfina, her older sister by just a year, followed suit. The two dark-haired girls ran up the street playing *tocca ferro*, a game of tag, expending their final burst of energy for the day. Emilia couldn't care less about playing tag. Weaving was her fun, and that's what mattered to her.

Emilia helped Lirua lug the chairs inside, arranging them around the kitchen table except for one, which she placed alongside a wall. She gathered up the strands and set them on top of the chair seat until tomorrow. Emilia was the last to leave.

She took the long way home. On Mondays the round-bellied man sold roasted chestnuts in the piazza, and she had a craving. Closer to the weekend he traveled to the city, he told her, but on slower weekdays he preferred to stay close to home. She figured Mamma wouldn't scold her if she bought a small bagful with the change in her pocket. She strolled down the hill past a row of white stucco houses with red tiled roofs. Clanking pots signaled womenfolk preparing the evening meal, and she caught a whiff of frying food. A chicken darted out in front of her, and as another chased it she watched, taking pity upon the first chicken's henpecked back, bare of feathers.

Emilia turned to chase her shadow until it collided with the intersection of Via Mancia and Via Colle. She followed Via Mancia straight to the piazza, even though this route led her past Germena's house—or rather, Uncle Aldo's house. She dreaded running into Germena, but she took her chances. To avoid the risk altogether and still arrive at the piazza, she would have had to set off from Lirua's house in the opposite direction, along Via Sette Ponti, a road that looped widely around the town. The unfamiliar route frightened her.

She headed along the familiar street, and as she neared the cast-iron fence that enclosed Germena's garden, Emilia heard crying. She stopped and listened, then recognized the sobs. She thought about knocking but decided against it. Uncle Aldo's buggy was parked alongside the house, and he knew how to calm her; besides, there was the lady friend next door who was like an aunt to Germena. Anyway, what would be the point? Germena never listened to what Emilia said to her. She had a way of twisting Emilia's well-intentioned words, of throwing them back at her. *Besides, it's probably just another one of her fits.* Emilia continued on toward the town center.

A nutty aroma wafted through the piazza as she entered it. She made a beeline straight for the source of the smoke and watched the seller scoop chestnuts, with their freshly blackened skins, into a hand-sized paper bag. Emilia sat on a bench, and as she ate the warmed meat she watched a woman with a baby on her hip disappear into the butcher's shop. Several miners straggled up the hill from the stone quarry down by the river and crossed the piazza. The daylight was fading. She set off for home, following the lower Via La Volta up the hill until it switched back, putting her on the upper side of the lane. Houses lined the street only on her left side because to her right a grassy ledge fell off into a bowl-like valley. Here, the town ended: fruit trees intermingled with rows of grapevines that ended in a meadow where she watched the shepherd with his dog steer several lagging lambs back into the herd. Above him, a road climbed to the hilltop hamlet of Artimino, where, as she had learned in school, the Medici had cultivated the surrounding forest to use as their royal hunting grounds and, centuries earlier, the Etruscans had lived. Fascism, her teacher said, took inspiration for its name from the Etruscan *fasces,* a bundle of rods that meant unity. Last week, her teacher had brought in an oversized book with pictures of Etruscan tombs around Tarquinia. It was a mysterious place to Emilia and her classmates. On the blackboard the teacher had written the lesson title, "Manifesto in Defense of *Italianità*." Emilia had copied the words in her uneven cursive letters into her notebook and then struggled to write several other big words: "The quality and essence of being Italian. . . . Evidence of Italian cultural supremacy . . ."[2] Never mind that the meanings were lost on her. As the teacher droned on about the greatness of the nation's legacies, she drew what impressed her: a picture of a spotted wildcat from the Tomb of the Leopards. She wondered whether such lean creatures had ever roamed these soils.

The late afternoon sun lent a golden cast to the yellow rapeseed flowers that blanketed the distant hillside. She picked up a stick and dragged it behind her. As her house came into view, the vines at the edge of her vision swelled like ocean waves. They stirred up memories, sharp and sudden. The distorted image jarred her into recalling the long journey last summer when she had accompanied her father to the sea after Count Michon Pecori had asked him to haul the food for their family's month of holiday. She wished she could have stayed, but she hardly had a bathing garment. Besides, the only common folk who went to the sea, Daddy had told her, were the sick ones that the commune sent off to the colonies to get well before it was too late and they wasted away. He said she should count her blessings that she was a healthy girl. She had stood at the sea's edge, closed her eyes, and breathed the iodine-laced air deep into her lungs for good fortune. Death had already touched her family. Daddy had lost his first wife to *la spagnola,* Spanish fever. He had told Emilia how the fever moved with the soldiers in 1915 and attacked its victims, as ruthless as war. Ersilia Lorri's body had turned hot as fire, then she had died. Just like that. It had struck her heart. She had left five children. Then Daddy had met Giovanna Paolieri, a sturdy woman with clear eyes, and together they had had another two babies, Emilia being the first of their union and her little brother Carlo the second.

Via La Volta dead-ended into the backyard of her family's farmhouse, a uniquely situated *casa colonica* with its back to the village, its front to the countryside. Most farmhouses sat in isolation, scattered throughout the countryside, an end point of one-lane dirt roads. Mamma always said her family was lucky to be so close to the town and the countryside all at once. Poggiola, named after the hillock where it perched, was a ten-acre *podere,* or farm, with a spectacular view that her parents and their kin had enjoyed not merely as a view from afar but as a landscape with which they had intimate contact—one they had sculpted with their own *braccia,* or arms, since taking up residence there in 1900.[3] On a clear day, from the edge of the olive grove in her front yard, she could see the red, dome-shaped roof of the Duomo in Florence. The kitchen, by contrast, was at the backside of the house and looked down onto Via La Volta, the V-shaped lane that divided town from land and villagers from peasants.

Emilia skipped up the grassy slope and took the postcard out from her skirt pocket. Clutching it, she walked around to the front yard and went inside. Mamma was leaning over the fireplace, shrouded in smoke, her face aglow from the fire and her wavy black hair pulled back in a loose bun at the nape of her neck. The fireplace opening was big enough for a grown man to sleep in, and it dwarfed Mamma. The problem was, it made smoke. It always had and always would, Grandpa said. The chimney didn't draw well, no matter how seasoned the firewood she chose for Mamma. The smoky smell mixed with the odor from the cows, which slept inside in the big front room during winter months to generate warmth. Signs of the animals' recent presence lingered from the chilly, early spring nights. Emilia had gotten used to their muddy, fecal smell against the tepid hay, heavy though it was.

"Daddy isn't home yet?" Emilia asked. Usually he was here a good deal before Mamma put in the pasta to boil. He hated it *scotta*, overcooked, and she was careful to please him out of pride for her role as the *massaia rurale*, the rural matriarch, as much as out of respect for his authority.

"He's over at Aldobrando's," Mamma said.

"Why, Mamma?"

"Fetch me some more wood," Mamma said.

Emilia was tired and had no desire to go back outside, plus she hated how Mamma gave her a chore rather than answering her, but she complied, dashing upstairs to slip her postcard under her mattress before heading outside. As she carried several pieces of split wood back toward the house, Daddy came up the driveway with Sergio and Osvaldo not far behind. Daddy smiled at her beneath his thick mustache, but Emilia sensed that something was not quite right.

Her older brothers headed upstairs. She followed Daddy into the kitchen, where Mamma now stood over a pot of boiling water and her half-sister Hamidie sat at the far end of the table, chopping the stem off the end of a dandelion green. At her feet, her little brother Carlo sat on the floor, rolling the lid of a pot like a wheel across the floor. He frowned as it spilled over and clanked to a halt, having hit an uneven edge of the worn tile. Emilia took a seat as Mamma tossed in the pasta along with some salt. In front of the girl were scattered several terracotta carders. Mamma used them to open, comb, clean, and straighten wool fibers so as to spin yarn for sweaters and such. They were rectangular with handles just long enough to grasp.

Mamma stirred the pasta, then walked over to the hutch and pulled open its door, the yellow paint chipped around the glass panes from years of use as the sole cabinet in the kitchen. She took out two small tumblers, retrieved a green bottle from beneath the sink, and poured Daddy a glass of wine. From a clear bottle, she poured Emilia a glass of water.

"Germena is beside herself," Daddy said, taking a sip of the red wine, a batch from last fall's harvest. "A telegram arrived this afternoon. Magdalena wrote that they aren't coming back."

"Well, what did you expect?" Mamma asked.

"Aldo was under the impression that his sister would come back for Germena," he said. "He was thinking she and Silvano might even make the trip this summer, but Magdalena doesn't want to travel alone, and it's just too risky for Silvano."

"Why is it risky, Daddy?" Emilia asked, looking up from her counting game.

"Oh Emilia!" said Hamidie. "The questions you ask."

"You know, Germena's dad was a communist," Daddy said, patiently. "It's not something that the Duce allows."

"He was hardly an assassin," Mamma explained. "He just didn't see eye to eye with fascism."

"Do we?" Emilia asked.

"I'm not fascist, or socialist, or communist," Daddy said. "He who lives, reigns." Daddy refused to belong to any party. He was a neutral man who put his family first. He didn't want to hear of politics.

"Things aren't how they used to be, Emilia," Mamma said. "Things have changed since you were born. You've only ever known one uniform, one pledge, one leader."

"I think his bald head is ugly," Emilia said. "The kids at school call him *crapa pelata*, the bald-headed man. I make myself stare at his face on the side of the school for five seconds every Wednesday morning. Asia says it's good luck."

Just then one of the carders dropped from the table's edge. Shards of terracotta shattered across the tile floor.

"You broke it!" Mamma scolded.

"Well, I broke it, Mamma," Emilia said, apologetic but defensive.

"You know how many of those you've broken?" Mamma said, scolding her.

"What's done is done," Daddy said.

TWO Abandoned

Five girls sat outside the house of Emilia's best friend, their chairs aslant on the cobblestone road. They wove furiously. It was late afternoon and they knew Uncle Aldo would arrive to pick up the plaits at any moment, and they were far from finished. The tip of Emilia's right index finger tingled from weaving so intensively. She glanced over at the pile of straw that remained to be woven. Just looking at it gave her a feeling of nausea, similar to when she had fallen behind in her schoolwork during the olive harvest last year, and she wondered now as she had then how she would ever get it all done.

Emilia turned to see how the other girls were faring. Asia and Natalina were still going strong. Asia gossiped about a cute boy in her class who had pulled a bottle cap from his pocket and given it to her.

"I think he likes me," she bragged, her smile curving so far upward it almost touched her chestnut cascading curls.

"Don't be so sure," said Natalina, who sat straight as a cypress when she worked, her posture a reflection of her serious attitude. "The cap was probably just poking him, so he gave it to you rather than toss it into the field."

Emilia sensed that Asia's thoughts were somewhere else. She turned to Lirua, who showed no interest in the older girls' conversation. The same age as Emilia but a little taller and of a darker, café-latte complexion, her best friend sat quietly. Her coal-black hair barely touched her shoulders, which drooped down, as did the edges of her lips. Emilia spotted weariness. Germena, on the other hand, seemed not to feel a thing. Ever the resilient one, she wove with unabated seriousness, her broad fingers moving as quickly as they could despite their stubby shape. She rarely chatted except when something irked her, and her feelings were not usually something Emilia or anyone else wanted to hear. She had already insulted the girls for falling behind in their work, and Emilia felt her stomach knot as Germena opened her mouth.

"You're too slow, Lirua. It's an embarrassment," Germena said, pushing her thick yet uneven brown bob of hair behind her right ear with a motion that emphasized the words *slow* and *embarrassment*. "I mean, it would be one thing if you made a perfect weave, but you don't. Look how you made a mistake here. You're going to have to undo the whole section and start over."

"Come on, you can barely tell—" Lirua said, trailing off and looking down at her knees, which she pressed firmly together.

"*Guarda* . . . Look, right here," Germena insisted, grabbing the plait from Lirua. "Just look at what a slipshod job you've done. They'll never accept it down in Florence. This is an important job, did you forget? Don't act the peasant that you are."

Lirua's hands froze, and her lips quivered.

"You're only making matters worse, Germena," Emilia said. "Why don't you just leave her be?"

"And who do you think you are? Just because Lirua is a patsy and her work is sloppy," Germena shot back. "Who are you to come to her rescue? Countess Emilia, the little girl weaver," she mocked. "Right."

"*Oh smettila!* . . . Cut it out!" she said, no longer heeding Mamma's advice to bite her tongue with Germena.

The distinctive walk-then-trot then-walk-again sound of the gait of Uncle Aldo's horse engulfed Emilia with conflicting feelings of relief as well as dread. His presence would quiet Germena, but he would find the job unfinished. Emilia liked to please him.

"You're going to pay for this," Germena said, ignoring her uncle's approach. She leaned over and yanked Emilia's strand. The two of them battled in a tug-of-war, which within seconds Germena won because she was the older, bigger, and stronger girl. Emilia lost her grip, and Germena landed straight on her rear end with a loud crash as a chair toppled over beside her.

"Hey! What's going on here?" Uncle Aldo yelled as he pulled the horses to a halt in front of the stucco house and jumped down.

Nobody said a word. Silence settled in like winter fog over the valley of Prato and camouflaged the scene of recent commotion.

"Cat got your tongues?" he asked.

Germena knew she was in big trouble. She pushed herself up from the street, brushed off the back of her dress, then let the girls have it.

"They're not doing good work, uncle," she said, putting on her whiniest tattletale voice ever. "It's just plain shoddy. Look. And they're not even done."

"Well, with this fighting, who can get work done?" he said. "Looks like you're nearly finished, girls. Just this one pile to go?"

The four girls nodded.

"Well, I've got something for you. I trust you all told your mammas that it might be a late night of working? So they won't be expecting you for supper?"

More nods.

He leaned into the wagon and reappeared with a loaf of bread, paper-wrapped prosciutto, a basket of figs, and a bottle of water. He took out his hunting knife and sliced chunks of prosciutto for each girl. With the spirit of a clever *contrasto* peasant poet, he said, "The count says to the peasant: 'Don't tell anyone how well cheese goes with pears.' To which the peasant replies, 'Count, you have no clue how good figs are with prosciutto!' "[1]

The girls giggled and their mouths watered. Emilia set her teeth into the white, wrinkly skin of a Carmignano fig, dried yet soft, sweet yet spiced with a hint of anise. There was nothing like the homebred variety. The local soil and lore made them that way. The girls took pleasure in the old sayings—and Aldo collected them. He was a shameless motivator. Anything to consign an order on time. Besides, the girls loved hearing grownups poke fun at the landowning nobility, who thought they were better than the peasants. Though young, the girls grappled with a sense of inferiority that sprang from their occasional glimpses of how the wealthy families lived, yet also a sense of pride that sprang from the secrets they cultivated and kept, whether these pertained to tending a fire, weaving straw, gathering wild mushrooms, threshing wheat, curing fresh food, or "robbing" a few grapes for their father's homebrew.

"Germena, why don't you come along home with me?" Uncle Aldo said, grabbing her around the forearm and foreclosing further discussion. Looking at the girls, he added with a gentle firmness, "I'll be back for the last of the plaits after supper."

Natalina, Asia, Emilia, and Lirua finished their light supper, put on their sweaters as the chilly night air settled over the hill town, and returned to their weaving. Their work spilled over into the *veglia*, the evening social time. Lanterns flickered down the road, and before long, Lirua's mother, Raffaella, appeared barefooted from inside the house. She might have been attractive, for she was slender with fair hair and oval-shaped green eyes, had she not had such large dark circles beneath them. It was hard to see the resemblance between her and her daughter, for the girl's face still shone with the brightness of youth. Wearing a faded blue apron tied at a slant around her waist, Raffaella carried a chair, placed it near the girls, and sat down.

"Patience," she said with a sigh, leaning over, her fingers skimming the top of the straw pile. "You need a lot of patience in life." The grown woman looked at Emilia, whose rhythmic hand motions created a sort of music without melody. "You girls, you work so hard. Problem is, one day you get old. My mother-in-law is so very old, and it falls on me to take care of her. You know, when we get old we smell. So I have to bathe her twice a week. Oh, what a job! If she still had her sense of humor, it would be one thing. But no. She lost her wit about the time Lirua acquired hers. My mother-in-law's character has hardened, like old brittle straw."

Emilia glanced up as she heard the shuffle of wooden clogs nearing. The mammas of Asia and Natalina approached arm in arm. The dusky light accentuated the difference between the two women's walk: Enza struck a solid stride that suited her sturdy build, whereas Tosca swayed at the hips with each graceful step. The two women were a contrast in movement and form, slender Tosca and robust Enza, but that was only the half of it. Tosca had a distinctively modern look, especially for a rural woman; her shiny auburn hair was parted on the side and pulled back into a neat, twisted bun. She was the envy of many village women. No wonder Asia was boy crazy, though her mamma wasn't the type to fuss over such things; she was a natural beauty who took her good looks for granted. Asia often told the girls of visitors who would come from the city, eat dinner, drink wine, and talk. Her mamma would send her and her siblings off to bed. Asia would listen hard, trying to stay awake late into the evening so she could hear what they said, but she could never hear anything from their conversations but an occasional muttering of the Duce this, or the Black Shirts that, all filtered through intense emotions. Then there was Enza, whose white headscarf framed her stoic exterior. The cloth formed a line where her hair met her forehead like the base of a triangle. She pulled the headscarf taut to the back of her head, where she knotted it at the nape of her neck, the flaps of the ties like bird wings. The look struck even the young girls as a strange holdover from life in the mountains.[2]

Raffaella disappeared inside the house to fetch another two chairs. The women lost no time gathering straw in hand to help the girls finish their order. The girls launched into a diatribe about how terrible Germena had been to Lirua.

"But you should have seen how she looked, lying there on the ground like a pile of straw, when Uncle Aldo arrived," Emilia giggled.

"That poor girl, what can you expect?" said Enza, adjusting her headscarf. At thirty-eight, she had already birthed eight babies, buried two, and worked as a wet nurse, only to have her heart broken when the child was taken from her. She knew the pain of loss and felt sorry for Germena. Of course, she had the perspective of a newcomer, as she and her family had only moved to the area earlier in the year. Her husband had not had a choice—their landlord needed the family to work a farm he owned in Carmignano.

"Her daddy never intended to abandon her," said Tosca.

"Intentions or not, he did, and just look at her," added Raffaella. She tired of Germena picking on her daughter, Lirua. "Not that she was an angel before, but she gets worse and worse with each passing year."

"It's from her ordeal," Tosca said. "She can be a little aggressive."

"Is that why they're not coming back for her? Because she's bad?" asked Emilia.

"No, *ninni*, that's not it," said Tosca, who had grown up with Germena's daddy and knew Silvano well because he and her husband had been deeply involved in politics together, and she had participated from the sidelines. "Germena's daddy risked everything to escape, and he'd be risking even more to come back."

"He escaped, Mamma?" asked Asia. "How?"

"Tell us the story! Tell us the story!" Emilia and Lirua cried in unison.

"You girls just remember one thing, Silvano Santini never planned to abandon his daughter," Tosca repeated. "Sometimes a person takes a path that leads to a place they never imagine, not even in their darkest hour."

Aldo Manetti was the mellow one of his four siblings, but that wasn't saying much, as they were all rebels in their own way. It was no accident that his sister, Magdalena Manetti, had married Silvano Santini, a longstanding member of the local cooperative and a devoted communist who played a pivotal role in organizing the grain strikes of 1920. Magdalena adored his risk taking. Aldo always believed she had gone a little too far in choosing Silvano, who followed in his father's footsteps as a wheeler-dealer who sold and bought hats for the transnational market. Rare was the deal in which Silvano did not secure a favorable margin of markup. His father had trained him well, achieving an outcome that was the envy of any master-apprentice relationship: the skills of the apprentice exceeded those of the master. Despite being the successful dealer that he was, Silvano's charisma also led him to have one weakness, at least as his brother-in-law Aldo saw it. Silvano's dedication to his work paled in comparison to his passion for politics.

Silvano's heart lay with the plight of the peasants and the agricultural day laborers, in particular, but also the miners. He paid frequent visits to the sharecroppers' houses to check in with the women weavers, especially during the fall months, the season for consigning the weaving of new sample styles. In that period, he would take time out to speak with the *coloni*, the sharecropping men. Most families could barely survive the sharecropping conditions. Sure, there were a few shining stars in the constellation of sharecroppers, and the landowners made a habit of holding them up as exemplary models for the others.[3] But everyone faced the salt tax. Most households dealt with constant debts. With the rise of transoceanic competition and declining wheat prices, Tuscan agriculture shifted toward commercial farming. Landlords sought to transfer the new costs of cultivation onto the peasants. These burdens created conflict. They introduced precisely what landlords dreaded: rural trade unionism. In a countryside whose hilly terrain had long discouraged mechanized equipment and organized workers, the market changes constituted a turning point in the lives of the supposedly isolated peasants.[4]

Silvano learned that the senior men were at their wits' end having to ask permission of their landlords for matters they felt they should have the power to decide: matters related to managing the farm but also to overseeing the family. It was insulting to have to ask whether or when a son or daughter could marry and whether or when a son could leave the farm to join the priesthood. Silvano listened closely to these complaints as his work took him throughout the countryside, and he had a way of drawing out even the quieter tenant farmers who put on a good show of contentment with their station in life. He was, therefore, ideally positioned to spread the word about plans for a strike. He was committed to advancing the cause. Until, that is, the situation worsened.

"Emi, you and Lirua were just babies," said Tosca, "but people in '20 were on a collision course. Have you ever ridden the carousel in the Piazza del Duomo, in the center of Prato?"

The girls nodded. They had done so once, together in fact.

"Well, imagine that kind of motion. Grown-ups were whirling with excitement."

Tosca explained to the children the political events of seven years ago but then found herself responding to Enza's questions. Emilia and the girls tuned in and out, working and talking among themselves. Tosca reminisced about how leftists had ridden a wave that had surged across Europe in the wake of the Russian Revolution. Labor struggles rocked the Italian peninsula from urban factories to rural fields. Workers dreamed of a utopian future. A factory council movement in the northern Italian city of Turin evolved into the most hopeful yet epic struggle of all. Workers in the huge Fiat plants sought to replace capitalist management with workplace councils, and they occupied factories in a monthlong strike. The state responded with a massive show of force.[5]

"Here in Carmignano even farmworkers went on strike," Tosca said, turning back to the girls. "February 1920. Now that was a month to remember. Your friends' daddies tried to get new contracts. They wanted a say in things."

"Farmworkers on strike?" Asia asked. "How?"

"*Bah!* They refused to go into the fields," answered Raffaella, Lirua's mamma. "After a few days, the *fattore* came around. The countess, now, she had a farm manager with a reputation. *Mangione,* we called him. The big eater. He was a hulk of a man. He had eyebrows so thick they nearly grew together like a single woolly caterpillar, a neck as broad as an olive tree trunk, wide shoulders, and a belly so big it would have taken two of you girls to reach around it. And did he ever have a temper! He was quick to blow. The only thing slow about him was his walk. He slogged along like a mule pulling a cart loaded down with demijohns filled with wine. His pace made him a keen observer, and it didn't take him long to see that the fields were empty. One afternoon during pruning season he showed up and knocked on Lirua's grandma and grandpa's door—my mom and dad. It must have been around 2:30, as Mamma was still washing up from lunch. Mangione fumed: 'Why was nobody out in the fields this morning?' Daddy just poured him a tall glass of Vin Santo, pulling out a kitchen chair. They sat and talked for hours. Daddy knew how to soften up the *fattore.*"

"So they won?" asked Emilia.

"*Ma che! . . .* Not hardly!" Tosca said, glancing over at Enza. "But the factory workers over in Prato got their eight-hour day. And so did the farmhands."[6]

"Imagine! Only eight hours!" Raffaella quipped. *"Che bella vita!"*

"Germena is a living testament to the fiasco—" Tosca added.

"As is the *podestà!*" Raffaella said.

"That socialist mayor would be in office instead if the Duce had given me the vote," Tosca said.

"You and my husband," Raffaella added.

"Why?" asked Natalina, who, as the newest girl to the area, listened closely.

"People were out of work," Tosca continued. "Food prices skyrocketed. Times were tough. The fascists spread their propaganda. They blamed hard times on the socialists in power. As winter gave way to spring," she paused, glancing over at Enza, "the fascists turned tragedy to their favor. It came after two *carabinieri* were murdered."

"Ma senti . . . Just listen. Who were these fellows?" asked Enza. "Did they have families?"

"One of them had three kids, the other four," Raffaella replied.

"Real opportunists, those fascists," Tosca continued. "They blamed two local socialists. Called them antipatriotic. Killing state policemen proved they were traitors, they said. Then the fascists vindicated the murdered officers: they set fire to the food cooperative. Also the local headquarters of the socialist party."

"Ma senti," said Enza. "What a story."

"Capito?" Tosca said. "The more violent things got, the more pumped up the fascists became. They stopped citizens from voting if they suspected they were socialist or communist. They blocked them from joining the electoral commission. They were crazy with aggression well into the summer until—"

"It was horrible," interjected Raffaella.

Emilia and Lirua were still as statues. Asia dropped her plaits. Natalina stared at Tosca.

"Tell us, what happened?"

"It is a very sad story," Tosca said. "Maybe I shouldn't tell you."

"No. Tell us! Tell us!" Emilia demanded.

Tosca paused. *"Va ben . . .* okay." Her voice lowered nearly to a whisper. "One night a group of fascists went to the house of a well-known antifascist. They went to his door. He opened it. On his threshold, well, they killed him. Right at the front door to his home in Poggetto. *Veramente* . . . Really."[7]

"Can you imagine?" Enza said, glancing down at her hands so that no one would see her face flushing with emotion. She was not easily moved to tears.

"It was horrible. For everyone. Especially for that family. *Povera donna* . . . poor woman," Tosca said. "People were afraid, and the fascists knew it. But not Silvano. He was a great organizer. Communist to the core. A real heart of gold. Always had the people at heart. You might say he didn't see eye to eye with fascism. But then the tide turned with the March on Rome.[8] You girls would have been two years old."

"Wait," said Emilia. "Marching?"

"*Bah!* The Black Shirts filled the piazzas and the bars," Tosca continued. "We were frightened. There were stories. Whoever defied the Duce disappeared. One by one. Abandoned on islands, penal colonies far out at sea, they said. *Capito?* Silvano had his family to think about. What would happen to his wife and children if he were taken prisoner? He began plotting his escape. Several close friends helped him."

"Who?" asked Asia.

"Even now, five years later, I can't tell you who they were. It's still too dangerous."

"But—" Emilia began.

"The fascists do not take well to those who disagree with them," Raffaella explained.

"That's right," said Tosca.

"But how did he escape?" Emilia said.

"Do you really care to know?"

"*Per piacere.* . . . Please. Tell us!" the girls said in unison.

"Silvano had lots of connections," continued Tosca. "His family had been in the hat business forever. Somebody put him in touch with a man in Florence, a shipping contractor who had a friend in the port of Genoa. He knew of a captain who had a shipment to take to America. They said Argentina.

"Silvano knew he had to act fast. The fascists were onto him. He could sense the crackdown. He had to be careful. He decided to travel on a Sunday. Can you guess why?"

"So he could go to church first?" offered Emilia.

"Communists weren't exactly the first in line to take communion," laughed Raffaella.

"So he could travel on a full stomach?" guessed Lirua.

"*Brava! . . .* Excellent guess!" Tosca said. "Silvano was one who liked to eat. But no. Fewer police were on duty on Sundays. Plus he wanted to blend in with the families traveling. So after *pranzo,* he left in the early afternoon. He took a train to Florence and then transferred to an express to Genoa. I saw him before he left, carrying just a small leather suitcase. He didn't want to draw attention to himself by carrying a lot of luggage. He'd sit in second class, the kind with the facing seats. He would have felt safer in the company of others.

"When he arrived in Genoa, you can imagine how his heart must have been racing for fear that word of his escape might have leaked. What he did was very risky. Silvano was quick to find his point man. He helped him board the ship. Another man helped him stow away in a crate of straw hats. The same kind you girls make. That's right, he was there right along with the hats, and that's how he fled to America."

"Does it take a long time for a ship to get to America?" Lirua asked.

"Did he stay inside that crate the whole time?" Emilia demanded.

"Well, I have no idea," Tosca said. "They just say he stowed away in the crate of hats, that's all I know."

"I bet he got out to eat," said Asia.

"I bet the captain snuck him food and water," Natalina surmised.

"Poor Germena," said Enza. "Just to think, here was her father, this Silvano, trying to do something right for his family, to avoid being abandoned on an island at sea. And then he abandons one of his own."

"Well, it was hardly an accident. You know, when he left, when he and Magdalena were deciding what to do—before she and the other kids set off to join him in America—Aldo said to him, 'Leave me the girl, at least—' and he left him Germena."

"Why not the other children?" Enza asked.

"I don't know," Tosca said. "Nobody around here ever talked about that much. But I think it was her character."

"Or maybe her age," Enza speculated. "I always thought if they had come to take my wet nurse baby away from me a few years earlier, it wouldn't have been as heartbreaking as it was. When a child is five or six, they're really attached to their mamma. The other kids were older, weren't they?"

"Yes, Germena was the youngest," Tosca answered. "She would have just been three."

"So maybe they thought she would be easier to leave behind," Enza said. "They thought she'd forget."

"Boy, were they wrong," Raffaella said.

Emilia thought about the postcards that arrived every so often with the stamps from Argentina. She could only imagine what it must be like for Germena to have been left behind. She almost forgave Germena for her ill temper. Maybe if her mamma and daddy came back for her she would change. In any event, Emilia would never forget what had led to Germena's destiny, and she, along with her friends, would grow up and pass these memories on to the next generation. Trauma would leave its traces on them as well.

Just then Aldo came up the road. The girls and their mammas had gotten carried away and had forgotten about finishing the job, but there wasn't too much left to do. He took a seat with them and saw the project through to its conclusion. Raffaella swept up the last bits of straw that lay on the street. They all said goodnight. Since it was now late, Aldo gave Emilia and the other two girls a ride home through the narrow roads lined with dark houses.

THREE Telling Time

Emilia heard yells and a loud thud, so she dashed across the yard and into the shadowy barn to investigate. Boys' voices surrounded her in the darkness. As her eyes adjusted to the dim light, her little brother Carlo came into focus, wavy bangs brushing across his big brown eyes. He pulled on the corner of a crate with a gash across the side. Amerigo, the scrawny neighbor boy with a hatchet haircut, climbed out with a bloody scrape on his shoulder.

"My turn!" Carlo insisted, pushing Amerigo out of the way with the force of a two-year-old whose will far outmatched his size. "My turn to hide."

Sergio seized a stick and held it like a gun. The quintessential big brother, he reveled in the role of playing the tough guy: "Fine, but I'm the police coming to take him to the island, where he can't spread his lies."

"I'm not pretending to row the boat all night long," protested Amerigo as he picked up a weathered, short plank of wood.

Emilia neared the action. "I'll play one of the men at the secret communist meeting."

"Forget it, you're a girl," said Sergio.

"So what?" Emilia's skinny seven-year-old arms were planted firmly on her hips, and her bony elbows created sassy triangles at each side. Sergio made her so mad when he acted as if he were in charge just because he was five years older than she was.

"So you can't play a boy," Sergio said.

"Then I'll be a communist girl at the meeting," she proposed.

"That's highly improbable," said Sergio. "The Communist Party isn't even allowed anymore."[1]

"Who says?" Emilia protested. "You just make things up to suit you. It's just like the last time we played. You ruin all the fun."

Carlo crawled into the crate and Sergio poked his gun into his side. "You're caught, dirty communist."

"No, no! Let me go," cried Carlo in his whiny little-brother voice.

"You bloody fool!" Sergio replied. "Hands up. Subversives like you must be removed from circulation."

Emilia, realizing that she had a dead-end role in this game, looked up in distraction. Against the doorjamb, a girl stood backlit, her arms crossed. Emilia's stomach knotted as she made out the silhouette.

"Germena?" Emilia asked, her voice shaking mid-syllable. "Uh, do you want to play?"

"Uncle Aldo has a job," Germena replied, her tone decidedly curt. She began to leave, then turned back. "He sent me to round up some girls. If you want the job, come soon." She left without waiting for Emilia's response, her gaze fixed forward and her walk swift.

Emilia felt a hole in her gut as she realized what Germena had seen. She turned to Sergio. "How long do you think she was standing there?"

"No idea," he answered, leaning on his stick and chewing a blade of straw. "But what of it?"

"You idiot," she said. "I quit."

"I'm going home," said Amerigo, tossing the wood overboard and abandoning ship.

"I want to play!" Carlo protested, emerging from the crate.

Sergio dropped his stick. He and the younger kids stepped out into the yard where Great-Uncle Giovanbattista leaned at some distance from his friend Maurizio against the cement wall that surrounded the well. Their uncle's wavy white hair glistened in the sunlight, and his leathery hands grasped the rock wall. His fingernails were thick and curled, yellowed and untrimmed, good for picking food out of his remaining teeth or for using as a screwdriver. Despite his unkempt appearance, he was hardly a typical peasant. Like his siblings, he could read. Giovanbattista's brother, who was Emilia's granddaddy, shared his convictions for education and had married a like-minded woman. The couple had made sure all the Raugeis knew how to read and write. That was no small feat back then. No public elementary school existed, yet Emilia's *nonna* had managed to send all of her sons to a priest who taught them to read and write. Despite the instruction, the kinfolk from the older generation had a thick and guttural way of talking. And they had some strange names too. Still, her uncle took pride in being from a literate family, and he passed this sensibility on to his kin for two generations, in particular his nephew Emilio Raugei, Emilia's father. He had his family to thank for his literacy, which for his cohort was as uncommon as meat at the dinner table.

Perhaps that's what had initially drawn him to Maurizio. A well-educated man, Maurizio worked as a notary for the county government and had managed to keep his position even with the regime change. Giovanbattista did not hide his resentment about Maurizio's new political allegiance despite the history the two men shared. They had worked together to establish the socialist food cooperative in the 1910s, and they had served on the co-op's board together up until five years ago, when the order of life had turned fascist. Ultimately, Maurizio had abandoned the cause to keep his job. As time wore on, Maurizio increasingly sided with the landowning class of people from which he came. Giovanbattista, on the other hand, was deeply committed to socialist causes. On occasion, he revealed himself to be a philosopher in his own right, capable of critical self-reflection as well as insightful analyses of local and even national events. As a bachelor, he didn't bear the headaches or responsibilities of a *capofamiglia,* the patriarchal head of household. He indulged himself in politics and the company of his like-minded friends—though that company dwindled with each passing year.

As the two men chatted, Emilia took a clue from the limited words being exchanged and the space between them that something was amiss. Uncle Giovanbattista stared straight ahead as he spoke. Maurizio left without even giving her uncle an *arrivederci*. Only later would the children fully grasp the source of the rift.

"Ermina," he called to Emilia as she and her brothers appeared from the barn. "*Che otta è*—what eight is it?"

Emilia ignored him at first, then cast him a sideways glance. She viewed his way of speaking as a backward dialect, it was so ugly and incorrect. At school, the teachers taught her proper Italian.

"If you ask me, 'What time is it?' I'll tell you. If not, I'm not telling you a thing," she replied, speaking in her updated dialect, which still carried a rural lilt, and addressing him with the formal *voi*, plural for you, to show respect.[2]

"Have it your way," her uncle said. "What time is it, then?"

Emilia stepped toward him as he held out his arm. "Two-thirty," she relented, looking up from his watch. "Two-thirty, Uncle Giovanbattista," and she giggled, glancing over at Sergio. They had both agreed that Giovanbattista, or John the Baptist, was a ridiculous name to give a child. How old fashioned! Besides, who could ever live up to that?

"Two-thirty. Let's go, then," he said. "Everyone to Maurizio's house, that selfish excuse of a man. The Duce is giving his Ascension Day Speech at three o'clock, and we'd be wise to hear what we're in store for."

"What is it, uncle?" she asked.

"Another blow, I can guarantee you, that's what we peasants are in for. Nothing less. You heard it from your old uncle first."

Mamma joined them, and Emilia with her brothers and her oldest sister, Hamidie, followed the two white-haired men up the lane and into the heart of the village to Maurizio's house. Daddy, with the excuse of his fieldwork, would not be coming. Carlo was napping and stayed home with Matilde and Maria.

Mamma and her uncle walked a few strides ahead, but the breeze was in Emilia's favor for eavesdropping.

"I worry about you, Giovanbattista," Mamma said. "You've hardened."

"The world I was born into is not the same. It's changing far too fast for my own good, not to mention the good of the children. The forces are stronger than me, than any of us. They're shaping not only our history but our relationships with others, like it or not. I may not be wise enough to be a certified organic intellectual, but you know I've always aspired to be, in my own humble way."[3]

"You're bona fide, all right." Mamma smirked. "Any more humble and you'd disappear into oblivion."

Giovanbattista had moved with his brothers to the hamlet of Comeana from the hilltop county seat of Carmignano when they were mere boys in the 1860s, the culminating decade of the great Risorgimento. His generation came of age learning songs that sang the praises of Garibaldi for organizing the rebellions that had unified the peninsula.[4] As he matured, Giovanbattista came to believe through reading editorials in his favorite newspaper that the hero of liberal nationalism had ultimately failed to stamp Italy's unification with a popular and democratic character.[5]

Giovanbattista kept abreast of politics for years as a regular at the co-op, where he'd read *L'Ordine Nuovo*, the journal of the Turin factory council movement, and, with even more frequency, *L'Unità*, before its founder, Antonio Gramsci, was thrown into prison along with two dozen other elected communist parliamentarians. That's when things began to deteriorate between the two men. Giovanbattista marked November 21, 1926, as the breaking point. The date was branded into his memory. He had stopped into the old co-op, long since converted into a fascist club. Maurizio was leaning against the bar when Giovanbattista took a seat at a table nearby, picked up the newspaper, and began reading aloud. "Listen to this, Maurizio, they've arrested Gramsci. Just listen to what the prosecutor said: 'We must prevent this brain from functioning for twenty years.' "[6] Maurizio didn't flinch. He looked up just long enough to cast a cold glance over the wire rim of his glasses. For Giovanbattista, that was it: he knew their connection was broken.

"You know, Giovanna, it's no simple feat to raise consciousness in the countryside, but it's not impossible either," he said to Emilia's mother. "The seeds are already there, and only a foolish count is blind to that.

The fear of standing up to the *signore* runs deep in our beings, to be sure. You know as well as I that rare is the *mezzadro* who can bear the thought of having his brethren thrown off 'their' land—all the more so if they've toiled it for generations."

"Show me a sharecropper who declines to submit half of the harvest or to deliver on his duties and deeds, and I'll show you a count who goes to the river to stir the ashes into his bed sheets!" Mamma said.

"That'll be the day! Best to just prepare the annual prosciutto, two capons, eight dozen eggs, and—what is it now—six new brooms?—than risk being thrown off the farm. Getting back at the *signori* calls for cunning. Show me a peasant who doesn't rob a little of the fall harvest for his own stash of Vin Ruspo, and I'll show you a day laborer who refuses to drink from a fresh mountain spring. Why last season we snuck the grapes and mashed the fruit right there with our feet. When the foreman wasn't looking, I hid the demijohn under the vines. In the dark of the night I went back for it. But hear me out: these sorts of actions are the seeds of protest. These are the kernels of reform. You're certainly not going to find it in the self-loathing peasant who gets himself a hand-loom, hides it away in his barn to make some extra lire, only to abandon the cause and become a social striver."

As they approached Maurizio's house, several neighbors advanced from the opposite direction. The green shutter was propped open to reveal the freshly lacquered wooden door with white lace curtains that covered the glass pane. Emilia and her brothers dashed ahead of their mother and uncle, stopping at the threshold to wait for the adults before heading inside.

Giovanbattista slowed to allow Mamma to go ahead and enter first. As she started through the door, she turned to him. "Careful, Giovan,'" she whispered over her shoulder.

Leaning toward her, he said, just loud enough for Emilia to catch: "The hottest places in hell are reserved for those who in times of great moral crises maintain their neutrality."

FOUR Fascist Folk

Emilia settled onto the chilly marble floor. Maurizio's house smelled of burnt garlic. She wrinkled up her nose to close out the offensive odor. Relief arrived as lanky Lirua walked in with her mamma, looking tired as ever. Emilia scooted over and patted the floor just in time for Lirua to plop down beside her. Emilia smiled, forgetting the bad smell. There was nothing like a best friend. She and Lirua shared so much: their toils, their troubles, their trust.

Several dozen people soon crowded into the living room. A brown, rectangular radio with curvy edges and a round inset speaker sat atop an end table. The guests gathered around it, and soon lively chatter filled the room, a testament to the excitement of partaking in a rare experience of listening to a human voice speaking to them from afar. Hardly anyone could afford a radio in their own home. Before long, the air became stuffy.

Aldobrando appeared with Germena in tow. He was as chipper as she was gloomy. Her round cheeks puffed up with poutiness. Emilia tried hard to avoid her gaze as the hatter and his niece neared the seated girls.

Aldo squatted down, his furry brown brows almost touching Emilia's pale forehead. "Mind if I bring by some work tomorrow?" he asked.

Emilia nodded, relieved that he hadn't said anything about the communist game. Aldo stood up and Germena followed him to find an empty spot across the room, where the pair sat down.

The mood turned tense as the adult villagers exchanged predictions about the policies the dictator would announce.

"As for migration, I'd put money on the Duce not budging one iota," Giovanbattista asserted.

"*A' voglia . . .* you bet," said Aldo. "If only it weren't the case."

Maurizio stepped through the villagers crowded into his living room. He was dressed for the occasion, his shirt collar neatly pressed beneath his lightweight pullover. He approached the radio, leaned over, and turned a black knob to the "on" position. Loud static assaulted the guests' ears.

"Doesn't always have the best signal," he apologized, then rotated the tuner knob. The station did not matter since the government required all stations to broadcast Premier Mussolini's speech. The world listened, too. The controversial content led it to be reported the following day on the front page of the *New York Times* and published in its entirety on Sunday. After all, the year 1927 marked five years of the world's first fascist regime. Its significance was still hotly disputed within the Italian Communist Party, international labor organizations, and political parties everywhere.

Uncle Giovanbattista and his friends spent many an evening arguing about whether fascism was merely a phenomenon specific to Italy or whether it would become an international trend. He argued that it was a way to suppress labor. Some alleged, and Giovanbattista tended to agree, that fascism could best be understood as a brutal instrument of big capital's dominance, but the jury was still out.[1]

Maurizio looked up from the radio at his full house of guests.

"At the fascist club this morning they said the speech will have three parts and that he will lay out his vision for a greater, more powerful, more resplendent Italy," proclaimed Maurizio.[2]

"At what price?" shot back Giovanbattista from an armchair.

A radio announcer spoke behind the cacophony of voices filling the room, which now rose to a formidable volume.

"*Silenzio!*" shouted Maurizio. "Quiet. It's starting."

A hush settled over the listeners as Mussolini's trademark charismatic cadence broadcast from the Chamber of Deputies in Rome, some 185 miles to the south.

"*How are we faring? What is the picture of our present situation? The Italian race, the Italian people in their physical expression, are they in a period of splendor or are there symptoms of decay? If development takes a step backwards what are the forecasts for the future? These queries are important, not only for professional doctors, not only for those who follow sociological doctrines, but above all for statesmen.*

"*So let me say that the picture in this regard is very gray.*"[3]

Uncle Giovanbattista shifted in his chair. "Fear tactics, he relies on fear," he scowled.

"Don't be so old-fashioned, old comrade," Maurizio scolded.

As still as a statue, Giovanbattista stared toward the source of the broadcast. Emilia sensed her uncle's discomfort. She caught a glimpse of the profile of an old man, a distinctive bend on the bridge of his nose, high cheekbones, and deep-set dark eyes, and she imagined that he might have once been handsome. Daddy had always said that he had been painfully shy as a boy and that when he wasn't working in the fields or tending to his secret stash of aged wine he was at the club. Daddy accused Giovanbattista of wrapping himself in the "protective cloth of politics." For Emilia, the phrase conjured up the image of a man wearing a heavy, black woolen coat on a wintry night.

Emilia watched his pained expression as the fascist leader warned of worsening social maladies and boasted about public health improvements.

"*Under the direct charge of the organs of the Public Health Department, 10,000 ships have been disinfected and ridden of rats which carry contagious diseases from the East—from the East which brings us so many pleasant things like yellow fever and Bolshevism."*

"Just listen to him!" objected Uncle Giovanbattista. "Likening Bolshevism to yellow fever and rats. The struggles of the working classes, he's assaulting them."

"Hush!" Maurizio commanded. "Those days are finished. You know you cannot speak that way, Giovan."

"Where's the dignity? Talking about our struggles as though they are a contagious disease? What of my cousin who joined with a thousand workers in Prato to sign the salary agreement of 1919 with the owners of ninety small textile firms of Prato? They were *all* socialists.[4] Listen to what he's saying! Carriers of the fever he would have us all."

Giovanbattista knew better than to speak so directly against the Duce, but he couldn't help himself. No one said a word. His family and friends let it go, turning their gazes back to the radio and their attention to the Duce's words.

"We must seriously watch the destinies of our race. We must cure our race, beginning with maternity and infancy. This is the precise object of the National Foundation for the Protection of Maternity and Infancy. From a lack of funds there sprang the idea of the tax on bachelors, which may in the not very distant future be followed by a tax on barren marriages."

Lively comments and assenting voices from the Chamber of Deputies filled the airwaves.

"Do you really believe that I introduced it merely to raise money? No. I merely took advantage of this tax to give the nation the lash of a demographic whip."

Giovanbattista rose, reached his fist over the opposite shoulder, and feigned dramatic lashes of self-flagellation. "And I already have the welts to show for it," he said.

Emilia, Lirua, and their mammas laughed. Everyone knew how it irked her uncle to have to pay a tax when he had been a bachelor all his life. Now, as he neared his sixth decade of life, marriage was not even a remote possibility, and the annual tax of eighty-five lire felt, as he colorfully described it, like a dead-center kick in the balls.[5]

"Some intelligent people say we are too many. The majority of intelligent people reply, we are too few."

Murmurs of assent from the chamber led Mussolini to pause for several seconds before resuming his speech.

"I affirm that the fundamental, if not the absolutely essential datum, for the political and therefore the economic and moral power of nations is their ability to increase their population.

"Let us speak quite clearly. What are 40 million Italians compared to 90 million Germans and 200 million Slavs? Let us turn toward the West. What are 40 million Italians compared to 40 million Frenchmen plus the 90 million inhabitants of France's colonies, or compared to 46 million Englishmen plus 450 million who live in England's colonies?

"Gentlemen, if Italy is to amount to anything it must enter into the second half of this century with a population of at least 60 million inhabitants."

Maurizio stood up and joined the cries of assent from the Chamber of Deputies. Emilia and Lirua giggled, then glanced at their mothers, who looked puzzled.

"The fact remains that the fate of nations is intimately bound up with their powers of reproduction."

"Did I hear that right?" muttered Raffaella to Paola and Tosca.

"If he thinks I'm about to start having more babies to populate his army—" Tosca began.

"Little Italians are taught to respect the Duce," interjected Sergio, ever the authority figure as the oldest boy in the family. "We have to make sacrifices. We have to be as tight as the fasces of ancient Rome."

"Ah, you are a well-educated boy, I see," piped Giovanbattista. "From our Little Italians, what more could we expect?"

"Enough already," said Maurizio. "You were invited to come and listen. *Silenzio!*"

"The five-year period of the greatest birth rate was between 1881 and 1885, when it stood at 38 per 1,000. Since then, we have been decreasing steadily and have now reached 27. . . . The regions which are still above this figure are, first, Basilicata, and I send her my sincere congratulations because she thus shows her vitality and her strength. Evidently Basilicata is not yet infected with the pernicious currents of contemporary civilization."

Lively comments filled the Chamber. Several adults in Maurizio's living room began to whisper among themselves.

"The regions which are below the 27 mark are Lombardy, Tuscany, Piedmont, Liguria and the Provinces of Trento and Trieste."[6]

"Ah, so no longer is the South the ball and chain of the North but the North is the sterile ball and chain of the South?" challenged the uncle.

"Giovanbattista!" Maurizio said.

"Come on, we all know that the North was like an octopus, using its tentacles to take from the South," he continued. "To modernize, what agenda is this?"

"I'm warning you . . ." Maurizio's face was grape-red.

Emilia glanced at Hamidie, who looked concerned, then leaned over to Lirua. "Do you think he'll report him?"

"He's sure fired up," Lirua said, looking at Maurizio.

"I have to admit," Emilia said, swallowing before she continued, "I'm frightened."

"Nor is this enough. There is a type of urbanism which is destructive, which renders our people sterile. It is industrial urbanism.

"Do you think that when I speak of the ruralization of Italy I do so only out of love of beautiful phrases which, instead, I detest? But, no, I am like a doctor who does not neglect symptoms, and these are symptoms which must give us furiously to think. And what do these considerations lead to? First, that industrial urbanism leads to sterility of population, and, second, that small rural property leads to the same result. Add to these two factors the infinite moral cowardice of the so-called upper classes of society, and you have a complete picture."

The deputies from Rome once again began to cheer, and Giovanbattista took it as his cue.

"If they hadn't arrested Gramsci and the other leaders of the Communist Party you would be hearing cries of dissent," he said. *"Ma dai . . .* Come on. Do you really think he has any intention of helping the working class to achieve dominance?"

"It takes fascist courage to speak like he does," Maurizio shot back.

"Che coraggio! Courage my ass."

"If we decrease in numbers, gentlemen, we never will create an empire, but become a colony. It was time that these things should be said, otherwise we would

continue to live in a reign of false and lying illusions, which must fatally lead to severe delusions. This explains to you why I do everything to help agriculture, why I proclaim myself a convinced ruralist."

Applause cut through the Duce's proclamation, and Giovanbattista stood up from his chair and clapped along.

"Ah, fascist folk we have become," he interrupted. "I too am a convinced ruralist. My good sister-in-law convinced me not to move to the city but to stay here on the farm. I suspect it was just because she likes my Vin Santo."

Everyone laughed except for Maurizio. His eyes were fixated on the radio. The topic shifted to political reorganization, a subject that interested him deeply given his employment for the county government.

"Meanwhile we have nominated podestas to take the place of elected Mayors in all municipalities. When we first mentioned podestas, there were not a few who shed tears over the disappearance of the old elective system . . . But the fact remains that all these podestas, or nearly all, are governing with the full, and often enthusiastic, support of their populations. . . ."

As Mussolini spoke of the state's police forces, of his crackdown on delinquency, of letters as well as telegrams received from the "healthy" members of the population who thanked the government for its actions, Emilia noticed Mamma whispering with Raffaella and Tosca. She could not make out what they said. Her thoughts drifted to an image of Mussolini's bald head on the front of the school building as he boasted about fascist successes, the work of *carabinieri,* police, and customs guards in their fight against criminality.

"On the whole Western frontier there are not more than 900 Black Shirts and they, alas, having nothing to do except with bad Italians who would like to leave the country and bad Italians who would like to re-enter it."

"This does not bode well for Silvano," Tosca said to Mamma, speaking now in a louder voice.

"I'll say not," Mamma said. "It's not exactly the best time to come home now anyway. You'd have to be a *bischero,* a half-wit."

"Hush," insisted Maurizio. "He's getting to the third part of his speech where he deals with political action. Remember the assassination attempt last October in Bologna?"

"I remember the *alleged* assassination attempt," Giovanbattista asserted.

"*Basta!* ... Enough! There was violent emotion all over Italy," Maurizio said. "The Duce had to take necessary steps for the good of the country."

"There was never any proof!" Giovanbattista countered. "Of course people went to the streets. The assassination was merely an excuse to take away our rights."

Maurizio glared, and his eye contact with Giovanbattista was enough to quiet him, but no matter, for the premier proceeded to outline the rights that had been taken away in the name of social good.

"It was necessary for our revolution to dig its toes in against anti-revolution. It was then that on this very piece of paper that I am now showing you I wrote in pencil a complete outline of measures which were to be taken. The withdrawal and revision of all passports for foreign countries, an order to fire upon any one attempting to cross the frontier clandestinely, the suppression of all anti-Fascist daily and periodical publications, the dissolution of all anti-Fascist groups and organizations, the deportation of all those who plot against the Fascist revolution or who illicitly wear the Black Shirt, the creation of special police in all regions and the creation of a special tribunal for investigation."

As Mussolini boasted about applying repressive measures "with intelligence," Giovanbattista sighed in disgust.

"*Che mondo* ... What a world," Giovanbattista snapped.

Maurizio looked on nervously. "Shhh. Listen, he's talking about the penal islands."

Mussolini was challenging the international press's claim that some two hundred thousand men had been sent to forced domicile in the islands. The Duce claimed the number was 1,527, a fraction of the rumored calculation; then he read from letters of prisoners promising to abandon all political activities and responded with laughter to their pleas.

"Some people talk of amnesty. No, gentlemen, there will be no amnesty. There will not be any amnesty before 1932, and then one will talk of it only if, as I sincerely hope, it will not be necessary to extend the life of our special laws for the defense of the State."

"It's a good thing Silvano left when he did," Tosca said. "Or else he would have surely been at sea until 1932."

"If he was lucky," said Raffaella. "Lucky for him and Magdalena and the children that they got out when they did. What with all the Black Shirts at the borders."

Everyone was silent. Emilia wondered if the others were thinking what she was: *Not so lucky for Germena.*

A scuffle arose from the other side of the room. Germena stood up. Her face was flushed.

"I hate them!" Germena screamed. "I'm not going there tomorrow. You can't make me."

Uncle Aldo forced a smile. "Now, now, Germena," he said. "Calm down. Nobody meant it like it sounded."

Germena turned and glared straight at Emilia. "You're awful. You're all just awful. I hate you all!" She ran out of the house and slammed the door behind her.

Uncle Aldo stood up and looked out at the gathering of shocked villagers. He shrugged. "I'd better go after her. Who knows what she'll do when she's this angry."

Lirua looked at Emilia. "*Cha ha?* . . . What's wrong with her?"

Emilia looked toward the door. "Oh, I don't know."

"She looked straight at you."

"Oh, well, you know how she is."

"Tell me, tell me, tell me."

"Well, there was just a little something that happened in the barn," Emilia confessed.

"Just a *little* something?"

"Well, all right, me and my brothers and the neighbor boy were playing this game."

"Uh-huh?"

"We were making like there was this communist guy who was captured and what not—"

"Yeah?"

"And Germena walked in."

"So?"

"So? She walked in just as we were playing catch-the-communist. Lirua, I've never seen her look so sad. I thought she was going to cry."

"Is this terror, gentlemen? No! It is hardly even severity. Is it terrorism? No! These measures are measures of social hygiene, of national prophylactics. I re-moved certain individuals from contact with their fellow-men, as a doctor would segregate one affected with infectious disease. . . .[7]

"*Opposition is not necessary for the proper working of a healthy political regime. Opposition is stupid.*"

"How can he expect anyone to buy that?" asked Giovanbattista.

"My friend," Maurizio said, looking almost sorrowful, "we fascists carry opposition inside ourselves."

"*Therefore, let nobody hope that after this speech he will see anti-Fascist newspapers appearing again or that we shall permit anti-Fascist groups to form again. Never!*"

Between Maurizio claiming the moral high ground and Mussolini leaving no hope for a future alternative to fascism, Giovanbattista was beside himself. Emilia had never seen him show such emotion. He stood, waving his arms, and shouted back at the radio.

"Calm down, calm down," Maurizio insisted. "Mussolini has ways of knowing what's happening even in the most obscure village. Sooner or later, he will reach out his sword and strike. The country needs discipline, it needs moral strength."

"Listen to what's happening," replied Giovanbattista, his breathing as desperate as that of an old man who had just run from the center of town to his farmhouse. "And the deputies cheer him. Outrageous. They are nothing but sheep."

"Sheep have brains."

"Chickens then. Squawk. Squawk. Squawk."

"Quiet, if someone should hear you."

"Oh what of it? I'm an old man. 'One must be somewhat ashamed of one's old age.' The Duce said it. What threat am I? Just an old bachelor, required now to pay that damned tax."

"Giovanbattista, don't be so critical. After all, it's for the women and children and the state. The country needs more people if it is to become a modern power."

"Like a chicken needs teeth."

As Giovanbattista forced himself to turn his last ounce of attention toward the closing words of Mussolini's speech, Emilia swore the Duce was speaking directly to her great-uncle:

"The generation of die-hards who did not understand the war and who have not understood Fascism will at a certain moment be eliminated by natural processes. Their place will be taken by young men, by workmen and peasants who are now in our battle organization, which gives us the means of controlling the life of the country from six to sixty years and creates the new Italian, the Fascist Italian. . . .

"Five years ago I thought that after five years I would have finished the major part of my work. Now I see I have not. I am convinced that, despite the gradual creation of a directing class, despite the ever growing discipline of the people, I must take upon myself the task of governing the Italian people for 10 or 15 years more, if necessary, not because I am lustful for power but because it is my precise duty. My successor is not yet born."

Loud and prolonged applause vibrated the speaker, distorting the broadcast.

"What?" interrupted Giovanbattista, who this time expressed the sentiments of surprise of everyone in the room.

"It's true," Maurizio said. "At the club this week there was talk of revolutionizing the state machine. It's to begin at year's end. The idea is to create a corporative state to solve the problem of parliament."

"The Chamber of tomorrow cannot resemble that of today. Today, May 26, we solemnly bury the falsehood of universal democratic suffrage."

Resounding applause from the radio broadcast again filled the room, almost hypnotizing the listeners.

"Perhaps things will be better," Maurizio said hopefully. "There will be less corruption without an electoral system of opposing parties. We will all work together. The Chamber of Deputies will become an organ of the corporative-state."

"And how on earth will the deputies be chosen?" asked Tosca.

"Instead of by the people directly, a Charter of Labor will create national corporations, and those corporations will elect the deputies."

"Fascists from top to bottom," Giovanbattista said. "Like onions. My eyes water. Layers upon layers of onions and as pervasive as parsley."

"Now, now, Giovan. Even the men and women in the most remote village of the country have their share of responsibility," Maurizio said. "To be true to the revolution is to concern ourselves with moral order. Elections breed opposition to the collectivity, to the State."

Mussolini moved on to promote the need to bolster and perfect the armed forces. He called for an army five million strong.

"Today we announce to the world the creation of a new, powerful, Unitarian Italian State from the Alps to Sicily. This State is composed of a kind of concentrated, organized, authoritative democracy. In this democracy people can settle down at their ease because, gentlemen, either you admit the people into the citadel of the State, in which case they will defend it, or you leave them outside, in which case they will attack it.

"Gentlemen, I tell you that in ten years' time Italy, this Italy of yours, will be unrecognizable to itself and to foreigners because we will have radically transformed not only its face but, which is far more important, above all its soul."

Prolonged cheers from the Chamber of Deputies were so enthusiastic they seemed to almost burst the radio speakers. The listeners imagined the deputies on their feet as they applauded the Duce. They broke into song, with visitors in the galleries obviously joining in the singing of fascist war songs.

"Oh *dio bono*. For god's sake," Giovanbattista pleaded. "Please shut that garbage off. I can't take it any longer."

Maurizio ignored him and let the bellicose songs fill the living room. Sergio sang along, seeming more man than preteen in his conviction, and the other children joined in. The boys marched about the room, pretending to be soldiers, laughing as they sang:

> Black flag
> Color of death
> Will be stronger
> And will triumph

Emilia glanced up and noticed Giovanbattista leaning over to Tosca. He cupped his hand and yelled over the singing, and Emilia managed to hear him.

"They've put new words to "Bandiera Rossa." Remember the old lyrics? 'The Red Flag / will triumph / long live Communism / and our liberty.'"[8]

Tosca nodded with empathy.

The old uncle looked painfully defeated. If a soul could feel pain, his surely felt it deeply now. He looked sapped of energy, and his weakened state seemed inversely related to the triumphal rejoicing of the Little Italians. Giovanbattista pushed himself up from his chair, shuffled to the door, and left without saying a word.

FIVE Giotto's Circle

Carmignano, 1935

Come Sunday Emilia woke up early, splashed her face with cold water from the basin, pulled a dark blue wool dress over her head, and sped down the stone stairway with the enthusiasm of a fifteen-year-old anxious for the evening to come. She said nothing of her thoughts to Mamma, whom she feared would only reprimand her for indulging frivolous feelings. Emilia was sensitive to things emotional and observant of things material. She immediately noticed the unwrapped packet of biscotti, a rarity in their household, sitting in the center of the large kitchen table. Emilia's mouth warmed with anticipation as she spied the insignia of her favorite baker's shop: Bellini's of Carmignano. The biscotti were baked from flour mixed with abundant eggs, butter, almonds, and a zest of lemon, then rolled into a loaf and sliced into bite-sized ovals. To her, the hometown variety topped even the famous originals from Antonio Mattei's *biscottificio* in Prato.

"Mamma!" she shrieked with delight.

"With Lent beginning next week," Mamma explained, "today we'll feast."

Mamma poured fresh cow's milk into a small pot on the wood-fired stove and heated it for Emilia's morning latte. The house smelled of tomato, onion, celery, garlic, parsley, and olive oil. Mamma was already preparing the *sugo* for the midday supper. The longer it simmered, the better. She'd add the wild asparagus last.

"Emilio, can you skin me a good-sized rabbit?" she asked. Babbo had managed to raise a good many rabbits despite the count's protests. The landlord expected his sharecroppers to devote their energies to tending the crops from which he was accorded his share. Mamma planned to make *coniglio alle erbe* for the family. Emilia and her siblings had grown, as had their appetites. Babbo was now the head of a household with ten people.[1] He and Mamma were grateful to have the rabbit for Sunday *pranzo*. Times were tough, and they could hardly afford to eat meat on a regular basis. Most days, they ate potatoes, pasta, or polenta—often with white beans. When they said grace, the parents reminded their children of their good fortune not to have the disfiguring ailments of malnourishment, as some of the precariously situated day laborers' children did.

Carrying a three-inch-long skeleton key in one hand and a knife in the other, Mamma headed to the front door. Emilia heard the familiar clank as Mamma turned the key clockwise to release the lock. She slid back the latch and pulled the red doors open to expose two more wood doors. With a swooping motion, she reached her arm up and pulled downward on a latch, then bent over and pulled upward on another. As she flung the doors open, the morning sunshine lit her into a silhouette. Emilia watched from the threshold as Mamma crossed the front yard. She cut off several sprigs of rosemary, then picked a handful of sage leaves.

Back inside, Mamma minced the herbs with a *mezzaluna*, its blade curved like a half-moon. She patted the flavorful bits onto the slippery, translucent skin of the pieces of butchered rabbit, then sprinkled them with salt and pepper. Her face flushed as she opened the hot wood-burning oven. She took out a loaf of bread, now finished with a golden crust, and, in its place, she set the pan with the prepared rabbit to bake.

As the meat neared perfection several hours later, she boiled water, then poured in a kilo of *tagliatelle*, a wide-noodle pasta that she had made fresh the previous afternoon.

"*A tavola!*" she shouted, just as the pasta was ready, at 12:20 p.m. The family assembled at one large wooden table, four on each side. Uncle Giovanbattista sat at the head of the table, Babbo beside him. Mamma's seat was empty at the other end, and the children filled in the other places—six now ever since Matilde had married and moved in with her husband's family last November. Mamma busily served the pasta, and everyone devoured the first course—as always, Carlo finishing first and Emilia last. Mamma got up to serve the herbed rabbit, placing beside each piece a spoonful of steamed radicchio and other greens that Babbo had gathered from the fields. Everyone's spirits appeared high, and why not? Nothing could erase troubles like a savory meal. No one ages at the table, the old folks always said. As stomachs filled, conversation flowed.

"Aldobrando says Germena's itching to go to America," Babbo said.

"With this government, she doesn't have a prayer," Giovanbattista said. "No one is going anywhere. Every man, woman, and child at his station, for work, for life, and for good. You heard it from your uncle."

"Does he want her to go?" asked Carlo, only ten but never one to miss the chance for an inquiry.

"She's a big help with the business," Babbo answered. "And that's no small matter these days."

"Is she ever," Emilia said. "All the girls are scared stiff about messing up their plaits. The other day, Vera, the Nunziati girl, wasn't ready with her consignment, and you should have seen how Germena yelled at her. She was plain unfair. I mean, Vera took in a blow of cold wind last week, a blow right to the neck, and she came down with a fever. A high fever. She hasn't been feeling well since."

"She should just do like her dad and board a ship and go," Carlo interjected. "*Vaffanculo crapa pelata.* Screw the bald-headed guy."

Sergio glared at his younger brother. The others kept their eyes glued to their plates.

"Watch your mouth, Carlo," Mamma said, as she unwrapped a loaf of fresh pecorino cheese from *il pastore,* the shepherd, and offered slices to each of the children, her husband, and her uncle-in-law.

They lingered over their meal for some time, enjoying the tender meat despite the underlying tension. Emilia was quick to fill up and ready for dancing.

"It's time for Vespers," said Mamma. "Come on!"

Emilia scowled.

"If not, don't even think about dancing," added Babbo.

After helping Mamma clean up from the meal, Emilia walked with her family down the lane. They rounded the corner to follow a street that hugged a rock wall, then passed the villa with the regal cypress-lined drive. They crossed the piazza overlooking the river valley and continued down the main road until reaching the church courtyard. Townsfolk and peasants alike gathered in their Sunday best. Emilia recognized many of them: *trecciaiole,* straw weavers, *scalpellini,* stonemasons, and *coloni,* sharecroppers; a fraction of the men were *braccianti,* agricultural day laborers, and a smattering of the women took pride in being simply *atta a casa,* housewives. She also saw the town's two seamstresses and the village teacher as well as the midwife.[2] Rare was a sighting of the three landowning families. They kept to themselves, arranging a private mass in their own chapels or doing whatever noble families did when they spent the weekend at one of their *palazzi* in Florence or at the seaside in Viareggio.

The Raugei clan arrived in plenty of time for the four o'clock service. Emilia couldn't wait until it was over so she could go dancing. How Emilia loved to dance. She had her eye on a boy with an intoxicating name: Parigi, like the French city, Paris. Mamma must have sensed her drifting because she suddenly nudged her. The priest, reading from the Book of Luke, reminded the parishioners of the coming of Lent: "Jesus, full of the Holy Spirit, returned from Jordan and was led around by the Spirit in the wilderness for forty days, being tempted by the devil," he said. "And He ate nothing during those days, and when they had ended, He became hungry."

Vespers dragged on for Emilia. The priest had barely uttered the final phrase of the closing prayer when she was on her feet.

Carlo walked Emilia to within a block of the social club, long since taken over by the fascists, as were all the leisure associations. "I'm off to the cinematographer's," he mumbled. She suspected he was headed to a secret meeting with the older boys, but she didn't want to hear the details. She waved him goodbye and caught up with her two girlfriends: Lirua, whose coal-black hair had turned curly in adolescence, its below-the-shoulder length giving balance to her tall stature, and Vera, whose large Romanesque nose, spattering of freckles, and broad yet curvy build attracted boys with unconventional standards of beauty. Emilia, whose complexion was the fairest of all, was the petite and bony one of the threesome. She didn't particularly like being so skinny, but it was one thing she didn't worry about much. She was just happy to be in the company of her friends.

Three was company enough to ensure safety when walking the dark streets. They laughed as they strolled and speculated on what would come of the evening. A dozen boys were already there, standing around in small groups in the big room with its dingy white walls and concrete floor.

Emilia blushed as she caught sight of Parigi Peruzzi. He stood in a group with five other boys. His arms were crossed over his chest. He wore a mischievous grin on his handsome face. She admired his stocky build. His pressed and fitted white shirt suggested a strong man. Emilia suspected her girlfriends had noticed her reaction, so she confided in them her crush on him. She was shy and doubtful anything would come of it.

"At least try to talk to him," Lirua encouraged.

"But I don't even know him," Emilia said. "I've only just seen him once before. I can't just walk up to him."

"Why not?" said Lirua. "This is hardly the Middle Ages."

"I have an idea," said Vera. "Look, my uncle is from Artimino. I've seen that Parigi guy before. I think he probably even remembers me. I'll introduce you."

"I don't know," Emilia said, fear filling each word.

"Oh come on," Lirua nudged. "What are you waiting for? The priest's blessing?"

Lirua and Vera each took hold of one of Emilia's skinny arms and, laughing, started pulling her toward the group of five boys where Parigi stood. Emilia felt mortified at the thought of the scene they would create if she resisted her girlfriends.

"Okay, okay," she whispered. "Just let me go."

The three girls, with their fitted dresses, walked in a line as they approached the boys. For a moment, Emilia thought Parigi noticed her, but she couldn't be sure. His glance was fleeting. In her gut, something strange and unrecognizable tightened. She felt a deep sense of regret that she had agreed to this meeting.

Lirua and Vera did the talking. Emilia couldn't even hear what her friends said, she herself was so nervous. The introductions over, Emilia suddenly realized Parigi was saying something. He was talking to her.

"I've seen you here before," Parigi said. "Do you come here often?"

"A fair amount," Emilia managed. "And you?"

"I like to, but the walk is kind of far," he said. "You know, I live all the way up in Artimino."

"Yes, that's quite the walk."

"Four kilometers." He nodded. "Especially on the way back. The hill makes for a steep climb."

Emilia drew a blank. She looked down at her black shoes and then back around. She suddenly realized that Vera and Lirua had walked off and left her alone. Everyone but Parigi and Emilia seemed to be dancing. She felt so embarrassed. What more was there to say? Her mind was as blank as a teacher's chalkboard at the start of the school day.

"Do you like to dance?" he asked. She loved the sound of his voice. It rang with confidence. She let it ring through her ears.

"Emilia, do you like to dance?" he repeated, the firmness of his voice jolting her back to the moment.

"Oh, sorry. Dance. Yes, uh. I think so."

"You think so?"

"I mean, yes, I generally do like to dance."

"Would you consider this to be a general time when you would like to dance?" He was smiling now.

She couldn't help but smile, too. His smile met hers. He put out his hand and she accepted it, hoping he couldn't sense her trembling.

They walked to the dance floor together. He smelled like the fields, yet clean and fresh as cut hay. She told herself this all must be just some dream as the two of them moved in tandem, gliding to the rhythms of a *ballo liscio*. At the end of dancing their fourth song, Emilia looked up at him.

"Are you thirsty?" he asked her.

"Sure."

They headed toward the bar and each had a fountain soda.

"So, how many of you are there?" she asked him.

"We're four, four men plus my dad, my uncle—"

"Only four?" she asked.

"I meant the men—to work in the field," Parigi said.[3]

"Are there any women living in your house?"

"Well there's my mother, of course, and I have two sisters, too."

"So you are six siblings then?"

"There are actually seven of us. We're five brothers and two sisters. But one of my brothers, Amaretto, he's gotten into hat dealing. He's a *cappellaio*. So he doesn't work in the fields anymore."

"A big patriarchal family but not as big as Torquato Grassi's," she said. "They live down by the creek at the Fonte. Do you know them? Past the shepherd's place. There must be twenty-one people all told living in that house."

Parigi nodded. "Speaking of the shepherd, I have this uncle, Nello, he's a phenomenon, he can't write but he reads the newspaper. And he knows everything. He's something else, I'm telling you. The other night he was telling me about Giotto, you know, the artist. Without him there wouldn't have even been a Renaissance."

Emilia perked up. She admired Parigi's excitement for something besides selective family arithmetic.

"Sounds like a clever man," Emilia said, her tone sincere with admiration. "So you're familiar with Giotto's circle then?"

"Of course!" he said. "Pretty unbelievable. I mean, imagine a guy who wins an art contest for St. Peter's by drawing a circle."

"Well, it was a perfect circle and he drew it freehand," she said. "A marvel to behold—"

"I've always been surprised that the courtier actually sent the circle to the pope," Parigi said, interrupting. "I bet he risked his life doing that. Any other pope wouldn't have gotten the ruse."

"Any pope who didn't see Giotto's talent in that circle didn't deserve to be pope in the first place," she countered.

"I've always heard the courtier thought that Giotto was making a fool of him," he continued, ignoring the bait. "Who knows what led him to go ahead and send the circle along with the drawings from the other artists."

Emilia resigned herself to agree, but only for the time being.

"You know," Emilia began, thinking she would impress Parigi with her knowledge of the great pre-Renaissance artist and architect, "when Giotto was tending the sheep as a little boy, along came Cimabue. Giotto took a small stone and drew one of his sheep on a rock, and it was such an impressive sketch that Cimabue wanted him in his studio."

"It wasn't a sheep," Parigi said dismissively, "it was a fly."

"Oh come on, a fly?" Emilia countered. "It was a sheep."

"Look, my uncle knows it all, and he said it was a fly."

"Oh, your uncle!" Emilia shot back. "Giotto drew that fly when he was in the studio of his master."[4]

"You sure are certain of yourself," Parigi said.

"And why shouldn't I be?" Emilia's shyness had vanished, her nervousness a faded memory.

"Because you're a girl."

"What did you say?" she asked, her words almost slow motion if that were possible, carrying a tone that was both edgy and sweet.

"Oh nothing. Never mind." Parigi shrugged casually.

She crossed her arms and looked away.

"Now, now," he said. She detected a slight quiver in his voice. "Would you, in general, consider another dance?"

She stood as motionless as an oak on a breezeless summer day. She cast her gaze steadfastly in the other direction, careful to hide the grin that was forcing its way onto her face.

"Come now, *signorina*," Parigi said, extending his hands toward her.

She turned back around, looked at him and unfolded her arms. She did love to dance. Soon, his strong arms were again wrapped around her slender waist. She felt heavenly being so close to him.

Before she knew it, Carlo reappeared in the doorway of the dance hall. He glowered at Emilia.

"*Allora io vo via!* So I'm out of here," he said abruptly, in his bossy little brother tone. "Grab your coat."

Was it already time to go? The evening had passed in a heartbeat. Well at least, she thought, she had gotten to dance with Parigi. Twice. Deep down she felt misgivings about how things had gone. It was a rather odd way to begin a relationship, if that's what this was. The argument left her wondering whether they were meant for each other. Then again, this mix of tension, closeness, and distance fueled her excitement for him and kept them both guessing.

Neither she nor Carlo said much on the walk home. She didn't care. She was lost in her own thoughts.

SIX

Blood Relations

Parigi woke up Monday morning with an idea he fancied as so brilliant it startled him. He sat bolt upright in his pajamas. He couldn't see a thing. His bedroom was pitch dark. The wooden shutters were securely shut. He pulled himself out of bed. His feet stung with cold as he walked barefoot across the terracotta floor to unlatch the hinged window covers. Dim light filtered into his room through the canopy of trees surrounding his house. The fog was dense and hung low. He fumbled around his room for a pen and paper. For a teenager with only a fifth-grade education, Parigi had a clean script. He wrote to Giorgio Gentile. He had not seen his distant cousin in some years, but the relative was still the best hope for carrying out his plan.

4 February 1935

Dear Giorgio,

We're still here on the farm. We work hard most days but Sunday. Babbo gets along well enough with the countess. Doesn't see her much. She's got sixty-five *poderi* now. Believe it! Not sure how one person can manage so many farms, but she has an awful mean manager. He treats the peasants with an iron fist. He's a force to be reckoned with. Something terrible.

Anyway, I have a favor to ask of you. I have a new girl. Would you mind showing her around the city sometime? Her name is Emilia. She's a pretty little thing and smart too. Has a special liking for Giotto, I understand. She sure would fancy a tour of Florence, and I would be grateful to you.

With affection,
Parigi Peruzzi

Parigi dressed in a shirt and sweater, then pulled on his heavy pants. The scratchy wool rustled loudly in the quiet house. He headed outside, down the driveway and up the steep road that curved through the old Medici forest. The regally cultivated landscape had endured even as royalty had given way to a republic and then to a dictatorship. A mosaic of flat-leafed oak, chestnut, elm, and walnut trees contrasted in form and texture with towering fir, long-needled pine, and majestic cypress.

Parigi came to a trail and took the shortcut. As he walked through the dense woodlands, he recollected the disagreement he'd had with Emilia about his uncle's version of the Giotto story. His uncle was dear to him. Occasionally, Parigi accompanied the elderly man into the forest to gather wild asparagus come spring and wild mushrooms come fall. His uncle knew the forest as intimately as Parigi knew the terraces. The old fellow brought to life Parigi's imagination of the glory days of Ferdinand I, who in the early *seicento* had stocked the hills with wild boar, hare, and pheasant for royal hunting excursions. Parigi saw the creatures dart in and out of the undergrowth: the green feathers of a peacock disappeared into the foliage, the red beak of a partridge slipped behind a tree trunk. He stumbled upon a stone wall, and the long snout of a hunting dog vanished into the shadows. The crumbling remains had once been an enclosure that extended some fifty kilometers around the entire hunting reserve.

Heading out of the woods and onto the road, Parigi neared the walled town center of Artimino. From here, he had a panoramic view of the dozens of chimneys of the old Medici villa. The terraced hills were covered with sculpted olive trees and robust grapevines that he and his brothers cultivated. It had taken him a quarter hour to walk from home to the tobacco and salt shop to buy postage. He licked the stamp, pressed it onto the envelope, then tossed the letter into the red postbox outside the *tabaccheria*.

Babbo would be up by now, wondering about his son's whereabouts, so Parigi headed home straight away, mulling over his own knowledge of Giorgio and contemplating what he had just done.

Giorgio was a middle-aged stonemason who had traded his job quarrying stone in the village cliffs for the less arduous trade of repairing stone stairways in public buildings. He had a reputation as a man who considered himself more clever than lucky, in that he had managed to move to Florence some years ago, before Mussolini's antiurban campaign made leaving the countryside difficult and costly. He had rather easily remained a bachelor, not that anyone could tell he was proud of it, particularly given the annoyance of paying the bachelor tax, but his unmarried status allowed him the freedom to cultivate a self-image as an artisan, even though he could be quite a rogue and, truth be told, liked his wine a little too much.

In the weeks after sending the letter, Parigi consulted with various family members and calculated that Giorgio's artistic merits outweighed his unpredictable deficits and hence qualified him as his best choice for a guide. He banked on Giorgio's relation of blood, even if diluted, as insurance for gentlemanly conduct.

Little did Parigi anticipate that his desire to impress Emilia would nearly lead their relationship to a disastrous end. Looking back, perhaps the incident was just the vinegar they needed to keep them together.

Parigi saw Emilia on occasion through the spring and most Sundays into the summer and early fall—mostly at the town dance. They became acquainted little by little. What was the hurry, anyway?

One evening in October, he and Emilia were dancing when they looked up to see his brother, Amaretto, flirting with Germena. She didn't appear to be laughing at his jokes.

"I don't think he has a chance," Parigi said.

"She doesn't look impressed," Emilia agreed. "She's a tough one to figure out. I've known her my entire life, and I can't understand her. She's so moody and hard-edged. What does Amaretto see in her?"

"I can't imagine," Parigi said. "Maybe he likes a challenge. He's always been a little different than the others. Besides, objectively, even if she is a big girl, she is pretty."

"Do you think so?" Emilia said, jabbing her finger into a ticklish spot on his side.

"Oh Emilia, stop," he said, squirming and laughing.

"Has he known her for a while?"

"Surely you know her uncle, Aldobrando, the hat dealer?" Parigi said. "Amaretto and he are friends. They work together sometimes. My brother has known Germena for years. He talks about her quite a bit. It's not normal. I've been suspecting for sometime that he was sweet on her."

"But he seems like such a nice guy, your brother," said Emilia.

"He is. He doesn't have a cruel bone in his body. At least I've never seen it."

"Boy, he'd better be careful or she'll rule him like David over Goliath, like nothing you've ever seen."

The next day, Parigi was out in the field with his brothers, Babbo, and his Uncle Nello. Even his brother Amaretto, his two sisters, and his mother had joined them for the olive harvest, as it was a bountiful if early crop. Parigi spread out a large net beneath a mother lode of a tree. Just as he was smoothing out the last lump, he heard a low-pitched buzz from the distance. He looked up to see a trail of dust following a small motorbike. The *postino* headed up the gravel lane and disappeared into the forest that surrounded his house.

With a small pang of guilt, the teenager excused himself from his work and ran home. It wasn't every day that the postman came up their lane. Parigi looked into the mailbox and sure enough found a letter addressed to him, postmarked Florence. He ripped it open and read a short note scrawled in a messy hand.

22 October 1935

Dear Parigi,

Excuse the delay. Been waiting for the new station to open. It's ready.
Send your girl down the first Sunday in November. That will be the 3rd.
On the afternoon train. I'll meet her there around 3 o'clock.

Salutations,
Giorgio Gentile

Parigi knew better than to leave his family out to finish the day's labor
without him, but there was only another hour of daylight left, he figured,
so what was the difference? Just this one time? He dashed down the hill,
running the whole five-kilometer stretch to Comeana, Emilia's village.
The road afforded him a bird's-eye view of Poggiola, her farm atop the little hill, but also other little estates whose names spoke to their location or
some special feature: Bosco indicated the nearby woods; Fonte pointed to
a gushing spring; Castagna named a grove of chestnut trees. The names
lent a sense of intimacy to the relationship between the landowning
padrone and the sharecropping peasant, false as the suggestion might have
been.

Parigi took the shortcut through the field where the sheep grazed and
headed up a rocky path that finished at the backside of Poggiola. He was
out of breath when he reached the front door of the Raugei household,
perched as it was over the valley. He knocked, and, lucky for him, someone came to the door. It was Emilia's mother, Giovanna.

"Signora, I must speak with you," he said with urgency in his voice.

"What is it, Parigi?"

Emilia listened from the kitchen, where she was weaving a small number of sample hats for Aldobrando.

"I have this relation in Florence, and I wrote to him some months ago,
asking him if he would be willing to show my *fidanzata* around. I thought
Emilia would love a tour of the city. He's said to know quite a lot about it.
He just wrote back today, and . . ."

Emilia had stopped listening to the details and was stuck on Parigi's
reference to his *fidanzata*, his girlfriend. She had never heard him refer to
her that way. And now, here he was making the casual reference to her
mother! She flushed. She bowed her head and wove furiously.

"Emilia?" Mamma called.

With trepidation, Emilia headed straight to the front of the house. Emilia had grown into a curious teenager who loved the idea of the city even if its anonymity intimidated her. She was from a town where she knew or at least recognized everyone. Florence was not only a world of culture and art but also a world of darkness and of unknowns. She wanted to trust in her new sweetheart—if that's what she could call him. When he showed up at her doorstep to offer the tour idea, she was impressed that he would have come up with such a plan. But then she got to thinking.

Did she like this idea? It was thoughtful, she agreed. But a trip to the city all alone, with a total stranger, made her anxious. She wondered what this Giorgio character would be like. And she questioned how much he knew: Did he know she was Parigi's so-called girlfriend? She was hardly comfortable with the idea herself. It embarrassed her to think that this man might know such an intimate detail about her personal life. Besides, what did it mean to be somebody's girlfriend? She felt loyal to her own family and rarely entertained thoughts of moving out of her home and into someone else's. How awful that would be.

The other problem went well beyond her misgivings. After all, she had to convince her parents to give her permission. Even though Florence was only a twenty-minute train ride away, they would not be keen on the idea of letting her tour the city with a stranger.

Parigi insisted he could not go. His family was involved in a particularly intensive olive harvest, and he just could not get away. Not even for a Sunday afternoon.

"Emilia, it will be so lovely," he said, his sincerity seemingly genuine. "You'll truly have a fine time."

Emilia wasn't so sure, but she didn't want to appear fearful. She wanted him to think she was an adventurous girl.

"Well, all right," she relented, "but I'll have to discuss this further with Mamma."

Parigi left hopeful, and she and Mamma returned to the kitchen. Mamma was unconvinced. Yet the more Mamma disapproved, the more Emilia pled her case.

"This could appear dishonorable, a girl going to the city alone," Mamma said severely.

"But Mamma, I won't be alone, I will have an escort. This man Giorgio Gentile, he's a blood relation of Parigi."

"I don't know, I just—"

"Plus he was born here in Comeana. People know him."

Mamma paused for a moment as she thought about the proposal.

"Well, I'd consider allowing you to go," she said, "under two conditions. First, your brother must agree to accompany you to the station. And second, this Giorgio Gentile must take you to visit someone on my behalf."

SEVEN Chains

On an overcast November day, Emilia shelved her fears of traveling to the city alone. She felt positively pretty in her hand-sewn blue dress, button-down wool sweater, and black-buckle shoes as she boarded the train at the one-room station of Carmignano. The tracks had never made it up to any of the hill towns. The passenger stop sat in an unpopulated though accessible spot down by the river on the very edge of the rugged and vast county territory.

At 2:35 p.m., the train crept out of the station past the cane that straggled alongside the riverbank. The engine chugged forward and afforded Emilia a glimpse of a shiny maroon Fiat coupe whose driver waited for permission to pass through the tall iron gates that secured the hidden industrial complex of the Nobel dynamite factory. The train momentarily gained momentum as it rounded a bend and exposed a majestic view of umbrella pines lining a road parallel to the tracks. Emilia recognized the slowing of the train as the only stop along the route: Signa, the heart of the straw apparel industry in the province of Florence. Emilia's grandmother, a native of the City of Straw, combined admiration and loathing when she spoke of the renowned Domenico Michelacci of Bologna. In the early 1700s he had introduced to these hills a unique variety of wheat along with special techniques of cultivating, harvesting, and producing it. Michelacci was known for his experiments. He sowed the seeds densely and cut the grain before it had matured. These innovations, along with other bleaching and curing methods, bestowed the gifts of pliability and durability on the otherwise rigid straw. He eventually built his house next to his shop where straw hats were manufactured. Demand grew with quality. The hats were shipped from the port at Ponte a Signa down the Arno River to the Tuscan seaport of Livorno, namesake of the broad-brimmed, flat-topped Leghorn hat that by the nineteenth century had become all the rage on the international fashion scene. Some said the "Bolognino" single-handedly had done more than anyone else to bring industry to the countryside. Her grandmother had a different take. In Nonna's Tuscan version of the Rumpelstiltskin story, the weavers wove the straw into gold for a handful of industrial *padroni*.[1]

At the station, new travelers boarded and Emilia gazed out the window, upward past the tile-roofed residences that rose from the river valley to her grandmother's house and its constant smell of ripening wheat. Mamma was from Signa, too, and as a girl she would go with her father to help him with the straw. The key, it was true, was to harvest the grain while it was still green. In the day, they would bring it into the house and at night put it outside so as to retain the humidity and keep the cuttings pliable. With all the fiber, Mamma and Nonna would make meters, meters, and meters of plaits. Then they would sew them together into the most expensive hats of all and ship them to America, they said. America was grand. Emilia knew full well that this method was key to her own livelihood; the local secret for creating softer straw made her weaving easier and her product more professional. But something about remembering that history unsettled her.

Her mind drifted back to a well-known story. Wasn't *villanzoni* the word Nonna had overheard a signore from town use to describe the peasants? "Those boors—" that man had said. They had been known to take the winding route near his house back in Michelacci's day, and upon seeing grain that grew, not high or lush, like the type they planted on the regular ploughed fields, but thick and uniform like meadow grass, they had been awestruck and confused. "Uncivilized and unmannered is what they are," Nonna had said, mimicking the townsfolk's disparaging remarks about the peasants. For the townsfolk, the peasants were backward illiterates whose gaping mouths might as well have been encrusted with dust, as progress, fueled by the forces of rationality and industry, sped on down the road, leaving them far behind in its tracks. Never mind the efficiency of the hard-working and compliant peasant workers. Not only did they grasp novelty, Nonna had protested, but also they had tirelessly evolved their own manufacturing secrets, which were rarely recognized. Such blindness to their ingenuity served class hierarchies and made the loathing directed toward peasants seem as inevitable as nature itself.

From her window seat, Emilia imagined the peasant sharecroppers of two hundred years ago, standing up on the hillside above the town, their mouths agape. The intensity of the villagers' scorn toward the peasants weighed heavily on her. So what if the Duce had declared himself pro-rural? What were eight years of affirmation compared with two centuries of contempt? She feared that in the city she would fail to hide her peasant upbringing.

There were other things to consider, she told herself. Think about your grandmother, so brave for having marched with one thousand other women from Signa in 1896. The massive strike had involved some forty thousand workers from the tight-knit towns and hamlets lining the banks of the Arno. "We were working for a *tozzo di pane*, a crust of bread, and we just weren't able to get by," Nonna always said.[2] "You would have done the same thing. The wages were only a pittance but they were essential for the family's survival." The strike was hard for Emilia to imagine, not only because of the solidarity and networks that must have existed back then, but also because of the courage of those weavers. To her, growing up as a Little Italian under a fascist government that had gotten control over the unions and made workers' protests all but illegal, the fascist working conditions were just the way things were.

The train lurched forward and soon reached a good speed. Within a short quarter hour, sets of tracks multiplied tenfold before the train slowed and pulled into the rail yard of Santa Maria Novella. The newly opened station in Florence stood within the old city walls. Emilia climbed down the steps from her coach, her palms clammy against the metal rail. She headed toward the end of the platform, where she caught sight of a scruffy, squat man. She quickly looked away, finding diversion in an expansive glass atrium that invited light into the central gallery.

Giorgio recognized her immediately. It was rare for a teenage girl to travel alone. Besides, she fit Parigi's description perfectly: she was petite and attractive with a bob of brown hair and bangs framing her face. He noted the distinctive stroll of a country girl who appeared confident but clutched her handbag a little too tightly. He gazed at the girl and called her by name as she neared him.

Her eyes met his, and she felt draped in self-consciousness.

"You're Parigi's girl?"

She stopped, then nodded with reservation.

"I'm Giorgio Gentile, pleased to meet you."

She approached him, forced herself to lean forward and greet him with a kiss on each bristly cheek, pulling her hips back to avoid letting her torso touch his belly hanging over his belted trousers. As she pulled back, she noticed that his salt-and-pepper whiskers matched the patch of gray around his temples.

"How was your trip?" he asked, scratching his bulbous nose.

"Fine," she managed, looking up again at the rectangular shapes of light that filtered through the atrium.

"So you like the station?" he asked. "They just opened it last month." He had acquired a brusque, working-class Florentine dialect from living in the city for so many years. "They say the atrium's design recalls the great iron train sheds of the past."

Emilia was unsure what to say, so she just followed Giorgio through the bustling crowd to the outside of the building. She wished Parigi had come along. The tour would have held so much more promise to be fun. She felt profoundly alone in the company of a total stranger.

"Giovanni Michelucci and his men designed it," Giorgio continued.

"Did you say Michelacci, as in Michelacci of Bologna?" Emilia asked, intrigued by the coincidence.

"No, no Michel*ucci*. He's a Tuscan, a real modernist. I don't care much for the work. To tell you the truth, I don't think the city is ready for such a stark design, it's just too—what's the word? They were saying it at the club yesterday. Too rational. But his team won the contest, and now we have to live with it."[3]

Oh, what was she thinking? *Don't act the country girl,* Emilia scolded.

They headed outside and across the driveway. It was the first time she had walked on slabs of pavement designed for modern automobiles. Something about it struck her. Emilia stopped. She glanced back at the putty-brown stone that matched the surrounding Renaissance buildings in color but not in grace. The austere style wasn't the Florence of her mind's eye. She found distraction and delight in the people. They passed purposefully, wearing fine, fashionable clothes. Several gypsies mingled about the vendors.

"Would you like to see Giotto's crucifix?" Giorgio asked.

Parigi must have clued him in. She didn't bother to answer but forced a smile and then followed her guide toward the backside of Santa Maria Novella, namesake of the new station. She found comfort in the soft, graceful lines of the Gothic-Romanesque structure as well as the joyous, syncopated dance of the gray-green and white marble exterior.

They entered the church, its nave engulfing them like a huge ship. It was surprisingly light and airy. Giotto's crucifix was suspended midway up the aisle, framed by slender ribs and arches that drew her eyes upward. She had never felt so close to heaven. She stared, following one archway's delicate rectangles of alternating dark and light marble, which seemed to her like a miraculous stone weaving. Her eyes moved from the arches back to the crucifix. Jesus's body, painted not onto canvas but onto a wooden cross, appeared to have real weight: his head slumping forward in exhaustion; the skin of his torso taut over his protruding ribs; his belly sagging from the earthly pull of gravity; blood spurting from his right rib cage. A translucent loincloth draped just above his knees. Her eyes settled on a single nail that attached his two feet, one atop the other, to the base of the cross. His posture struck her as the ultimate embodiment of earthly sacrifice. Emilia glanced to each end of the crossarm, where portraits of the tilted heads of Mary and John cast sorrowful expressions.[4] She was overcome with raw sadness and genuine awe.

"Some say Giotto outdid his master with this commission," Giorgio said, scratching his nose again.[5]

Emilia looked back up at the crucifix, embracing the moment one last time before continuing her tour through the church. The argument about Giotto that she'd had with Parigi came back to her. With several months now elapsed, she could barely remember what had aggravated her so, and the memory seemed more sweet than sour now. She walked past a pew with an old woman dressed all in black and chanting Hail Mary's beneath a fresco that depicted another crucifix. Jesus seemed to hang at the back of an arched room, where a gray-bearded God Almighty effortlessly held the cross; the loincloth of his Son was almost indecently low as it revealed a shadow of pubic hair. She quickly diverted her eyes upward to the painted ceiling, whose rosettes had so much depth as to appear crafted from stone rather than pigment.

"It's *The Trinity*, by Masaccio, a real masterpiece for its trompe l'oeil," Giorgio announced, sounding part pompous schoolteacher, part working-class Florentine. She hadn't been in a classroom since the fifth grade, so the tone struck more of a nostalgic chord than one of resentment. She recalled an outing to the Church of Carmignano in the fifth grade to visit Pontormo's *Annunciation,* but this was her first close-up look at Masaccio and Giotto, and she sensed a momentary religious awakening.

Beneath two robed, kneeling figures flanking each side of the crucifix lay a skeleton painted within a tomb. A faded inscription appeared in block letters as though chiseled above the bones:

"*IO FV GIÀ QUEL CHE VOI SIETE E QUEL CHE SON VOI ANCOR SARETE*"

"I was once what you are, and what I am you will yet become," Giorgio read.

Emilia had witnessed plenty of people pass away in her town. Each time someone died, the bells tolled and the streets filled with mourning villagers. She had never been comfortable with death. Perhaps she had inherited her fear from her father. He loved Mamma well enough, but losing his first wife had changed him. Everyone said so.

"On to Santa Croce?" Giorgio interrupted, and then mumbled something inaudible.

Outside, rain threatened, but they pressed on. Emilia followed Giorgio across the piazza of Santa Maria Novella and into the heart of the city. The storefronts offered an overwhelming array of goods and diverted her attention from Giorgio. His habit of mumbling when he wasn't lecturing might have been irritating had she cared to hear what he had to say. She found his mannerisms almost repulsive, especially his incessant scratching of his oversized nose, but she was resigned to keep her word and follow through with the tour.

Emilia's spirits lifted when they entered the Piazza of the Duomo. Giotto's belltower caught her eye. She leaned her head back and stared at the campanile for so long her neck might have cramped were it not for Giorgio's interruption.

Stepping close and taking her arm, he said abruptly, "And now on to Santa Croce." His breath was stale. She gently pulled her arm loose, settling on a pace that placed her not directly at his side but rather several paces behind him.

The two of them meandered down a side street and into a quiet neighborhood. The buildings were tall and the streets narrow so the light barely entered—probably not even on a sunny day, she thought. They stepped into an even darker street, and her guide's voice became hushed. He seemed anxious. Did she sense shame in his voice? The route frightened her. She wondered why he had chosen to take her this way. She felt unsafe and wished she had not agreed to let him serve as her escort. But Parigi had said Giorgio could be trusted.

So there they were, in Via della Morina. She would never forget the name of that street.

"Oh! Don't raise your eyes here," he instructed, tempering his command by lowering his voice.

"Why not?" Emilia asked.

"Because of the *catenine*," he said.

Emilia was confused.

"There are shutters with the little chains," he repeated.

"And what am I to make of those?" she asked.

"They can't be opened," he said. "But don't look."

Emilia tried not to raise her eyes, but since she was young and curious, her keen peripheral vision afforded her a glimpse of a tall woman with long, dark hair inside the window. A burgundy tie dangled loosely at the side of her silk robe, which was narrowly opened to the navel and revealed bare flesh and generous breasts. Emilia knew she was seeing something forbidden. Her cheeks flushed, her heart raced.

Giorgio picked up his pace and, although Emilia felt pressured to do the same she managed to linger behind. They entered a vast rectangular piazza, and Emilia knew it must be the famous Franciscan church of Santa Croce. The white beacon of a basilica stared down upon them. But she was so shaken from the incident in the street with the chains that she could hardly take it in. She looked over at Giorgio. He had a smirk on his face. He appeared happier than she had seen him all day. His mood disgusted her. He disgusted her. Surely he had seen the woman behind the shutters too. Surely he had found her easy on the eyes. Or maybe it was something else. Maybe he took pleasure in shocking a teenage girl from the country. In any case, she felt ashamed for what she had seen. She shouldn't have looked.

The two continued walking in awkward silence. If Giorgio was talking to her as they went inside Santa Croce, she didn't hear a word. She didn't think to say anything to him until a short while later, when they were back outside, crossing the piazza, heading into another neighborhood.

"Where are we going now?" she asked tentatively.

"We have an appointment with the *professoressa*," he said. "It's been prearranged. All part of the tour, so not to worry."

They arrived at a house with a formidable iron gate, and Giorgio rang the bell. They waited. He rang again. It seemed like forever. Finally the door opened.

Inside stood an elegant Florentine *signora*, her hair pulled neatly into a bun, her posture and physique perfect for the form-fitting, stylish navy boutique dress she wore.

"I've been expecting you," she said, in her high Florentine accent. "Come in, come in."

Giorgio introduced himself, as the two adults had never made acquaintance. The lady then turned toward Emilia and smiled the bittersweet delight of seeing a child after the passage of so many years. Emilia all at once recognized her. She was Beatrice Benveniste, the *professoressa* of piano, a great aunt by marriage. Now the memory came back to her. She had visited Emilia's family one time years ago. The *professoressa* had told them stories. And what stories! She knew so many important people. She had even taught the daughters of the king, at the imperial villa in Florence, when the Marchesa Gerini had paid a visit to the city. Imagine the life of a *professoressa*. She had even drunk tea with royalty. Beatrice Benveniste certainly looked the part.

Giorgio and Emilia followed the *professoressa* through a hallway lined with oil paintings: some realist scenes of the countryside, others abstract representations of objects, still others portraits of beautiful, even exotic people. Arriving in the parlor, Giorgio sat himself down with a thump, his legs opening wide like scissors, on an overstuffed, tan armchair. Emilia and the *professoressa* settled themselves onto a divan with velvety sage green and rust stripes.

"I showed her around, even took her in the lane with the *catenine*," Giorgio boasted, "and I told her not to raise her eyes." He seemed oddly pleased with himself. Emilia stared at his rough face; he really was quite ugly.

"Just listen to where you brought her!" Professoressa Benveniste said.

"I didn't raise my eyes," Emilia assured her. "I kept my head down."

The *professoressa* lowered her glasses to the tip of her slender nose and cast him the fiercest look Emilia recalled having ever seen. "I'm sure you are a very busy man with much to do after having spent so much of your afternoon with this young lady," she said tersely.

"Actually, I'm fine," he said, looking quite comfortably settled into his chair. "You'd just about have to see the stone stairway of the Leaning Tower of Pisa collapse before you'd find me working on a Sunday."

Beatrice Benveniste realized she was dealing with a man incapable of even a minimal degree of subtlety or good taste. She was not a woman to be crossed, so she told him without wasting a vowel, "You've served your purpose for the day, *signore*." She stood up, arms folded, and glared at him.

"Fine then, I'm off," he grumbled, performing the role of a wrongly accused innocent man, and in one motion pushed himself up, then yanked his jacket down into place. He mumbled *arrivederci* to Emilia before trudging down the hallway behind the *professoressa,* who showed him to the door, leaving Emilia alone to listen to its hinges creak open, then shut. The teenager then followed the delicate sound of the woman's steps making their way toward the other end of the house.

Emilia sat in wonderment, taking in the parlor, its grand piano, hand-carved furnishings, and original artwork. She stared at a lovely porcelain vase with blue and orange birds in flight that sat atop a marble-topped, round end table. The *professoressa* returned with a tray of tea and cookies. She set it down on the coffee table in front of the divan and sat herself beside Emilia.

"How many sugars?" she asked Emilia.

"Two, please."

"Lemon or milk?"

Emilia hesitated.

"Take the milk. It will soothe your stomach."

The *professoressa* swirled a small sterling silver spoon around in the delicate teacup and handed the prepared tea to Emilia. The girl found comfort in the hot drink.

"Thank you, *professoressa.*"

"You can call me *zia* Beatrice if you like," she said. "I am, after all, an aunt, even if distant by marriage and generation."

Emilia smiled politely, uncertain she could call such a woman anything but *professoressa.*

"My dear, are you all right?"

Emilia nodded.

"You know what you saw today, don't you?"

"I think so," she answered, then looking down at the elegant tile floor added, "I'm so ashamed."

"That man took you by a 'protected house.' Women live there and certain men go to seek them out," zia Beatrice said, sipping her tea. "Men like Giorgio."

Emilia raised her eyebrows and tilted her head back in a quick gesture of understanding. She had heard mention of such places.[6]

"Well, never mind. You are nearly a woman now, and it's just as well that you know about such things. A woman has to know lots of things. Especially nowadays—what with Mussolini meddling in our affairs. I had only one child to spite him, you know."

"Really?"

"Why, of course. Better to avoid having the children you don't want than to find yourself in an 'interested condition' and then do something drastic."

Emilia felt confused but tried not to show it.

"One girl I knew a little bit, a few years older than me, they sent her to prison," Emilia said. "Nobody would talk about it much. Some folks said she violated the state or some such thing."

"That Mussolini, making abortion a crime against the race," zia Beatrice said, shaking her head. "There are more abortions than ever. It's gone underground. So many women using knitting needles or parsley stalks. Some bleed to death, poor things. Don't be fooled by the talk of those fascist legislators. Just the other day one argued that interfering in the private lives of women was a way to overcome 'liberal democratic and individual rights'! If a woman doesn't even tell her husband when she's getting an abortion, you think she's going to listen to Mussolini when he tells her to have children?"[7]

Emilia looked down at her lap and smoothed her dress. She didn't want to admit that she had never given the matter much thought. She took a bite of her cookie.

"Oh my dear—it's not true that you're from the country!" zia Beatrice exclaimed, then sipped her tea. "How is your mother?"[8]

"She works hard, and has my sisters and brothers to tend to all the time, then the farm and all the cooking. But she's in good health, so we count our blessings."

"I remember her as a little girl, always busy weaving, such a serious and well-behaved child."

The two sipped their tea for some time, and Emilia began to feel a little at ease. She managed to display at least a modicum of enthusiasm for the famous sights she had seen, and they chatted about some of those highlights and then turned to the worsening weather.

"Well, it is getting rather late, I'm sure they're expecting you home for dinner. We'd better get you to the station."

"Yes, I promised Mamma I would catch the 6:30 train."

"Come along then. I'll accompany you to the station."

The November days were short, the cold air blew in from the mountains, and it was already dark when the teenager from the country and the *professoressa* from the city headed outside into the drizzle. The *professoressa* opened an umbrella, held it with her right arm, and put her left arm out for Emilia to take. The women walked arm in arm into the dank evening across the wet cobblestones to the train station. The drizzle turned to steady rain. They kept their arms locked at the elbow. The backs of their dresses, their legs, and their dark shoes took the water. Emilia's feet were soaked by the time they reached Santa Maria Novella.

"It was lovely to see you again, Emilia, after so many years. Send my best wishes to your family. Your mother in particular."

"I will. Thank you for the tea."

"Have a safe trip, and in the future steer clear of men like Giorgio Gentile. His kind are nothing but trouble."

Emilia forced a smile and waved her aunt goodbye, relieved to find the track for the Firenze-Pisa-Livorno line and to step aboard the dry train car, digesting much more than tea and a cookie during the twenty-minute ride back to Carmignano.

The next weekend, Emilia was nervous about the dance at the social club. She was unsure of her feelings toward Parigi. She couldn't quite blame him for what had happened, but then again, what did the tour of Florence say about his judgment? Could he be trusted? She convinced herself not to be angry with him, and she played out a number of different scenarios in her mind. Their interaction was nothing like she had imagined.

"So how is my city girl?" he asked right off in his mischievous way.

"Well, she's just fabulous," she said sarcastically. "But she's a little puzzled."

"Oh, what about?" his curiosity verging on sincerity.

"About the tour, the 'tour of chains,'" she shot back, surprised by her own forcefulness.

"You didn't have a nice time?" Parigi asked, perplexed. "He didn't show you Giotto's crucifix?"

"Of course we saw the crucifix, but that's not all he showed me," Emilia said, looking right through him with her wakeful eyes. "What were you thinking to have such a man show me around?"

"What do you mean?"

"He took me past one of those protected houses."

"How interesting, but what of it?" Parigi asked. "They take us there all the time!"

"What?" she asked, stunned.

"The head of our fascist group took us all to Florence and showed us the brothels. We boys learned a lot from that field trip," he laughed. " 'There's this one here, and this other one there,' the Black Shirt leader said as he walked us around. They say when they send us off to the military, we'll already know a little bit about how things work."

"Well, they used to teach *us* gymnastics at school," Emilia replied, flustered.

"That's old school," he said.

"Oh be quiet!" Emilia shot back.

"Oh you be quiet," he retorted, paused, then smiled and with a change of tone added, "*Carissima*, my sweet! Consider it education."[9]

He had a lot of gall, she told herself, to lay on the charm while trying to put a girl in her place. He was just like the other boys, always thinking they were better than the girls. Just name one who worked harder than she did. Emilia might have been a peasant girl, but she fancied herself an artisan and demanded her due respect. She decided to cut the evening short. She convinced Vera and Lirua to leave with her. She made a pact with herself and refused to speak his name aloud as they walked home.

EIGHT

Rations

March 1940

Something about that young man from Artimino won Emilia over every time. Her anger melted like sugar in coffee. Before long, she found herself dancing with him on and off the dance floor. Friends now referred to them as *fidanzati,* engaged. It was an informal engagement that would endure a long time. Unexpected events had a way of making time pass, and life as they knew it was unraveling faster than they could make sense of all the loose ends.

One unseasonable cold, windy afternoon around five o'clock, when the war was on and hunger threatened, Parigi knocked at the door of Emilia's house. He brought news that would result in the first of many interruptions to their life plans. In other places, in other times, the couple might have gotten on with their life. But not Parigi and Emilia.

Their upbringing as peasants taught them patience, their experience with a changing market instructed them in the lessons of uncertainty, and their exposure to a world at war instilled in them a yearning for better times.

"May I come in?" he asked Emilia's mamma as he stood on the other side of the threshold. A strong March wind blew the chilly evening air.

Giovanna looked surprised to see him so late in the day. "Of course, Parigi, come in." Even her languid half-smile made her wrinkles deepen.

As Parigi followed the woman into the kitchen, he couldn't help but notice the messy strands of hair falling out of her bun of dark hair. The kitchen had only one window and at this hour was dark. The late afternoon sun hung low in the sky. Parigi sat at the big table and stared at a gaping crack that ran its length.

"What can I offer you?"

"Nothing. Really."

"A glass of wine?"

"No, no, I'm fine. I only wanted to speak with Emilia."

"I'll go and fetch her," Mamma said.

Parigi waited. He rubbed his knees.

Several minutes later, Emilia entered the kitchen alone. She looked concerned to see him. It was a strange time of day for Parigi to drop by. He normally came right after lunch, around 2:30, or later in the evening, after supper, around 8:30, not during the afternoon work hours.

"What is it, Parigi? She said, sitting across the table from him.

"I've received a letter," he said, reaching into his pocket. He unfolded the envelope and placed it on the table in front of Emilia.

"Something is wrong." Her voice sounded shaky.

"It's from the military."

"I suspected as much," she sighed. "I suppose it was only a matter of time."

"They've called me to Prato for training, then I'll be sent to Florence." He glanced down at the letter.

Emilia reached for the envelope. The official letter was brief and indicated the date he was called to serve in the Italian army: March 14, 1940. She stared at the letter and read it again, lingering over each word.

"I must leave very soon."

Emilia fiddled with her apron. "How soon?"

"Three days. They've given me three days to prepare."

"That's very soon," she said with resignation. "I'm sorry."

"Me too."

"At least you will be nearby." She forced a smile.

"Yes, it's only Florence after all."

Her hand trembled, and he noticed, so he reached over and held it.

"Emilia," he said, smiling now, "I have something else to tell you. I have some news about Amaretto and Germena."

"Don't tell me."

"They've decided to marry." Excitement filled his announcement.

"So soon?" Emilia had a hard time feeling elated about this news.

"Well, Amaretto is several years older than me, you know, and Germena doesn't have her *mamma* or *babbo* anywhere near, so I think she's ready for a new life."

"Where will they live?"

"Back in Comeana, with her uncle," he said, matter-of-factly.

"I see," she said, trying to hide her relief that at least Germena would not be moving into the Peruzzi household.

"Emilia," he said, looking at her with intent eyes. "When I return, shall we marry?"

She thought about his question. She could not find it in her heart to make a commitment. Who knew what would happen? Who could say what the future would bring? Everything felt deeply uncertain, particularly the future.

"All things in time."

The next morning pink clouds stretched over the valley behind the farmhouse like virtues of the dawn. The roads were free from shadows as Emilia headed directly to Lirua's house. She walked with intention until she reached the doorstep. Through the lacey curtain she could see Lirua's silhouette seated at the kitchen table. She didn't bother to knock. Lirua chewed a piece of day-old bread with a spread of apricot jam.

"My cousin got a letter yesterday, too," Lirua said through her mouthful of bread.

"What can I do? I'm all nerves. I can't eat a thing."

"Now's as good a time as any," Lirua said, the hint of a smile pushing its way forth as she reached for the knife to cut her a slice.

"It's not funny, Lirua."

"I know, I know. It's not funny. You're right. Let's think." She wiped a crumb from the corner of her mouth and pursed her lips together like she was pretending to think hard. "We'll join 'em."

"That's no part of anything," Emilia shuddered. "And how would you pretend to do that, anyway?"

"We'll go apply to Nobel. It's not such a far walk, why I bet we can get there in forty minutes, it's just past the station. Make more money making gunpowder than we do weaving all day and night."

"That's the most outlandish thing I've heard yet. Do you know how dangerous it is over there? That would scare me to pieces to be around all those explosives."

"It's not exploded yet."

"What does that mean?"

"It means what it means."

"It means as much as . . . as wine gone to vinegar. And you know it."

"What do I care?"

"Maybe you care that they're a bunch of fascists over there?"

"And what of it?"

"Not anything I care to be part of. I know from my *nonna*. That Sestini, he's in charge over there in Signa, he's a real *fascistone*, a fascist of the biggest order. My *nonna*'s friend, this Gianna, she had four children and a sick husband. She wove straw, too, she'd been a weaver her whole life, but there came a point when she just wasn't making it any more. The way things have slowed and all. And who was going to give her a dime? So this fellow, this Sestini, he must have heard about her because he comes up to her one day and asks if she'd like to work at Nobel. Well, like I said, he was in charge, so she had to do what he said. She was afraid to disobey him. "*Volentieri*," she told him, "Gladly." And so she went. And what of it? Well, she kept her family alive, but by and by she had to stay home at times and tend the family, so her money was short. On occasion she'd go down and line up for a little packet of food, you know, on Saturdays, the little packets of olive oil and breads, and little things for families who are down and out. Well this Sestini put one in charge who was a real *fascistaccio*, truly a wicked fascist, and he had been the landlord of this Gianna's family back when they were working the farm, he was their *signore*, and this wicked fascist guy together with the other fascist who was in charge of Signe would put her name on the list, but then he'd look around at everyone, look at his list, and staring straight at her would say, 'This one doesn't need a packet,' and he'd cancel her name. Just like that."[1]

"Now why would anyone do such a thing?"

"*Perché gl'era un cattivo,* because he was a bad man. Simple as that, Lirua. Those are the kind of folks in charge down there at Nobel. In case you haven't heard."

"Oh now, calm down. I'm not going to force you into anything."

"Get that straight."

"How about some bread and jam."

Emilia stretched back in her chair and broke her morning fast as the sun warmed the chilled March air.

Parigi set off for Prato as any young man in his early twenties might have done. Travel was a new sensation for him. Other than a few outings with the fascist youth club, his peasant upbringing did not allow for much in the way of family vacations. He waited in the piazza of his small town with several other guys. They cracked jokes as they waited, continuing even as the military bus pulled into the square. It drove down the hill, honking its horn loudly before rounding each sharp curve. The vehicle made stops in several other villages and then descended into the valley. The men's voices created a ruckus as many of them sat next to their friends. Parigi felt very little fear as the bus went by expansive fields of wheat that grew in the rich river-bottom soil. Carrying its load of live cargo past the factories with their billowing smokestacks that smelled of burned wool, the bus then entered the army compound. The newly drafted young men piled out of the bus. A guy with short curly hair and a cigarette dangling from his lips told a fascist joke. This wasn't going to be half bad, Parigi thought. Who could take the Italian military seriously anyway?

He found the habits of the men in uniform to be more of a story than he could have even imagined. The officers smoked as if there were no tomorrow and gossiped as if it were a profession. The whole scene fueled his sense of humor. His wit got the best of him the following day during a placement session where he had to produce a writing sample.

"Listen," he said to one of the black-shirted officials, "if my hand gets cramped, can I just go on home?"

"No!" barked the official. He took several steps toward Parigi and glowered down at him, dragged on his cigarette, and then raised his eyebrows.

"Not a bad hand for a smart-aleck. If you can shoot half as well, maybe they'll put you on the front lines."

Before long Parigi was riding the train with a few of his new buddies to Florence. After a spell, the commanding officer sent him off again, this time to the port at Livorno to board a ship. He sailed all night across the Tyrrhenian Sea to Sardinia. Once there, he realized he had gotten lucky again. Some 80 percent of the boys in his unit couldn't sign their name, and since his calligraphy wasn't bad and he'd already had experience, he landed another assignment in a military hospital office. Shuffling papers and assisting medical staff was fine by him. He got used to the odors of cleaning ammonia and healing wounds. He also grew accustomed to the sound of people coughing. It was a particularly bad winter for bronchitis.[2]

Parigi wasn't the fighting sort, particularly on behalf of Mussolini. Ah, the Duce. He did a lot for his soldiers. Selling or advertising contraceptives to civilians was illegal. Exceptions were made for persons with medical conditions that could be sexually transmitted, but for the most part Mussolini was steadfastly opposed to Malthusian measures. This was part of the dictator's grand plan to increase the birthrate.

The military was another matter. Mussolini encouraged soldiers to have sex to prove their virility.

Parigi's first Monday morning in Sardinia, he groggily opened his eyes as a low-level recruit stormed into the bunkhouse.

"Special delivery!" he shouted.

A soldier on the bunk across the room immediately sat upright in his bed, arms outstretched. The recruit tossed him three little packages. He then threw the little gifts right onto the face of a sleeping kid on the bunk beside Parigi's. He twitched. The recruit laughed, then met eyes with Parigi, who was looking confused.

"Use them wisely, boy," the recruit commanded, and then winked. "That's it for the week."

The young Parigi was taken by surprise when his ration landed on his white bed sheets. The other guys sensed his shock and razzed him.

"Don't fear, Parigi," they laughed. "They won't bite you."

Whatever happened to the condoms on the island of Sardinia stayed on the island of Sardinia.

NINE

War Country

March 1944

Emilia missed Parigi but kept her feelings distant. Wartime brought austerity and plenty of other worries. There was hardly time for sentimentality. As a mature twenty-three-year-old, she feared not only for him but for herself and her family. Emilia was grateful for his assignment in a military hospital rather than on a battlefield. She was not so delighted with her situation. She and her family were no longer inhabitants of a quiet countryside but of a war zone. Boiled meat, chopped eggs, or pea soup became common meals. How ironic that while Parigi had been sent far away to serve in the war, the war had found its way into her backyard. Guns and swastikas were as common as the straw and rags of local commerce, just more menacing.

Ragpickers combed urban neighborhoods and rural lanes for any old clothes. One fellow showed up at the farmhouse door every Thursday, pushing his wooden cart. A blue cap covered his head, revealing only salt-and-pepper sideburns. He wore his mustache trimmed. His shirt, frayed on the bottom, and his pants, patched at the knees, were probably pickings from his rag collection. He reeked of musty clothes and of unwashed flesh.

She turned him away and returned to a scant lunch of white beans from the stock pile and salad greens from the field. Emilia followed Carlo outside and took a seat on the cement ledge next to the fig tree. The ground beneath the olive trees was covered with *borragine*, a calf-high weed with a pretty blue flower that you could eat and leaves that were prickly to the touch but delicious when dredged through an egg-flour batter and fried in olive oil. Mamma had managed to keep three pots of geraniums blooming despite the tough times. A fresh spring breeze blew. Emilia's dark hair was disheveled. Carlo's had grown long and covered the nape of his neck. He had matured into a nineteen-year-old man, handsome despite his scruffy appearance. His white shirt was soiled from working in the fields. Two of their younger sisters were assigned to kitchen cleanup. Emilia broke from her weaving to talk with Carlo. All the wartime commotion had her feeling weary, confused, and frightened.[1]

A military jeep bumped across the valley below, leaving deep tire tracks in the muddy meadow. The herd of brown sheep moved out of its way, parting like the sea. Emilia tried to cancel the image. The scene was hardly biblical.

Carlo stared out at the hills, sprouting with green. He seemed jittery.

"What's going on?" Emilia asked. "Is it Sergio?"

"Russia is a long way off," Carlo sighed.

The wind picked up.

"Sometimes at night I think I hear troops marching and motorcades moving across the valley," Emilia said, her voice almost dreamy it was so laden with pauses. "It's all so overwhelming."

"You don't know the half of it," Carlo blurted, standing up abruptly.

"Do you know something about Sergio?"

"Wish I did."

Emilia stared at him, her slender face stern. "What then?"

"They're building—building the front. Word is . . ." Carlo hesitated. His eyes darted this way and that. "It's horrible up there for the resistance."

"What would you know about it?" she asked, skeptical that he was so well informed. He pretended not to hear her.

"Emilia," he said, and finally looked straight at her. "Swear you won't ever say a word of this to anyone?"

"I swear."

"Swear to the Madonna."

"I swear to the Madonna."

"Come with me." He grabbed her arm, and they walked down the lane to the intersection, where they followed the stone wall ten meters until he stopped and faced a small, rectangular shrine built into the wall. Emilia looked at the blue-and-white ceramic sculpture of the Virgin Mary, six swords piercing her heart. An unlit candle sat adjacent to a vase of freshly arranged purple wildflowers and three miniature pink roses. Carlo reached into his pocket, retrieved a small box of wooden matches, and lit the candle.

"Now swear on it," he said vehemently.

"What has gotten into you?" Emilia resisted.

"Just do it," Carlo insisted.

"But Carlo, you're hardly religious."

"I don't care. Just do what I say."

She stared at her brother in disbelief. He stared back.

"Fine," she relented. "I swear on the Madonna."

"Look, I need you to swear that you will keep this to yourself."

"I swear that I will keep this to myself. On the Madonna." And she crossed herself.

"All right, then. You know about the closures, don't you?"

"You mean of the factories?"

"You know the Germans closed more than two hundred textile firms last fall when they occupied the city? You realize that they left six thousand workers without work?"

Emilia had heard such figures. She felt fortunate to have any work at all. She knew it was the small artisan shops that had been hardest hit, those that specialized in single phases of transforming rags into raw wool: spinning, warping, weaving, dyeing. Some of the larger establishments churned out military-issue blankets made from recycled wool. As the war effort revved up, there were soldiers and laborers to keep warm, especially those in the mountains. As for the autonomous workers, she had heard gossip about some who hid their machines and material in storage rooms, confident that they would be able to resume production at some hopeful point in the future.

"It wasn't just a coincidence that they targeted the small firms," he continued.

"Nothing is ever a coincidence with the Nazis," she said.

"That's for sure. Well, they don't realize what a mistake they made in closing the small firms. They thought concentrating production would increase efficiency. They figured it would give them more control over the workers. They have no clue what they're up against. They have no idea of how things work in Prato. The networks connecting the artisans and the go-betweens are so extensive, they don't have a chance of controlling us, no matter how aggressive their actions."[2]

"What are you getting at?"

Carlo leaned over, cupped his right hand, and whispered into her ear. "There's going to be a general strike."

"How in the world are they planning anything with troops everywhere?"

"The *impannatori*, the go-betweens. People like Aldo. They're working the networks."

"Do you really think they're trustworthy?"

"Look, the middlemen may be clever as foxes and just as likely to exploit your grandmother as a child, what with their lending schemes and all, but ultimately they are speculators and they want the economy back more than anybody else. And they are Pratese."

"I don't know," Emilia said, shaking her head. "It sounds dangerous, Carlo."

"Are you kidding? Of course it's dangerous. But we don't have a choice. Ever since the Nazis took over the factories in Prato last fall, the situation has gotten worse and worse."

"I don't like the sound of it."

"I'm telling you, we don't have a choice. You can't believe what they're up to in the mountains."

Emilia's eyes widened as though to say: *What are you waiting for? Tell me the rest.*

"Hitler thinks the Italians are swine.[3] And what can you expect? He thinks his own people should rot if they cannot win the war.[4] He's obsessed about keeping the Allied forces at bay. They've broken through Italy. He's losing his dream of his Fortress Europe. So all those trucks and troops you think you're hearing, well you are." Hitler had launched his plan to construct a line of defense along the Apennine Mountains that divided central from northern Italy. Carlo described the formidable fortification of the Vernio Pass, north of Prato, and the Futa Pass, above Florence.

"It's unbelievable, Emilia. They say the line stretches all the way west to the Mediterranean Sea, at Massa Carrara, and east to the Adriatic, at Pesaro. It's crazy. Two hundred miles long and twelve miles deep. And get this: he has named it the Gothic Line."[5]

"The Gothic Line?"

"Yeah, it's to inspire his soldiers with images of ancient Germanic peoples who founded kingdoms throughout the Roman Empire. The whole thing is just a facade, though. The soldiers are weary. Do you realize they've retreated almost three thousand miles since early 1942?[6] He's looking right at his destiny, but he can't see it."

"Or maybe he sees it but refuses to accept it," said Emilia.

"His empire is crumbling. But one thing is clear: the Führer is not going to surrender without a good fight. The Germans are preparing for a major battle. Right up in the Apennines, they've enlisted two thousand Slavic technicians and conscripted fifteen thousand Italian laborers. They've evacuated the villages up there. Those Nazi bastards are filling the landscape with gun turrets and steel shelters. They've put defense nooks inside rock tunnels and they've dug deep minefields. It's a veritable military obstacle course. Partisans are trying to sabotage them, but the Germans lash back. It's harsh. They shoot and hang hostages, and they've even burned an entire village. The antipartisan Black Brigades are brutal."[7]

"How do you know all this, Carlo?"

"That's not up for discussion," he said, leaving no doubt that he meant it. He turned his back to her and headed down the hill toward the field, but then stopped and turned around again to face her. "Just trust me. I'm telling you the truth."

Emilia headed up the driveway. She heard voices and was startled to see three armed men in uniform talking with her father. They stood near the cement well in the grassy courtyard. The strangers wore calf-high lace-up boots and light brown pants with belted shirts; red bands encircled their upper arms with a striking black swastika centered inside a white circle. Babbo's face drooped with concern. He nodded compliantly as he disappeared with the Nazis into the darkness of the barn.

Emilia tiptoed over to the side of the farmhouse. She leaned against the white, rose, gray, and brown stones that formed the wall, but she was numb to the sharp edges. She held her breath as she prayed the Germans would not notice her there. She stood as motionless as a marble statue. She had heard horrible stories about the Nazis and what they did to people in villages. Gory images of dead bodies raced through her mind. She fought to push the bloody thoughts away. What if they killed Babbo right there in the barn? What if they hauled him off to a camp? How would they survive? What would become of her? She felt dizzy. From her hiding spot, she heard more talking from inside the barn. She told herself to breathe and listened to her own breath. She made out her father's voice. His tone was calm, if compliant, and that settled her down. She caught a glimpse of him as he walked back outside into the grassy courtyard and watched just long enough to see him nodding "yes." She sighed with cautious relief. As the men turned toward the driveway, Emilia took off in a sprint round to the other side of the house, which backed up to a footpath. She leaned against the wall, caught her breath, and let her racing heart slow. Hearing the engine of the Nazi's jeep, she froze, and once she could hear the vehicle race off down the driveway, she headed back to the front of the house, where she met her father just inside the front door. Her cheeks were bright red, and he couldn't help but notice. She sensed sorrow in his expression as he headed inside to round up her brothers and sisters, sister-in-law, uncle, and of course Mamma. Everyone gathered around the table.

"We've been through hard times before, and we are all the stronger for it," he began. He drank water from his glass. The children waited for his words but heard only swallowing. It seemed loud against the silence. They waited, no one daring to speak.

"What I have to tell you, I say with a heavy heart," he finally continued. "You have all worked hard. You have helped make our family strong. You all do your jobs and show due respect. These are good qualities that you can draw upon now. The coming weeks will try all of us in different ways. The men, the women, the young, and the old, the stubborn, and the gracious. Each of us will face a different challenge, and we will have to look deep into ourselves to rise to that challenge. We are going to have some company. It is not company that I invited, but it is company that we will have to welcome. I have given permission to the Nazis to use the barn as a kitchen for their soldiers."

"But what about the livestock?" objected Carlo.

"We'll make do," said Babbo firmly. "We'll bring them in the house if we must."

"Emilio, this is not a good idea, you start negotiating with those Germans and we're finished," Uncle Giovanbattista interjected.

"Believe me, I had no choice," Babbo shot back. "They gave me no alternative. They—"

"They are not to be trusted, that's what," Giovanbattista interrupted. "Ever since Mussolini's arrest, what is it? Eight months now? Hitler is sour on Italians. You can't trust the Germans. They sense our defection. They think we'd rather lay down our arms or, better yet, sell them, than fight against the Allies."

"Not a bad idea," agreed Carlo, cracking the lone smile in the room.

"Hitler is obsessed," Giovanbattista said, not finding humor in Carlo's comment. "He'll do anything to avoid yielding to his enemies."

"Anything," Carlo echoed, pursing his lips and looking down at his untied shoelace.

The family did not waste time worrying about the well-being of their animals or other goods. The Germans took everything they needed when

they needed it: horses, cows, grain, olive oil, wine. Luckily, Uncle Giovanbattista had insisted that Babbo dig a hole in the dirt floor of the basement
and bury a stash of food. Meanwhile, in the barn, military cooks prepared
food, and delivery boys shuttled the meals to their fellow soldiers posted
who knows where on the front. Bombers filled the skies, unloading explosives on the station and factories of Prato. German officers issued a decree
requiring the delivery of massive quantities of grain.[8]

Stories of the impending general strike in Prato spread. The Nazi
presence became increasingly intrusive. Organizers relied on antifascists
to print up flyers. On the morning of March 4, 1944, the residents of the
city of rags awoke to walls painted with red words—*Operai Scioperate!*—
commanding the textile workers to strike. Men and women, old and
young, filled the streets. They carried signs. They sang songs of the resistance. Well-connected people like Uncle Aldo played a key role, and
within days peasants in Carmignano launched a strike in response to the
German demand for grain. They refused to hand it over.[9]

The Nazis reacted ferociously. It was much worse than anyone had
imagined. Hitler ordered that at least 20 percent of all the strikers be
rounded up and deported to German camps. The fascists of Prato showed
no hesitation in enforcing the order. It was, some figured, a twisted, face-
saving gesture. They searched the houses of suspected antifascists and set
up roadblocks. They obliged firms to furnish the names of workers who had
participated in the strike. The fascists had a quota to fill: the Führer wanted
1,900 able-bodied men to work for the Third Reich. Terror was on the loose.

The next day Emilia was outside fetching water from the well when
Carlo came up the driveway.

"I told you a strike was too dangerous, Carlo," Emilia said.

"We didn't have a choice."

Word was the Nazis and their fascist conspirators indiscriminately
rounded up just about anyone they found wandering the streets of Prato
and deported them. The story was they were taken to Germany, but who
could believe it? In times of war, truth traveled with the victims.[10]

German soldiers infested the countryside like wasps come springtime.
News of the Allied advance reached the village through planes, airwaves,

and gossip. Uniformed men brought their dead and lay them on the hill-side just beyond the kitchen window. The sight of those young men strewn across the grass gave Emilia a fright. Her stomach churned. Even if they were Germans, Emilia felt sorry for them. Some of them were good-looking boys. Each one of them was some mother's son.[11]

Before long, though, she came to resent their presence. Living in a state of occupation was like living in an open prison. Even in the countryside, food was growing short.

One evening a Nazi soldier knocked at the door. "Let me in, I just want to talk," he said, speaking softly as though to plead with her.

Emilia came to the door wiping her hands on her apron. "Well, I was just leaving." She untied her apron and headed out.

His voice turned sharp. "You're afraid," he said.

"No I'm not," she said, searching deep into her gut to feign strength. "I need to go to my sister's house, that's all. She's expecting me. Her husband is a prisoner in Germany."

Emilia waited for him to leave and then headed toward her sister's house. Her steps echoed as she walked. Noises swept down upon her like so many bats. She wondered if the soldier was following her. She stopped and listened. Silence shrouded her. She began walking again, taking quiet steps. Listening hard, she glanced over her shoulder. Still nobody was there. At her sister's house, she knocked hard on the wooden door. After a long silence, shuffles echoed across terracotta. Her chest tightened as metal rubbed metal and a key unlatched the lock. The door opened and Emilia rushed in. Her heart raced so hard she thought she would faint. She wished the war over. If only Parigi would come home.[12]

TEN Resistance

June 1944

The house was dark and quiet except for a summer rain that fell like pellets on the terracotta roof tiles. Just past one o'clock in the morning, a deafening noise woke Emilia with a jolt. She pulled her covers tightly into her fingers. An ear-piercing explosion followed. Windowpanes shattered onto tile floors. The blast ricocheted off walls of the village houses like waves crashing against a fleet of boats on a stormy sea. The loudness rang for minutes.

When the noise subsided, Mamma's shouts echoed through the house: "Watch the glass!" In a flash and without a thought, Emilia found herself barefoot in the living room with all of her family members.

Carlo slipped into his shoes and headed straight for the door.

"And where do you think you're off to?" asked Babbo.

"I'll be back," he said, and he disappeared swift as a swallow.

In a daze, Emilia followed her siblings, clad in their white sleeping gowns, outside, down the driveway, and into the lane, where a collection of neighbors had begun to gather. The sky was dark, the stars and moon shrouded by low-hanging clouds.

Speculation abounded.

"The Nazis dropped a bomb on the town hall."

"Far too forceful for that."

"We're under attack."

"No way. It stopped too soon."

"They've blown up the munitions plant at Nobel."

"Impossible!"

"That must be it!"

Emilia was scared. Whatever it was, it was bad. Her older sister and some of her own friends worked at the plant. She knew boys who were forced to work there as part of their military service. She spotted Lirua in the crowd and went to join her best friend. Emilia trembled.

"Do you think that's possible?" Emilia asked, her voice shaking. "Weren't they working three shifts?"

"I'm not sure," Lirua said.

"I hear they have four thousand working there now."

"Four thousand, that many?"

"That's what they say," Emilia said, her arms crossed to fend off the chilly night air. "They need lots of explosives for the war. Mamma went and my sister Maria went. Did I tell you that? One said 'yes' and the other 'no.' Mamma went for two days and then she told me, 'I'm afraid of the gunpowder.' Me, I never went. I was too afraid."

"That place scares me to death now," Lirua said. "Especially since the Nazis took it over."

The girls shivered in the misty, smoke-filled air.

The chattering of the neighbors dissipated. Emilia noticed as everyone turned and looked down the lane. Carlo ran toward them waving his arms and shouting.

"It's the Buricchi brothers, the Naldi boy, and Bruno Spinelli," he gasped, almost to the point of tears.

"Son, calm yourself," Babbo said, visibly forcing himself to be calm. "What are you saying?"

"At least three of them are dead. Down at Poggio alla Malva. Naldi was blown to smithereens. All that was left was his railroad pass. They found it next to a rock, down by the station."

Emilia felt hollow. She crossed her arms and squeezed her fingers into the flesh of her upper arms. She didn't know Naldi, he was only twenty and a student in Florence. But she'd heard of Bogardo Buricchi. He was in her same class, born in 1920, though in Carmignano proper, and would have soon celebrated his twenty-fourth birthday. His younger brother was only nineteen. She knew of Spinelli. He had worked at the factory and lived in the little town up the road called La Serra. At forty-three, he was the oldest of the group.

"My God."

"Pray to the Madonna."

"What happened?" asked Babbo.

"All I know is—" Carlo said, his heart racing through each word. "Those train cars that were pulled out on the tracks yesterday? They were loaded with explosives. Just loaded to the brim. A group of partisans found out they were headed to Prato to blow up the city."

Grief, then fear, shot through the villagers.

"Spinelli is injured real bad," he continued. "They doubt he'll make it. But what a hero. All of them. They sabotaged the Germans."

"What bravery," Uncle Giovanbattista managed, rubbing sleep from his eyes. "But how in the world? How did they ever get past the German guards to pull off such a thing?"

"Apparently, the soldiers were off duty at their Saturday night dance," Carlo said, his words more level now than a few minutes earlier.

"They must have had quite the plan," Giovanbattista said thoughtfully. "I wonder what went wrong."

"Nobody seems to know," Carlo said. "They had TNT and a bomb. They were watching the eleven train cars that had left Nobel. The cars were parked a suspicious distance from the station. The Nazis were planning to bomb the factories in Prato. The men must have climbed up onto a car. Some of the other guys said they expected several minutes' delay.

Something went wrong. From where they found Naldi, it's clear the guys had barely made any distance when the bomb exploded."

The villagers stirred. The news spread. Grief mixed with excitement.

"The partisans have saved the factories of Prato."

"The Nazis will be furious."

"They will retaliate."

A young boy in the crowd began to cry. A cacophony of voices blended. Several women stirred and gathered around his mother.

"Take him to the Rossi girl, she will cure his fear."

"Yes, Milena Rossi is a young but competent healer."

The mother frowned and lifted her crying son to her hip. Hearing mention of the Rossi girl, Emilia and Lirua joined the circle of women. They offered to accompany the mother and her son up the road to the Rossi house the next day, since they were good friends with Milena's sister, Natalina.

The crowd dispersed and Emilia went to help her other family members clean up the glass debris scattered beneath the windows throughout the house. Shards glistened in the candlelight. The job would have to be completed with daylight. Emilia headed to bed, then tossed and turned through the night. She couldn't recall ever having had such a restless night's sleep.

Word of the fatal partisan act spread like battle smoke on a windy ridge. People were quick to come to conclusions. Gossip in the town held that the partisans had been paying particularly close attention to German activity at Nobel, even though the hilly ridge where the munitions plant was tucked away made it difficult. The Germans had taken over the plant and calculated that it would serve them well in their battles against the encroaching Allied forces. The sabotage would later become known as one of the most important acts of resistance in Tuscany.[1]

On Monday, after lunch, Emilia and Lirua wove groggily as they waited for the neighbor woman and her son to arrive at the house. "I hope she has some herb left," Lirua said.

"Why wouldn't she?" Emilia asked.

"Don't they usually collect *erba della paura* at the summer solstice?" Lirua said. "Why, we're almost upon a year."

"I saw several of the bouquets the other day when I was over there weaving," said Emilia.

"Are you sure?" asked Lirua.

"Have you ever seen one?" Emilia shot back. "They're unmistakable. They're shaped like a fist, 'to strike the fear.'"

Soon, the mother and her son arrived. The boy, a skinny little thing who looked even smaller in the daylight, was about eight years old, Emilia figured. He stood close to his mother, his bony hand grasping her hand.

"How is the little fellow?" Emilia asked. As she looked at him, he buried his pale face in his mother's dress.

"You can see, he's suffering from some trauma," she said.

"Let's go, then," Emilia said.

The foursome crossed the town and followed the curves of the road until they reached a steep unpaved driveway. They took it, wending their way to a stone farmhouse that perched at the top of an olive tree–covered ridge. They were grateful for the light breeze, a welcome respite from the weekend rains, for it moved the humid midafternoon air. The farmhouse was so still it seemed abandoned.

"*C'è nessuno?*" Emilia called. "Is anybody home?"

"Do you think she'll mind us coming?" the mother asked, her son whimpering now and again.

"Milena feels a calling to treat people," Emilia reassured. "She'll be happy to help if she can."

Finally Natalina came to the door.

"Are we disturbing you?" Emilia asked.

"No, no," Natalina said. "Come on in."

Emilia explained their reason for coming.

"Milena is just finishing up with the dishes." She motioned to her friends, the mother and her son to follow her into the kitchen.

"Can I offer you something?" Natalina asked.

"No, we're fine."

"Are you sure? Coffee? Vin Santo?"

"No, no. Really."

"What about the boy? At least take something for him."

"All right, perhaps he'd drink some water after the long walk," the neighbor said.

Milena, who was standing at the kitchen sink, ladled water from a vat into a glass and handed it to the boy.

"And you ladies?"

Lirua wiped sweat from the crease of her nose and smiled at Emilia. "I guess we are rather thirsty, too. I would gladly take a glass."

The women quenched the thirst they had denied. Their hosts pulled around a half dozen straight-backed chairs and everyone sat.

"In the evening," the mother began, "when it gets dark, my son starts to cry. 'What's wrong? What's wrong?' I ask him. And this child says, 'I'm afraid for Babbo, that something might happen to him, something bad, to Babbo, something horrible might happen. I'm afraid. Why doesn't Babbo come home?' And so, it's been like that. He stands at the window, crying, always with the thought of his father. I put my son to bed each night, but he won't sleep. And now, with this big explosion, he's gotten even worse. Just filled with fear, poor thing."

Milena nodded then disappeared outside. Shortly, she returned with a nearly empty basket containing a dried plant with long, spindly stems and small flowers. She boiled a pot of water, then steeped the herb in it to make a fresh infusion. The women talked as they waited for the brew to cool. The boy sipped his water.

"What's your name, child?" Milena asked, her voice as soothing as salve.

"Vittorio."

"Come, sit by me, Vittorio. Tell me if the water is too hot." Milena dipped a cloth into the infusion and asked him to hold out his right hand. She pushed back his short sleeve, to the tip of his shoulder, and gently dragged the cloth across first the top, then the underside of the length of his arm. The herb effervesced on his soft skin. She repeated this action on the boy's limbs one by one. Milena then blessed him with sacred words. It was different from the priest's benediction, part Catholic, part magic in its invocation.

"For this to work, we have to do the washing three times," Milena explained to Vittorio's mother. "And it's best if we do it on a Monday,

Wednesday, and Friday. So return on Wednesday. By the third washing, the herb should no longer fizz on his skin if it has done its job."

The mother thanked Milena. She and her son, along with Emilia and Lirua, headed back toward the town.

A few days later, the two girls walked down the long driveway to where Lirua's mother stood on the side of the lane hanging laundry on a line that overlooked the valley.

"That's strange," Emilia piped up.

They watched smoke billow from the top of the big hill. As Lirua and Emilia helped Raffaella hang out white shirts and bedsheets, the postman came down the road.

"It's the Peruzzi place," he said, looking straight at Emilia.

Emilia dropped her clothespins and took off like a startled horse.

"Wait, where are you going?" Lirua shouted.

"To check on Parigi's family," Emilia said.

"All alone?"

"Come if you like. But let's go."

Lirua took off after her. The young women sprinted down across the vineyard toward the hill that climbed to Artimino.

A good half hour passed before the girls reached Parigi's house. They could smell the acrid odor of smoke and burned goods as they neared. It looked as though the fire had even charred some of the trees. Parigi's mother, Ida Innocenti, stood in the front yard of the house, her arms crossed, just staring. Germena stood beside her, her toddler on her hip. The blaze had burned the house to the ground.

"Inside, we'd stored every God-given good: grain, wine, oil," Ida said, shaking her head. "Oh! And in times of war."

"What on earth?" Emilia said.

Ida seemed not to hear her. "He called himself a partisan," she said, turning toward the girls.

"What?"

"A partisan, he said. He heard a German soldier was holing up inside our house and decided to do something about it."

"Was there a soldier in your house?" Emilia asked.

"I wish," said Ida. "At least he might have stopped that *bischero*, that idiot."

"Did you check the house?"

"Nobody was inside," Germena answered. "We're sure."

"There's nothing worse than a fake partisan," said Lirua. "I can't think of anything less gallant."

The man had been intent on killing a Nazi. Although he had had no proof that there was a live "Ted" staked out inside the Peruzzi household, he had nevertheless set fire to the house—not an easy feat given that the *casa colonica* was of stone and beam construction and had survived five centuries.

Emilia searched her thoughts to offer some words of comfort. "Surely, the *contessa* will rebuild the house. This has been a good estate for her. Not even the worst landlord would blame the sharecroppers for such an ill fate."

"And what would he have done with a 'Ted' had he found one? And now what am I to do?"

"We will move forward. We will help you. At least everyone is alive and unharmed," Emilia offered, hugging Ida.

As dusk fell, she and Lirua headed back down the hill.

"Look at them," Emilia said as she turned to Lirua. "They have nothing save the clothes on their backs. Do you realize? They were eight living in the house: Parigi's mother and father, his two sisters, a brother and his wife, their two kids. That poor woman. She's got her other four sons off in the world, fighting a senseless war—and then to be left with nothing. To think of the goods they had so carefully stored: wine, oil, grain, linens, clothes."

"I've never heard tell of such a *bischero*," said Lirua, echoing the favorite Florentine term for idiot. The label was particularly appropriate given the local lore for the term's genesis: a Florentine family had refused to sell their house to the city for a good price, only to find their home burned with no right to rebuild; land was held in common, so the city seized the lot, ashes and all. The anti-Nazi *bischero* today would lose only his reputation, whereas the Peruzzi family had been left empty-handed, dependent on their wealthy landlady's goodwill.

"They had everything in that house," Emilia said.

"And in times of war," Lirua repeated.

"What of our plans to marry after the war?" Emilia said as they reached the bottom of the valley. She forced back tears. She didn't want to cry in front of anyone, not even Lirua. But she felt her face flushing, and she knew her friend noticed. Nothing escaped Lirua. "I'm sorry. I'm being so selfish."

"Maybe it's not as bad as it seems, Emi. The *contessa* will help them out."

"Everything's bad lately. Who would expect anything more at this point?" Emilia breathed deeply and wiped each eye with her right palm. "With this war everywhere, I feel half dead. I'm not sure who I am any-more or what road to follow. Glass shards on the floor, jeeps in the fields, planes overhead, bombs all around. And those Germans in our barn. Who can feel at home in their own house? And then there's hardly any food. I'm hungry all the time, Lirua, but I don't want to say anything. What would be the point? They know. We all know. We're all hungry. They're trying so hard to ration the food."

"We'll get through this, Emi, you'll see."

The house was dark but for one candle flickering in the kitchen. On the table, Mamma had set Emilia's bowl of pasta at her place, with an-other bowl over the top to conserve the heat. Emilia's stomach was in knots from the long walk and all the emotions, but she managed to eat. Chewing each mouthful seemed a huge effort and took tremendous con-centration. In a half-conscious state she walked up the stairs to her bed-room, where her three other sisters were already asleep. She collapsed. The future looked bleak and impossible. She felt lonely. She buried her head into her pillow and cried. Maria, ever a light sleeper, rustled in the next bed over. Emilia held her breath and forced her outburst to stop. She lifted her head and took in a deep breath of the cool night air. She refused to despair. *I will be strong. I will be patient. I will wait for Parigi and we will wait for the right moment to marry.* There was no hurry, the world couldn't possibly get any worse.

ELEVEN

American Chocolates

August 1944

The tanks arrived from Florence. They did not always follow the major thoroughfares but advanced northward like boars. They traversed fields, passing giant cone-shaped stacks of hay that brushed the roofs of the peasant farmhouses. They stirred up clouds of dust as their giant tracks cut swaths into the cultivated earth. The countryside teemed with movement. Columns of trucks clogged the main roads, and jeeps moved swiftly through the piazzas. Men lingering outside the local bar warned the boys to be alert in their play. The military vehicles marked a new season. Villagers everywhere felt a collective if apprehensive sense of relief about the coming of the Allied troops.

Come nightfall, the mountains lit up. From a distance, the fires appeared as flickering campfires rather than the burning belts of hell that they really were. The sound of birds singing in the otherwise quiet countryside was merely a distant recollection. Bombers roared overhead.[1]

Emilia sought out Carlo but could no longer rely on him. He had become withdrawn and forlorn. He disappeared for days at a time. Twice, a pair of men wearing black shirts had come knocking at the door in search of him, and nobody could say where he had gone. She turned to Tosca, who remained the most politically engaged of the older generation of women. Emilia could always count on her for updates. Tosca had kept an ear open for politics ever since the days of her acquaintance with Germena's father. She seemed to have a direct line to the activity in the mountains, though she was careful not to mention names. Everyone had to watch their backs these days, and Tosca was a prudent gossip.

One afternoon as Emilia and Lirua were sitting in front of the barn, working up an order of slippers, Tosca ambled up the driveway. Now well into middle age, she was as sturdy as ever. Her hair had grayed graciously, leaving enough of the auburn of her youth to give it a sunburst effect. Emilia still remembered how Tosca had been the one to tell her and the other girls the truth about Silvano Santini's escape when they had been just seven years old. Tosca had always expressed such empathy for him and for his family. Not all adults entrusted children with precious knowledge. Tosca had a talent for knowing what to say, when to say it, who to tell, and how to tell them. The young women were always happy to see Tosca. They put trust in her words. Plus they could always count on her humor even in hard times.

"Well just look at you two," Tosca said, putting her hand on the back of the chair and propping up her body. "Back here, working away."

"No more cocks in the barn," Emilia said, cackling as she spoke. "The Nazis have fled the coop. It's been some days now."

"I don't know how your family did it, "Tosca said.

"My tongue is numb from biting it."

Tosca let a smile slip out. "How is it you ladies always manage to stir up some work?" she asked. "The ships could be blocked at the ports, and you two would still be working furiously on some job."

"We're mindful that blockades are temporary, and the ships may embark on their voyage at any time, so we just keep our fingers dancing and our hearts hopeful," Lirua said, smiling back at her.

"Honestly, it's been quite slow," Emilia added. "This is the first work we've had in weeks. If the factories get back to full force, I'm thinking of going to work on the inside. The piecework just isn't paying anymore. Hats one day, slippers the next. The only constant around here is change. So, Tosca, what news do you bring?"

"Oh, not much, unless you haven't noticed the Americans all over the place," Tosca said.

"Don't know a thing about it," said Emilia, smiling and feigning ignorance.

Lirua shrugged in agreement.

"There's quite a crew of them, down at the station," Tosca said.

"Really?" The girls smiled at each other.

"They sing this little song, 'We are the D-Day Dodgers, / In sunny Italy.' "

"The D-Day Dodgers?"

"These boys had barely slept two nights after taking Rome when the other Allied troops launched the D-Day invasion. All the press went to Normandy. The poor boys fighting here in Italy try to make up for being passed over. They sing silly little songs."

The young women looked at each other and giggled at the thought of the young, handsome American soldiers so nearby.

"Word is, the troops are repairing the train tracks before heading up to the mountains. They'll make a major push to the Gothic Line, and they'll need the tracks to move supplies up from Florence and Nobel. This is the last obstacle between them and the Alps. Breaking through Hitler's defense line up in the Apennines is going to be a major test for these troops. They've slogged eight hundred kilometers to get here. Success will devastate the Nazi hold. Everyone knows the stakes."

Emilia and Lirua seemed unable to help themselves; they continued to exchange smiles.

"You girls had better behave yourselves," Tosca warned, her tone turning humorless and stern. "The ending is not a happy one for foolish girls who fall for soldiers. Even ones who sing little songs."

Tosca headed off, then turned back. "*Arrivederci*," she said, her wave more like shooing off flies than gesturing goodbye.

"I've heard the British and American armies even have soldiers from India," Lirua said. "I've seen a picture of one wearing a turban."

Emilia looked back down to her lap and wove faster. The girls worked quietly for a while, making up for lost time. After about an hour, they heard a twig break and looked up in unison to see a teenage boy. He stepped off the footpath and headed straight over to them. It was Luigi Martelli, the light-haired, heavy-set trickster who lived just down the hill.

"How are you two?" he said, smirking.

They glanced up at him suspiciously.

"And what, pray tell, brings you to these parts?" Emilia asked.

"I have a surprise for you."

"Oh yeah?"

"I met the American soldiers when they passed," Luigi boasted. "You know the ones? They've come to repair the tracks. They've brought other things, too. Do you want a little American chocolate?"

"Give it to us!" the young women demanded in unison.

They set their work on the ground beside their chairs, and he handed them a little, flat, square package. It fit in the palm of Lirua's hand. She looked it over carefully, then passed it to Emilia. She turned it over. Funny, it didn't look or feel like a chocolate. Unless in America chocolates were squishy.

"*Gli è un poppino, bischero*—it's a rubber, idiot," Lirua finally said to Emilia.

They both glared at Luigi.

"*Accidempoli a te!* Damn you!" they shouted.

Luigi buckled over, dying from laughter.

"Get out of here, you sneak," Lirua said.

"Give me back the rubber," Luigi demanded.

"Forget it. It's ours now," quipped Emilia.

"The American chocolate is ours," Lirua added.

Luigi could see he was outnumbered, but he wasn't about to give in quite so fast.

"And what intentions might you two have with a *poppino?*"

"That's for us to know and you to find out," Lirua shot back.

What could he say? He lumbered off down the path, only half-satisfied that his little joke had worked.

The girls picked up the strands of straw as well as their partially finished slippers. "Have you ever used one before, Emilia?"

"No, I've never even seen one before."

"It's modern, you know."

"Must be. The townsfolk probably know about them. How did you know what it was, Lirua?"

Lirua grinned. Emilia could detect some blushing despite her dark cheeks.

"Lirua? You little devil you."

"Well, I don't want to have a bunch of kids. What do you take me for? That's for backward peasants, not for girls like us. What about you?"

"Maybe two. Maybe I'll have two. Three at the very most. But honestly, I haven't given it much thought. To tell you the truth, I'm not in any hurry to become a mother."

"What's the hurry, anyway?" asked Lirua.

"Besides, now that the war *seems* to be ending—" Emilia said.

"Seems to be ending?" interrupted Lirua. "Come on, it is ending, don't be a pessimist."

"Fine, now that the war *is* ending," Emilia continued, "I want to go get a job in the factory. This piecework isn't good for much anymore. It barely pays, there's hardly any of it. I need to save some money for when I get married. I can't expect his family to have much for us. What do you say, want to go together? Down to a factory in Signa? I bet we could round up a couple other girls."

"I don't know."

"Come on, what are you afraid of? Gunpowder? It's not Nobel, for God's sake."

"It's just that, I don't know, it seems so far from home."

"Look, if there are four of us, there will be nothing to fear. We'll be together."

"I'll think on it."

April 1945

Carlo returned with reports of thousands of white crosses dotting the hillsides of mountain villages, marking the graves of fallen soldiers. Town cemeteries expanded as Nazi retribution exacted vengeance with no regard for age or sex or station in life. With so much suffering and hunger that had taken its toll, it was hard to read the signs even as they all pointed to the end of the war. Word spread fast of Mussolini's demise.

Emilia headed into town for bread late morning. In line at the *panificio*, she ran into Tosca, clutching the newspaper under her arm. Without uttering a word, the woman slowly unfolded the paper and held up the front page. Emilia grimaced as her eyes focused on a gruesome photograph: two lifeless bodies hanging upside down, gasoline pumps in the distance. The eerie yet modern backdrop stirred up memories of the previous August, when the Germans had shot fifteen Italians in a working-class district in Milan.

"It's the same piazza," Tosca said, matter-of-fact. "Just imagine, Benito and ladylove Claretta at the border, thinking they were just steps from freedom."

Tosca summarized the article. After Mussolini and his mistress had joined a convoy of German personnel, Communist partisans of the Fifty-second Garibaldi Brigade had halted the vehicles. The partisans approached the enemies as several Germans hastily moved Mussolini into a truck, where he threw on a military greatcoat. The partisans soon made their way back to the truck. They inspected its human cargo. Right away they recognized the poorly disguised couple and took them to a farmer's house. The next day, the duo was tried, executed, and transported to Milan for public display.[2]

The news sent shockwaves through the towns and cities of the peninsula. Emilia herself experienced a whirlwind of emotions. She had grown up a Little Italian, and all those teachings had proved false. What a waste of human lives! She knew the wounds of war would not heal overnight. She vowed that she would proceed with caution, protecting herself in an emotional coat of armor that she had learned to wear during these long, lonely years.

Deep down, Emilia dared to allow herself to think that the Duce's death signaled the beginning of a new era. She rejoiced for Tosca. It was finally safe for her to speak her mind. Things might even improve for Germena; perhaps she would at last have the chance to reunite with her kin in America. As the days brought distance from the gory finale of fascism, possibility swirled in the rejuvenating airs of spring, and she felt a new outlook taking shape. She asked around in her networks and before long landed a job in a textile factory working the looms with two other friends. The hours were long, but the pay was better than they had known during the war-torn fascist years. They had their first brushes with union politics as various leftist parties struggled for their support. Emilia didn't take much to politics. Her father's words echoed in her memory, "He who lives, reigns." When her guard was down, she let herself revel in a new sensation: the chance to get on with her life.

TWELVE

Only One

November 1949

Inside the stone walls of the dim Church of San Michele hung a wooden cross above a vase that grew plastic flowers. The priest's hands were as wrinkled as the Bible's spine was tattered. At just past three o'clock, the groom stood before him, gallant in a tailored, handsome suit. To little fanfare, the bride entered, wearing a neutral-colored dress with long sleeves and a mid-length hem. The couple faced each other with a sense of shared fate as they exchanged simple wedding vows. Emilia and Parigi had waited a long time for this moment. They counted fifteen years of engagement. No one questioned the marriage. They were almost thirty, plenty old to start a family.

Parigi had returned from the war with only his military-issue shirt and pants to his name. It was no way to start a life together. Getting one's affairs

Figure 1.   Emilia Raugei   *Figure 2.*   Parigi Peruzzi

in order took time. Five years passed without incident—until the defining incident. As Emilia stood at the altar, her body felt oddly foreign.

In the introductory rite, the priest recalled Parigi and Emilia's baptisms and then blessed the guests gathered as witnesses. He offered inspirational readings from the letters of several apostles. The duration of the ceremony made Emilia light-headed. Parishioners here and there chatted. Lirua turned to see who was making the noise in the pew behind her. As the priest moved on to the matrimonial liturgy, friends and family gave their full attention to the bride and groom.

"My dear Parigi and Emilia, you have come into the house of the Lord, before the ministry of the Church and before the community, because of your decision to join together in holy matrimony to receive the stamp of approval from the Holy Spirit, source of faithful and inexhaustible love. I only ask now for you to express your intentions. Parigi and Emilia," he said, looking down at her pallid face, "have you come to celebrate this marriage without any constrictions, in full liberty, and aware of the sacrifice—or rather—" (his interruption here caught the listeners by surprise) "—the *significance* of your decision?"

"Yes."

"Are you prepared, following the path of matrimony, to love each other and honor each other for your whole lives?"

"Yes."

"Are you prepared to welcome with love the children that God will donate to you and educate them according to the laws of Christ and his Church?"

"Yes."

"If this, therefore, is your intention to unite yourselves in marriage, give each other your right hand and express your consent before God and to his Church."

The bride and groom joined hands. As Parigi said his vows, Emilia lingered over his every word. The priest turned to her. She breathed deep through her wooziness and managed to say her part.

"With the Grace of Christ I promise always to be faithful, in joy and in pain, in sickness and in heath, and to love you and honor you all the days of my life."

The priest looked directly at Parigi, then Emilia, acknowledging their promises and, without lingering, moved the ceremony along. "The almighty and merciful Signore confirms the consent that you have demonstrated in front of the Church and offers you his blessing. Man does not dare to separate that which God unites." Rings were exchanged, the couple was blessed, and all joined in prayer, invoking Mary and the saints Giocchino, Anna, Zaccaria, Elisabetta, Giovanni Battista, Pietro, Paolo, Rita, Stefano, and Martino, and then professing their faith in one God.

After the ceremony, the guests put on their wool coats and headed to Artimino. They gathered in an intimate courtyard. Even with the flat lighting of an overcast afternoon, peasants who worked these hills appreciated the panorama. Beyond the reception, to the left, eyes set upon a regal lane of cypress that led to the old Medici hunting villa with its roof of cluttered chimneys. To the right opened a spectacular vista of terraced hillsides. Alternating patches of grapevines and olive trees lined flat ridges and clung to rugged hillsides, stopping only where they came up against the forest. The cultivated landscape in miniature softened memories of sweat and toil. From on high, the effect was nothing short of grace.

A modest spread of traditional fare covered a table. The guests kept their distance from the food until the newlyweds appeared, mingled, and greeted their kin and the friends they had known since their youth. Parigi's brother Urbano and his wife, Loretta Lunghi, were particularly anxious to greet the couple given that in a few hours they would all be living under the same roof.

Parigi nudged Emilia, and they excused themselves to make their way over to the refreshments, which no one had yet touched out of respect for the guests of honor. The favorite biscotti from Bellini's bakery formed a mound on two platters. Homemade Vin Santo from the Peruzzi cellar filled several clear bottles with its amber hue. Beside the brew the hosts had arranged several dozen small, simple glasses. Emilia nibbled on a crunchy *biscotto* and lifted a small glass of the sweet, strong wine to her mouth, only wetting her lips. Nausea swelled in her gut, and exhaustion overcame her.

Parigi noticed her wan face. "Wait here," he said kindly.

He returned with his brother Amaretto. He and Germena had wasted no time after their marriage several years ago to profit from the postwar boom. They had a dashing new Fiat to show for Germena's shrewdness.

Emilia and Parigi climbed in the back. The seat was chilled from fall air, damp with fog.

"How are you feeling?" Parigi whispered as he scooted close to his bride.

"Not so well," she said. Color rushed out of her face as she gazed out the window. She folded her arms over her coat. "I'm going to be sick."

"Slow on the curves!" he yelled to his brother. Then to Emilia, "We'll be there in just a minute."

"Better," Emilia sucked in a long, deep breath as they headed down the straight *vicolo,* or lane, that led to the Peruzzi home. She loathed the idea of getting sick on her wedding day.

Arriving at the Peruzzi house brought relief. She excused herself and followed the dark hallway to the bedroom that had been designated for her and Parigi. The trunk with her dowry inside had been sent up to the house the day before. She spotted it at the base of her new bed, then lay down, pulled a wool blanket up to her chin, and fell into a deep sleep.

She awoke disoriented and unclear of her whereabouts. Her new sister-in-law stood above her. In the pale light, Loretta looked ghostly.

"Are you revived?" Loretta asked, her voice gentle and comforting. She was aware of Emilia's condition and took interest in it.

"I feel so strange," Emilia said groggily. Dense woods surrounded the house, and trees shrouded the light.

"Come and show me your dowry. I'll help you get settled."

Emilia opened the trunk. On top were the linens for the house, neatly folded and pressed. She pulled them out and set them on the bed: perfect squares of white sheets, pillows, blankets, towels, and tablecloths. Loretta touched the corner of a pillowcase, admiring the beauty of the decorative handwork along the edges. As she opened one of the thick cotton sheets, so firmly pressed they seemed starched, she smiled.

"We'll have to do some recruiting to find virgins to make the nuptial bed!" Loretta teased.

"Oh, virgins!" Emilia shot back.

"You've waited so long to marry, surely none of your friends qualify," Loretta smiled.

"And what of it?" Emilia asserted.

"Well, they say it brings good luck to have virgins make the bed."

"That's so old-fashioned," Emilia shrugged. "Should I care?"

"You never know," Loretta replied. "I'll take all the luck I can gather."

Emilia turned back to the trunk, bent over and reached inside. Further down were her personal items: skirts, shirts, sweaters, underwear, nightgown, socks, shoes, a scarf, hat and gloves.

"Did you make all of this?" Loretta asked.

"For goodness sake, no. I made some of it and I bought some of it. I earned the money to put my dowry together. I worked nonstop before the war, making straw hats. We even managed to find work during the war, Lirua and I."

"You worked with Germena some, too, didn't you?"

"Yes, for her and her uncle, back when he was young. The things he would do to encourage us girls to work for him!" Emilia said, smiling as she recalled her days as a young girl. "The last few years, though, I'd been working the looms with several other girls in Signa. Now with the baby coming, I'm back doing piecework."

"Yes, there's work to be found again," Loretta agreed. "It's good to have Amaretto on your side. He's so calm, a great brother-in-law. Makes up for Germena. She's such a *crostino*, as hard as a stale bread crust."

The two laughed, and the laughter put Emilia at ease. Loretta helped her put away the linens and clothes before she left to tend to her chores. There in her new room Emilia confronted the promises of her new life and the dilemma of feeling oddly out of sorts. Even with the security of Parigi's arm draped across her, she slept fitfully.

Moving into a household of ten called for a major adjustment as *moglie,* wife, and *nuora,* daughter-in-law. Emilia had been living with only her mother and brother, Carlo, ever since her father had passed away and her other siblings had moved out. As the newcomer, she took her mother's advice to heart and tried her best, at least initially, to keep quiet. Being the newest daughter-in-law called for patience and sacrifice. At home, she had grown accustomed to the status of being her mother's eldest daughter, and that position had brought with it comfort as well as responsibility. She had provided emotional bridges between her hothead brother and her half-siblings, who, even if no longer at home, were still present in their lives. Now, in a new household with so many people, she had to get used to new routines and relationships. She set out to remake herself.

One morning she brought her weaving into the kitchen and took a seat at the big kitchen table beside Loretta. They worked on a new consignment of wool berets.

"You sure are quick," Loretta said.

"Well, you're good too," Emilia replied.

"But you're faster. I can see that it's easier for you to finish a few more than me. I'd rather cook than weave any day."

"Not me," Emilia said.

"I can see you love working with your hands, don't you?"

"Look," Emilia said, changing course. "You know what I'll do? If I make six hats, we'll each get three."

Loretta smiled approvingly. The task of preparing meals fell on the two daughters-in-law. Emilia did not exactly have an aversion to food preparation, but she lacked passion for cooking.

"You stay put then," Loretta said. "You're a little bit faster."

Emilia wove while Loretta cooked. This arrangement freed Emilia from household tasks. She increased the earnings for both of them. They remarked how clever they were to devise such a scheme. They joked about how they would confuse the state official when he came to inquire into their occupations. They made the best of each other's skills and preferences, and they were able to keep each other company while they worked. Emilia often sat in the kitchen while Loretta prepared a sauce, hashing out each day's happenings and imagining how their futures would unfold.

The next Sunday, her sister-in-law made a special meal: *crostini,* slices of bread topped with liver paté; *gnocchi,* a delicate pasta made from potatoes and flour, lightly covered with a tomato sauce; roasted rabbit with greens; and dried figs and pecorino for dessert. With each bite, Emilia considered how lucky she was, and she hadn't even had a virgin make her nuptial bed!

July 1950

The day before her thirtieth birthday, Emilia added a third new role: that of mother.

On July 14, 1950, Emilia gave birth to a baby girl. She did not go to a hospital. She had the baby right there in the house, with her own sheets and towels. And she wasn't ashamed of it either.

Patrizia, she called the baby. Patrizia Peruzzi. She liked the ring of it. Parigi agreed the name was poetic. Emilia's adoration for her daughter was matched only by her anxiety. Being a new mother brought countless new sensations and required endless tasks. Having a baby eased the loneliness that came from being the newest family member in a house so isolated in the countryside. But the infant created new worries. Emilia did not take well to nursing. She was used to working and being busy with her hands, and having to sit still did not come easily. She worried about her milk. She weighed the baby before and after every feeding as the pediatrician advised, and when the intake of grams did not measure up, she began to top it off with sheep's milk. She worried about whether she was cut out to be a mother. Loretta had taken to humming "Toys and Perfumes," and the refrain put her on edge even if she was hardly the selfish mamma of the song:

> "Mamma!"
> murmurs the child,
> her eyes welling up with tears,
> "for your little one, you never buy toys . . .
> Mamma, you buy only perfumes for yourself."

She was hardly prone to major indulgences, but the little she did enjoy worried her. She had been a single woman for so long. And she did not feel great warmth from her in-laws. She had hoped they would appreciate her more after she had given them the gift of a grandchild.

"You know," Emilia ventured, one evening as she finished a beret, "our in-laws like you better than me. And I'm the one with the baby!"

"But you know *la bambina* is the idol of the house," Loretta said.

Emilia continued to weave, consenting to her sister-in-law's suggestion to not dwell on such perceived differences. "Look, Loretta! I've made six hats. We'll each take three."

Emilia and Parigi plodded along at their lives, he helping his father work the land and she picking up consignment jobs thanks to her networks, including Amaretto and Germena. Emilia's energy waned, and she tried to ignore it, but the pain was more of a struggle to deny. One morning she confided in her sister-in-law.

"The pain has gotten really bad," Emilia said.

"Where does it hurt?" Loretta asked.

"Here, down low." Emilia touched her abdomen.

"You should go and see a doctor," Loretta urged. "I'll watch the *bambina* while you go. It will make the trip easier on you."

Emilia accepted her sister-in-law's offer. Amaretto offered her a ride to the station of Carmignano seven kilometers down the winding road. Taking the train to Florence brought back mixed memories of her youth and of that strange day with Giorgio Gentile when she had been just a young woman. What words she would have had with him now that she was wise! She laughed uncomfortably at her old self. As she did so, she clutched her sweater around her waist to ease the pain.

The walk from Santa Maria Novella to the hospital seemed far given her condition. Cars and *motorini* filled the city streets, and the noise was dizzying. She reached the stone steps of the hospital and passed through the towering doorway. A middle-aged man sat at an information desk reading the newspaper through thick eyeglasses. A dozen people waited in the sterile room with bare walls. Emilia approached the counter.

"Excuse me," she said. She searched to be patient, but the pain made it unbearable.

"Sir! May I check in?"

He slowly looked up from his newspaper, then set it down as though he were going home for the day. He moved his hand around the counter, his gaze following, searching for something almost in slow motion. Looking up at Emilia with a pen in his hand, he finally asked her name and symptom.

"They'll call you," he said, looking back to his newspaper.

The strong odor of ammonia made her queasy. Each minute dragged on as she waited for her name to be called. She eavesdropped on conversations, then nodded off in her chair. Hearing her name called startled her.

She walked toward a nurse who stood in a doorway with dark hair bobby-pinned to a white cap. She led Emilia into a large examination room with four beds, two on each side, flanked by privacy curtains and several chairs. She directed Emilia to have a seat, then listened to her heart and took her blood pressure.

"The doctor will be right with you," she said coldly as she left the room.

Before long a doctor appeared in a white coat. He was about her age. His face was clean-shaven, and he had exacting features: sculpted eyebrows, a slender nose, thin lips, and a pointy chin. He smelled like Marseille soap. Emilia fended off anxiety. She was not accustomed to city doctors and hospital routines.

"So what's the problem here?" the doctor asked, each word beautifully enunciated in a high Florentine that made her feel like a schoolgirl.

"It's been a piece since I've been feeling bad," Emilia told him.

"Can you tell me about it?" he asked.

"For two years now, I've been living with my husband's family," she began, speaking quickly. "They're ten in all. Up in Artimino. Do you know it? The town of the Medici palace with the hundred chimneys? We're a large family. During the war, the house burned. The man fashioned himself a partisan, he did. A *bischero* of a man. It was during the war. The house burned. So we took some time preparing everything before we married. And then I had the baby right away. She's two now—"

The doctor shined a light in her eyes, listened to her heart, and scribbled on his clipboard. "I see you're a little nervous," the doctor said. "You're having a bit of an *esaurimento nervoso,* a nervous breakdown," he concluded, patting her shoulder.

"Well, I was used to living with my mamma and my brother, and then to find myself in a house with ten people, it seems—*di sopraccapo,* like my head is going to explode."

The doctor stood up and, without offering any further diagnosis or cure, sent her on her way.

On the way home, Emilia felt frustrated. She could hardly believe what had happened. The doctor had not even considered her pain. She began to doubt it herself.

Back home, she sat at the kitchen table with Loretta. "The doctor said it's my nerves," she said. "What with the adjustment to the big family. I'll just have to bear the pain. It does come and go, after all."

Loretta recounted the cute and naughty things the baby had done while she was away. Emilia managed a laugh.

"You know how doctors can be wrong," Loretta said cautiously and then turned to the baby. "*Che tesoro,* what a sweetheart."

"I would like another baby," Emilia admitted. "Even if I am thirty-two. I'm hardly too old to have another baby."

"You're still good and young!" encouraged her sister-in-law. "If I had been blessed to have children, I wouldn't stop with one either."

"We'll see," Emilia sighed, rubbing her belly.

Six months passed, the pain persisted, and Emilia worried that something was wrong. She thought she might have a tumor. She decided to take a gamble and return to the hospital. This time, the nurse gave Emilia a white gown, showed her to a bed, and pulled a hospital curtain closed to give her some privacy. A different doctor entered the room. He was younger and stockier than the first. He sat down on a stool and felt her belly with his chubby fingers.

"You're pregnant," was his diagnosis, quick and confident.

"But if I had my menstruation just the other day?" Emilia asked.

He ordered a urine analysis, and the result was negative. She was right: She wasn't pregnant. She went home again, uncured and unsatisfied.

One day six weeks later while sitting on her chair, weaving a beret as Loretta prepared the mid-day meal, Emilia buckled over. The half-finished woolen beret and knitting needles fell to the floor.

"What's wrong?" Loretta said, startled.

Emilia didn't look up as she spoke. "These are the worst cramps ever," she cried. "I can't go on. If it's time for me to die, so be it. But I can't go on like this."

Loretta offered to accompany Emilia to Florence. The baby, now almost three, stayed with her *nonna*. At the emergency room, a diminutive doctor approached her and began rattling off questions: "Ma'am, have you had children?"

"Yes!" Emilia said, mentioning that her daughter was now nearly three years old.

"Abortions?"

"No! I've only had one baby and I did it on my own," she asserted. "I had her at home with all of our belongings, the sheets and everything, and I'm not ashamed to admit it!"

"*Fatta bene?* A healthy child?"

"As for defects, my daughter doesn't have any," Emilia snapped, her patience wearing thin. "Look doctor, could it be that I have a tumor?"

The doctor looked at her straight on. "Well, it's unlikely to be a tumor."

"*Allora, icchè?* Well, what then?"

"Now, we'll see," he replied, self-assured, and sent her upstairs to an operating room. She lay on a stretcher waiting. The pain was sharp. In walked the specialist, *il professore*. He was older than the others, gray hair, bright eyes, and a cheerful demeanor. He was gentle and reassured her as he proceeded to perform an internal exam.

"An ovarian cyst, signora," he said. "Not a tumor. This is not a cancerous tumor." The cyst had grown bigger than her fist. "We'll have to remove it."

"When?"

"Immediately."

He called in the nurse and an assistant. Emilia looked up at a naked bulb, and it faded into a blazing sunburst. The next thing she knew she was waking up bleary-eyed, the specialist standing at her side.

"*Pastasciutta,*" he instructed. "Eat a lot of pasta." And it went down well. For twelve days she stayed in bed all bandaged up. Eating pasta.

"You see, it wasn't true," Emilia said to Loretta when she came into the room. "My nerves weren't to blame. The big family wasn't to blame. It was the illness I had."

"Thanks to the Madonna they finally found the problem," Loretta said.

"That last doctor, you should have heard him! 'Anything but a tumor.'"

"What a story."

"And all the questions. I told him straight away that I had one healthy child, at home, with all of our belongings. I wasn't ashamed to admit it, either," Emilia sighed. "Now look at me. I'm all open, from here to here." She pointed to her belly.

Unaware that she had a captive audience in the other women sharing the recovery room with her, she was startled to hear a catty voice.

"You wait and see," said a woman from across the room.

"They've done you here, they've done you there," said another roommate.

"They've done you top to bottom," interjected another woman, leaning back on her elbows from the bed next to hers.

"Yeah, you just wait," laughed still another. "They've given you a total."

Emilia's eyes began to water. The room began to spin, stainless steel blurring with the stark white of the walls.

"Don't listen to them, Emilia," Loretta assured her. "The doctor will be here soon."

When the doctor returned to her bedside, she confronted him: "These women tell me you did a total, that you took out everything."

"I didn't take out anything. You can have another ten babies, at thirty-three years old; you can have another ten, until you're forty years old. In forty days, your regular menstruation will return," the specialist assured her. "Signora, it'll be six years before you return strong like you were, but you will, because you have good blood and a phenomenal heart." His predictions were precise. Exactly on the fortieth day, her period came back.

Emilia's desire for wanting another child, however, waned with each passing year. The truth cut deeper than her health problems. The thought of regaining her health only to go and have another child seemed hardly worth the effort.

Talk about the future became incessant around the dinner table. There were the rumblings of change and talk about Italy becoming "modern." Babbo said there was no future to be had in being a sharecropper. The *mezzadri*, or peasants, wanted a better share of the harvest, and the new government was making headway. But it was doubtful that even reforms would be enough to make it worth advising the young generation to devote themselves to a life of farming, and without them, how could the old folks keep up with the crops? Loretta and Emilia mused over the shifting world.

Maybe the Peruzzi household would move to another farm. Maybe they would leave Artimino. Maybe some of the sons would leave farming altogether and find jobs in the factories. There wasn't much money to be made in farming, at least not on this farm, not now. The senior Peruzzi reasoned that living closer to a town like Comeana would give Parigi and Urbano a better chance of finding work. Emilia's in-laws could sense the restlessness, especially among their sons.

La regina, or the queen, as they called the countess of those sixty-five farms in Artimino, found herself in a desperate situation. She offered to pay people to stay and work the land. Families were abandoning houses and farmland left and right, fleeing the countryside for the city, assuming jobs in the booming textile factories. The peasants did not rise up and struggle against the queen—she had too much authority. But she could not stop them from walking away.[1] For people who had lived their entire lives under the thumb of such a powerful woman, that was a remarkable turning of the tables. The countess became desperate. She offered free rent if only they would stay. It was a sign of things to come.

July 1954

Shortly after the family had celebrated the baby's fourth birthday, the senior Peruzzi announced the decision to move everyone down to Comeana to live in the old Raugei house. The Raugei family had grown too small to farm, and they approached the count about a change in hands. The Peruzzi household soon switched patrons: from working under a countess who oversaw sixty-five *poderi,* or farms, to a noble landowning family who had only twenty-one farms.[2] Landowners with fewer farms had more personal relationships with their tenants. The senior Peruzzi figured he could negotiate a favorable situation.

Emilia was able to renew her networks to ensure a steady flow of consignments as an artisan weaver. She loved being back home, where she could walk the lanes of her girlhood. She ran into friends and dealt with familiar shopkeepers on her errands. Parigi felt mixed about the move. Comeana, with a couple thousand people, was three times the size of Artimino. Granted, it had much better access to cities, and the location allowed him to take a job working for a Pratese industrialist who had a nylon factory, some twelve kilometers to the north, in Pistoia. But working in a factory wasn't like working the land. The land required care and knowledge in its cultivation. He pined for the landscape of his boyhood. For him, the steep climb up the road to the summit of Artimino was a journey into God's country, and he felt this way despite being a believer more in the teachings of the Communist Party than in those of the Church. It was no accident that the art-loving Etruscans had settled here eons ago, only to be followed by the Medici in the early *seicento,* the 1600s.[3] He fancied himself a partial heir to that legacy until a run-in with his new overseer served as a rude reminder of his station in life.

With fewer than two dozen farms, the count could keep close watch over his sharecroppers. Word slipped out about one of the Peruzzi boys who had a side project of raising rabbits, which technically was against the rules. Peasants were permitted to raise only animals that fell under the sharecropping contract. But rabbits bred quickly and served as a good way to make a little extra money for the family coffers, and Parigi enjoyed raising the little critters. Late one afternoon, when he was in the barn cleaning a rabbit pen, the diminutive count showed up with his hulky *fattore*, or farm manager.

Parigi heard footsteps and looked up at the doorway to see the silhouettes of the two men's contrasting statures.

"We're here to take a census of the animals," the manager bellowed.

Parigi approached with a shovel in his hand. "There's nothing to count here."

"You well know what the contract stipulates!" the manager barked. He reached into a leather satchel, pulled out a document, and began to read from it. "'At all times it is forbidden for the sharecropper to keep rabbits in the hayloft and in the stalls.' That is clear as the day is long."[4]

"The Duce is dead," Parigi challenged.

The man stepped closer to Parigi. "Get your obligations straight. That space is for cows and cows only."

"We haven't had cows for years," Parigi said.

"It is cows that fall under the contract, not rabbits. Did someone give you permission to raise rabbits?"

Parigi glared at the man.

"Let me count those rabbits!" he insisted. "We'll see how you've been short-changing us." He grabbed Parigi by the shoulders. Parigi's lips tightened and brow furrowed. He clenched his fists.

The count could see the two men were about to come to blows. Even though his father had served as a mayor under Mussolini, he fashioned himself a supporter of the old Republic and its values. He was a man of letters and did not take well to the idea of brute force.

"Enough!" he said, calling off his manager as one would call off a guard dog. "Let's go."

Emilia watched from the window as the two drove off in the count's forest green Fiat Cabriolet. The assault did not have to get physical to leave a lasting mark. It had gouged deep into his dignity and self-worth as a man, and she sensed it. She expected the incident would sting for the rest of his days.

Parigi was fuming as he came into the house. "If I want to raise rabbits, by God, I'll raise rabbits. It's honest money."

"Shake it off," she said.

"If I can't carve out one iota of autonomy in this life, then it's hardly worth living," he reasoned.

"Oh now, let's not blow smoke. What do you expect? You may have found your niche in the factory, but we're still under the count. Even these days, a count is a count just like a doctor is a doctor or a mother-in-law is a—"

"What in the world does that have to do with anything?"

"Everything. You can bet your last lira on it."

"Oh Emilia!"

"Those doctors, they didn't listen to me. They took me for a peasant from the country, living in a big patriarchal family, like some kind of throwback. *A nervous breakdown!* What a crock. Do you know what that specialist told me in the end? 'You'll be just fine to have more.' He assured me of it. 'You can have another ten babies, at thirty-three years old; you can have another ten, until you're forty years old.' As if! Like some kind of rabbit. What did he take me for? And what good would that do me anyhow? It's not like it's got me anywhere with your family."

"Oh now, don't start in with that—"

"Look at Loretta. She never had any children, and your folks favor her, always have and always will. So what difference does it make? Even in the moment, with that specialist, I said to myself. 'I don't know. *Gli è meglio aver paur che toccarne*—It's better to have fear than to touch it.' When I went back to the doctor for my postoperative, I told him, 'No, you'll see, *se mi riesce*, if I manage, I'm not having any more."

Parigi let it go. For both of them, the encounter with rabbits would serve as an antidote to the nostalgia that, as life wore on, had a way of rising up unexpectedly like mist on a muddy river.

PART TWO **Memory Encountered**

THIRTEEN Neighbors

On a crisp October morning in 1996, Chris slid the final suitcase into our compact Fiat 127. It fit like the last piece of a jigsaw puzzle. Satisfied, I turned and locked the door to our basement apartment that had become our home, dank though it was, and took Hollis upstairs to say farewell to our widowed landlady, her two grown daughters, and her son-in-law. They had worked their way into our hearts in the thorny sort of way that only family can manage, and we into theirs, especially my daughter, whose plump five-year-old cheeks had proved an irresistible target for certain women's pinching tendencies. We left in silence and drove down the little incline, away from the sweater-making neighborhood, its garage-sized workshops and computerized looms that wove all night, spewing out stretches of sweater lengths onto concrete floors and leaving a vapor of tinged wool, acrylic, and nylon fibers. We turned onto the main thoroughfare that binds Pistoia to Florence, with crossroads to Prato. Our car was still peppy after nearly two decades of motoring and took the curves well through the trafficked town of Poggio a Caiano and on toward the unfamiliar village where we would once again be strangers. Starting over brought mixed feelings: the sadness of abandoning familiar rhythms, the emptiness and even betrayal that comes of leaving friends, and the anxiety but also the excitement of beginning fresh.

Friends in the industrial zone of the commune kept telling me to "go to Carmignano." They pressed me to talk to people in the older hill towns. My gut told me they were right. I had spent the first year of my project in a thriving industrial-residential neighborhood investigating a distinction that Italians had earned in the early 1990s: of having the world's lowest fertility rates. The move to a rural setting was born of my desire to become intimate with peasant memories of a time when the contours of life were so different as to be otherworldly. I was not chasing the exotic. I was after the unconventional. Perhaps here could be unearthed the cultural roots of Italy's "quiet revolution," the rapid fertility decline that had begun in Europe in the 1870s.[1] Massimo Livi-Bacci explains in his *History of Italian Fertility* that the earliest and most rapid decline in Italy occurred in the northern and central regions of Piedmont, Liguria, and Tuscany. By 1910–12, these regions had registered a 25 percent drop in marital fertility. By 1992, Italy's total fertility rate had become, along with Spain's, the lowest in the world, hitting its lowest point, in the mid-1990s, of 1.2 births per woman.[2]

If cultural setting was key to influencing how many babies women had over their lifetime, my challenge as a cultural anthropologist was to explain what shaped people's beliefs and informed their practices. Memories of the period during the onset of such dramatic changes, I reasoned, could shed light on the experience of family change. Memories might hold important clues to accessing a truth that involved more than the commonplace explanation that women were choosing work over motherhood and hence not having babies. The ways in which women—and men—reproduce partly have to do with personal choice. But they also involve broader influences. Those influences provide the grooves into which memories become engraved and lives unfold. Memories are

Figure 3.   Children throwing confetti in the countryside of Carmignano. Photograph by Betsy Krause.

anchored in history and provide people with fixed points for orienting themselves to their social worlds. They are loaded with symbols, meanings, tensions, and consequences. Memories are not just what people say, not just what people store in their minds; they reflect and impinge upon what people do and how they feel. People hold memory in their bodies, in their emotions, in their senses, even in their muscles. In short, memories are not only socially situated but also deeply embodied. They inform people's sensibilities in terms of who they are and who they should be, of how they conform to and resist social norms.[3]

Loaded into our compact car, we sped along a two-lane road past a Madonna statuette at a small intersection, big-box warehouses that stored sweaters, the iron gates to a small cemetery, and a signpost marking an Etruscan tomb. In the distance, beyond a field of tall grass, rose cypress along a driveway that led to our new landlord's villa. We followed the narrow street into our new hamlet, passing Hermada's hair salon, the Banca Toscana, and the butcher shop, turning right at the piazza, passing a gas pump and the Co-op Market, and continuing up a hill, where we made a sharp V-turn to the left. Here the town ended. The road yielded to a panoramic view of a valley below. We slowed as we drove down the quiet lane of attached stucco houses in muted yellows and soft whites, topped with terracotta roofs. Some houses had stairs that stepped directly onto the street, others offered patios in miniature. The road dead-ended into a cement wall that bounded the backyard of the farmhouse. We zipped up the driveway and pulled around to the grassy front yard. The house sat up high. From the edge of the olive trees, the red-tile Duomo in Florence was visible in the distance. I was smitten with the view: vineyards below, olive groves beyond, stone walls all around.

Inside, the house was bright and spacious compared to the subterranean apartment we had left. The farmhouse offered a dry, airy, and simple home. Furnishings were sparse yet tasteful. I fell in love with the old, wooden kitchen table, complete with cracks and carvings, and the cupboard with its mustard-orange chipped paint. The three bedrooms were without closets but contained towering postwar armoires and laminated wooden dressers. Down a long hallway, the updated bathroom had a large if narrow tub with a hand-held shower. We would not miss the mold of our old apartment that had fuzzed up on the walls as the fall rains settled into the valley that cosseted Prato. We would be free to entertain guests without disturbing anyone, particularly important since many of our guests arrived with musical instruments. Unable to practice overseas as a veterinarian, Chris relied on his violin to create a life for himself and hence cultivated relationships with various players from Florence to Pistoia and ranging in genres that spanned jazz, gypsy swing, blues, and bluegrass. Would the anthropologist be seduced into a life of bohemian leisure and become a "luxury mammal" basking under the Tuscan sun?[4] Or would loneliness and newfound inspiration lead to hidden histories?

The neighbors were slow to warm up to us. They watched our every move as they walked the lane, hung their laundry, and swept their porches. The mood was an artful blend of pure skepticism and studied indifference

Figure 4.   Chris Brashear and Maurizio Geri playing music in the farmhouse, 1997.
Photograph by Betsy Krause.

as they tried to figure out who we were and why we had come to live at the
end of the lane.

One day in early December, I set out to purchase a block of fresh
pecorino cheese from an old peasant woman who was said to live at the
opposite end of the lane. I didn't get very far. At the bottom of the backyard on a cement ledge sat an elderly man. White hair fringed his face,
and white whiskers bespoke several days of growth. He caught my eye
as I passed.

"*Buon giorno,*" I said.

"*Buon giorno,*" he returned.

"How's it going?" I asked, smiling and stopping, eager to have someone converse with me.

"It's going, but at my age not too well," he admitted, rubbing his knee.
"The pain is tremendous. *Non ci vorrebbe proprio.* It's exactly what you
wouldn't want. Oh *lei,* you still have your youth."

"It's true, I know I don't have anything to complain about," I said. "But this morning I didn't even want to get up."

"Yes, that can happen, too," he said, empathetically. "*Che viene?*"

He spoke with a rural cadence that was initially lost on me.

"My wife is here now too," he added.

Ah, he was inviting me in. He was deflecting any possibility that a young woman might think he was making inappropriate advances. I explained to my neighbor, somewhat apologetically, that I hadn't been around much since we had moved in. My role as parent representative of my daughter's first-grade class had kept me busy attending to school politics. I was also putting in time at the local historic archive and nurturing relationships I had made the first year of the project, when I worked for several months in a sweater factory and then a family sweater-finishing firm. He seemed delighted when I accepted his invitation.

My elderly neighbor stood up slowly and favored one leg as he headed two doors down. I followed him across the threshold into his house. We entered a small kitchen. We sat around a square table in faded light. He introduced me to his wife, Emilia. She wore an apron over her housedress. Even with the layers, she appeared a feather of a person. She was skinny with bony hands. Her eyes, though, shone bright, and her voice conveyed attitude. Her last name was unusual and I didn't catch it. His name was Parigi Peruzzi, yes, like the city in France. They apologized about the smallness of their house—the downstairs consisted only of the kitchen—and their small bedroom was up a narrow stairway on the second floor.

The couple spoke over one another, interrupted each other, and bickered with ease. They had accrued two lifetimes' worth of practice.

"I was born in that house," Emilia told me of the farmhouse where I was living. "I lived there until I was twenty-nine years old."

The coincidence struck me as uncanny. I listened closely. Emilia and Parigi spoke so fast and with such a rural lilt that I had trouble following them. They had both worked as peasants under *il signorino*, who was now our landlord. They used to be sharecroppers, giving half of the crop to the *signore*'s family, which was large. It was a family of five, two brothers and three sisters, but only one of the brothers had ever married and moved away, to Milan. The other brother and his three sisters all lived up in the big villa. I wondered why none of them had ever married.

"They're obviously not ugly people," I ventured. They were small, attractive, well-educated, old-moneyed folks.

"You see, someone lower was not an option for the *signorino*, who is actually a count," Parigi said. At first I took him to mean lower in stature, but then I realized he meant lower in status.

"But they are *brave persone*, good people—*veramente grande di testa e grande di cuore*, generous and warm-hearted," Emilia chimed in.

"What do you think?" Parigi asked, his bright eyes still. I felt put on the spot, yet the invitation to gossip enlivened me.

"I have nothing bad to say," I said. "They have been very gracious." So often in my work I crossed lines of social class that piqued people's curiosity.

They asked about the house, what it was like inside. As they anticipated my answer, their expressions struck me, but I could not with certainty pinpoint an underlying emotion. I suspected it lay somewhere between nostalgia and curiosity. The line between the two can be very thin, it is true, and I surely did not know them well enough to intuit a reading. I realized I should invite them up, and did so, but they seemed hesitant to accept.

"I bet it's been a good thirty years since I've been inside," Emilia said. I was amazed that she had lived two doors down from the house and hadn't set foot inside it in three decades. She might not have moved physically far from her house of birth, but emotionally she might as well have moved to America. It also occurred to me that the updating of the house had transformed it into something very different from what it had been in her youth. No longer was it a stigmatized peasant dwelling with no running water, no central heating, no electric lighting—in short, no modern conveniences. It was now a destination for temporary residents, tourists, or other outsiders seeking a picturesque yet convenient location in rural Tuscany.

Before long, conversation turned to my reason for moving here. I was an anthropologist studying the transition from large to small families. Immediately, they seemed to claim themselves as my "subjects." They freely offered details from their lives.

As we talked, they told me that they had left the peasant life for factory work. Both were from large patriarchal families of seven children. Together, they had had only one child. Their daughter had done some piece-work over the years, mostly finishing sweaters, but did not do much anymore. Their son-in-law owned a lighting factory and had done well for himself. They had two grandsons, and Emilia marveled with cynicism at how many things her daughter and son-in-law bought for the boys: cars, motorcycles, a boat. I sensed disapproval in the way she spoke about the consumer habits of the new generation. The shift from a generation of producers to one of consumers was dramatic and hard to fathom.

"Parents today, they have so many worries," Emilia said, her hands animating each opinion. In the old days, fear was contained—it was something right there in the town: the fear of the bogeyman in the attic, of hail ruining the olive harvest, of sickness itself. Nowadays, parents had much more to fear: drugs, violence, accidents.

Her critical view of consumerism intrigued me. My own love-hate relationship with money and merchandise had initially attracted me to anthropology and its social criticism. I had grown up in St. Louis, a city of commerce, the daughter of a father who not only wanted to make money but also deemed financial success the bottom line of existence. While I was a journalism student in the college town of Columbia, Missouri, words, ideas, music, and art found their way into the core of my being. Money for money's sake seemed as bankrupt to me as sex for pay.

The late anthropologist Eric Wolf observed in his *Europe and the People without History* that modern people judge each other by their ability to consume. Acquiring stuff becomes the way that people demonstrate success. The flip side is also true. Just as an ability to consume signals social success, an inability to buy the "right" goods signals social defeat.[5] I sensed that Emilia shared a similar discomfort about the consumer values that the postwar boom had given her descendants.

A lot more talking would have to be done. The morning was wearing on, hunger pains were stirring, and I did not want to take up any more of my neighbors' time. I thanked them for inviting me in and talking with me, and I headed back up to the farmhouse—to their old house—empty handed but full of thoughts.[6]

After lunch I continued my mission to buy some fresh cheese. Half a kilometer down the lane I came to a stone pathway that lured me past a throng of cats milling around an old farmhouse that had been split into apartments. Beyond a weed-covered door lived the commune's controversial counselor of culture and public instruction. Her taste for the avant-garde present and the Etruscan past did not put her in good graces with regional social historians who sought to document, expose, and validate the peasant past. The path continued to the opposite side of the rambling structure. It was hard to know whether I was at the right entrance. I knocked. A haggard woman opened the door. Fermenting milk soured the air. She invited me in, and I followed her through the dark hallway into a darker kitchen. She flicked a switch, probably for my benefit, not hers. She took a seat beneath the bare, glaring bulb whose dim light barely shone beyond her corner. She invited me to sit too.

She explained to me her *destinaccio*, her awful destiny. She was a widow and lived with her only son. She had given birth to a second child, but it had been stillborn or had died shortly thereafter. She had a strong rural dialect, even more so than Emilia and Parigi, perhaps because she lived here rather isolated among the cheeses and the sheep. She began telling me about my own landlords, that their property was called Calavria because of ancestors who had fled the boot heel of Italy in the 1200s. How history was alive here! How memory weighed on the present![7]

Her only son, a bachelor heading into middle age, walked into the kitchen and without making eye contact joined in the conversation. He did not hide his dissatisfaction with following in his late father's footsteps as a shepherd. Were they under the same landowner as us? I asked him.

"I wish, I wish," the son said.

"Why?" I asked.

"*Perchè sì. Perchè lui è grande di testa e di cuore.*" It was the same phrase Emilia and Parigi had used about the count being thoughtful and kind.

"And yours?"

"SHIT!" he said emphatically in English.

His mother turned to me. "What did he say?"

I hesitated. Her gaze penetrated me. It felt cruel to leave her out. "He said *merda*," I replied, embarrassed and sensing that my translation of this particular word was also serving a dual purpose of mediation between the two.

Their former countess had died childless and had left her estate to her husband's nieces and nephews. It was a disaster, since the heirs were selling properties as fast as real estate agents could deposit commissions. The situation placed the cheese-making mother and son, as well as the sheep, under pressure. I imagined how a wealthy industrialist from Prato would love to get his hands on their old farmhouse and transform it into a rural grandeur it had never known.

The woman must have registered my interest in history. She suddenly came out with a story about an award her mother had won around 1927 for her skills as a *massaia rurale,* a rural housewife. Schoolteachers had judged women on behalf of the commune in the name of the fascist state. What mattered was how people kept their things, how linens were folded and such. People had been neat before, she said, but the recognition of precision motivated women to pay greater attention to the details of the house. A similar award was granted for how grains were kept in the *granaio,* the barn.

The conversation lulled, and before it could become awkward she took me to the dank cheese room and invited me to select a block. What did I know about such distinctions? She noticed my eyes settling on a smallish form and placed it on a rusted, old-fashioned scale, jotted down a price, then wrapped the cheese in paper. Part of the contract of buying and selling in these parts was an unspoken agreement to give some of your time, some of yourself, to cultivate a rapport before making an exchange.

A massive Siberian blast froze our pipes and left the farmhouse without heat on December 30, 1996. The house had heating throughout, and unlike our apartment, where our landlady had authority over the thermostat, gave us our own control. Autonomy, though, came at a price. Down in the cellar, which dated to the 1500s, inside a little metal box, burned the pilot light that powered our "modern" heating system that, as we soon learned, might just as well have been medieval. The temperature dropped into the subzero Fahrenheit range within hours of the freeze, and the heating gas flowed so slowly that the pilot light fluttered to a premature finish. Our antique fireplace, with its cavelike opening, sucked up all the warm air from the kindling, and the fire itself made so much smoke we had to open the windows to let in breathable air. Our flawed yet desperate decision meant letting in frigid winter air. Shivering and afraid, aggravated and alone, we realized how unprepared we were for such severe weather. Whatever had happened to warm, sunny Tuscany? I had never been so cold. We layered all the sweaters we owned. We were grateful for our good fortune in having many sweater-making friends who were generous with their soft, wool-blend samples.[8] We gathered up all the blankets we could find in the house. Our daughter snuggled into bed with us. We had never slept with so many layers, so close together. Body heat was the surest source of warmth we had.

The thaw came soon enough. On New Year's Day 1997, while outside hanging up laundry on a drying rack, I spotted Emilia walking up the driveway. The ground had softened, leaving a good slick of mud to glimmer in the newly returned sun. She wore a jacket over her shoulders and slippers on her feet.

"I came to collect some *malva*," she said, referring to *Malva sylvestris*, or mallow. "It used to grow right over here." She headed toward the corner of the stone barn next to where we parked the car on a small slab of concrete. "It seems it's all been burned from the cold weather. We're not used to this cold."

I was excited to see my neighbor coming into my yard. It seemed a good omen. Her daughter suffered from colitis, she told me. " 'Mamma,' she says, 'make me an infusion of *malva?*' "

Emilia's eyes were fixed on the ground as she searched for evidence. Her bony body arched over like a fishhook. "Ah! There *is* some," she said, bending down to reach the ground, then standing up with a handful of the curvy-leafed herb. From inside the house appeared Chris, holding a plastic bag.

"No, no. Use that for the trash," Emilia insisted. "I only need this little bit. You see, *malva* is good for inflammation, especially indigestion."

I followed Emilia toward the sealed well that protruded from the yard midway between the farmhouse front door and the grove of olive trees.

An abundance of *malva* and *radicchi*, or greens, had once surrounded it, she told me. I glanced toward the unrestored part of the house that was normally locked. I had seen its cavernous interior for the first time several days earlier after a workman had left the door ajar. The ceilings were pitched with the old beams exposed; the original terracotta tiles were dirty but still intact.

"I was born up there in that bedroom." She pointed to the corner room, where she had lived until after the war. She headed to the edge of the driveway, where she told me a sage bush had once grown. "Oh look! There's a little sprig of it still left. Why, it used to be huge. Sometimes I use sage to make a tea. Or I use mint. I mix mint with the *malva*." She turned and headed back down the driveway. "Look at me!" she snapped, turning back toward me and shaking her head. "I wore these slippers. We're not used to this cold."

"Happy New Year," I said.

"Let's hope it's a good year. I'm afraid it won't be, though. Look at all the things happening: family members killing one another, trains crashing, the machinists dying because of the train track mix-up." She headed down the driveway.

"Say hello to Parigi for us," I called as she parted. It seemed a large foreign object had lodged its way into my throat, blocking the barrage of questions I wanted to ask her.

FOURTEEN

A Weaver's Tale

Emilia and Parigi's gift of gab made my job relatively easy. I asked them if they would be willing to sit for an interview, and they seemed flattered that a researcher all the way from the United States would take an interest in their lives. On January 28, 1997, with my toaster-sized equipment bag slung over my shoulder, I strolled down the farmhouse's driveway the short distance to the couple's house. Their green shutter was propped open; I barely knocked and Emilia was at the door. I set my nylon bag on the table and took out my Sony tape recorder, clipped the mini-microphone to the edge of the bag, and asked the couple's permission to be recorded. Emilia raised her slender shoulders and smiled with slight embarrassment but then agreed. The tape began running as they launched into a marital tiff over the best topic for the interview. Even my best efforts to explain my project did not get far,

Figure 5.   Emilia Raugei and Parigi Peruzzi at their threshold, 1999. Photograph by Betsy Krause.

and as we began she insisted we use the informal *tu* form of address. It went like this:

EMILIA: I'll tell you, I'll use the *tu*. I'll tell you how—

BETSY: Okay. Fine, go ahead and use *tu*.

PARIGI: If not, she can—could also talk about the berets recently—

EMILIA: Come on! If she wants to know about the straw, she doesn't want to know about the wool.

PARIGI: Well, because now they've been making berets, my brother used to make them.

EMILIA: No! They still make those.

PARIGI: But she—

EMILIA: But she wants to hear about before. Let it go, let it go!

PARIGI: Yeah, but isn't she interested in the berets?

BETSY: Her—? The—?

PARIGI: The berets for women.

BETSY: Oh, berets.

EMILIA: They still make berets. Berets of wool. They still make those.

BETSY: I'm interested in the work—

EMILIA: of the straw!

BETSY: of the—but more of women and how it has changed—

PARIGI: Eh! Bah!

BETSY: together with how you make a family. Because now there's this idea that before women were housewives.

EMILIA: Yes. Housewife. Yes. We used to put a group here in this house; there would be five, six, seven, eight women.

BETSY: Yes?

EMILIA: Yes.

BETSY: No, really?

EMILIA: Yes, yes. You bet! Oh! But oh!

BETSY: But when? In what era?

EMILIA: Eh, also before the war, much before the war.

PARIGI: Yes, but she is also interested in berets—

BETSY: [laughter]

EMILIA: Oh be quiet! The berets!

PARIGI: And madam, you be quiet!

EMILIA: She wants to know about the weaving now. She doesn't want to know about the berets.

BETSY: Why? You also made berets?

EMILIA: Me yes!

BETSY: Really?

EMILIA: I made turbans.

BETSY: But because the straw—

EMILIA: No! The berets are made of wool. After the war, the straw disappeared in the postwar. Nearly everything disappeared, hardly anything was left. So we did other work. With a sort of straw that we called rascello.

BETSY: Rascello?

(A changing market gave way to new materials, such as synthetic straw, and Emilia discussed the new challenges before changing the subject to women's artisan work.)

EMILIA: It was women's work. And we earned a fair amount. I made my-self my entire dowry.

BETSY: Oh yeah?

EMILIA: You know, a dowry, I mean the linens, working before the war. After the war it went and disappeared—

BETSY: Oh, I see.

EMILIA: from women. It was a lit—It was an artisan thing. All artisans. His brother, for example, his brother's wife, her uncle had his own business, he'd ship to America.

BETSY: Oh yeah?

EMILIA: Yes, he used to ship to America. Because she had her dad in America. He fled during the period of fascism.

BETSY: Oh yeah? Because he was—he didn't see eye to eye with fascism?

EMILIA: He was communist.

BETSY: Yeah?

EMILIA: Her dad. Oh! It's important that I tell the truth. He was hardly—

BETSY: Certainly, but—

EMILIA: an assassin. He didn't agree with the idea of fascism—

BETSY: Certainly.

EMILIA: since there was the dictatorship in Italy.

BETSY: Oh yes.

EMILIA: And so he was being persecuted, this person. He had *three* children.

BETSY: Ah.

EMILIA: Three children. He fled to America, he embarked at v—at Genoa.

BETSY: In what year?

EMILIA: Well, the exact year, it had to have been in 1922, '23.

BETSY: Oh! Early, so early.

EMILIA: Eh! When it, when fascism came to Italy. Fascism began in 1921. I don't at all remember the exact date. I was already a Little Italian. At school we had to be Little Italians: little white shirt, little black skirt, little beret, little black tie, little white socks, and little black shoes.

BETSY: Oh yeah?

EMILIA: At least they used to hand them out. We were the Little Italians of Mussolini. Have you ever heard mention of Mussolini?

BETSY: Yes, yes! Of course.

EMILIA: So the dad of my sister-in-law fled to America and was shipped
          in a crate of hats. They say there were hats inside along with him.

BETSY: Oh, I understand.

EMILIA: Because if after—they could have taken him, they'd send him to
          the border. They'd send them to the borders, to islands, in the
          middle of the ocean, they sent lots of them there. They sent the
          president, Pertini, of Italy, that's how it was, back then. Fascism.
          Then after the war this—the plaiting wasn't around any more, it
          wasn't around. The women began to go work in the factory. I
          went to the factory too.[1]

Emilia's narrative was rich in detail yet partial. Furthermore, her style
of telling anchored details not so much temporally as in a web of social relations, and the references to people I did not know, and contexts whose
significance I did not understand, together with the dialect, presented serious challenges of comprehension for me. Nevertheless, I felt called to
make sense of it. My training had ingrained in me the conviction that
cross-cultural work holds little value when the interpreter is seduced into
taming variability. Valuable work comes from struggling with the differences that one encounters and trying to make sense of them on their own
terms.[2]

I sought help from a local research assistant. Her perspective proved
priceless. Matilde, a university student in her mid-twenties studying theater history and literature in Bologna, was an interesting choice for the
job of transcribing the interview of an old peasant weaver precisely because she was the antithesis of Emilia. At times she burst out laughing at
the former peasant's way of putting things. Though I had expected her
decidedly modern identity as a progressive leftist to be associated with a
respectful attitude toward peasant culture, that respect reached its limits
when she encountered Emilia's rural dialect, and on one occasion, when
we attended a political event on immigration together, the slur "Che contadino," what a peasant, slipped from her mouth before she caught herself.

I met Matilde and her family through my networks. She lived with her
parents in a large, pristine, three-story house in a new-moneyed hamlet
in the province of Prato. From the beginning of our acquaintance, I was
fascinated by her contradictions and intimidated by her Mediterranean

beauty. She had gorgeous wavy black hair, wore only the finest Italian styles and fabrics, proudly professed her political affiliation with the Rifondazione Comunista, the far-left communist party of post-1989 Italy, and smoked as heavily as my first newspaper editor, the late Forrest Rose, a columnist and upright bass player who had spent the better part of his abbreviated but influential life in Columbia, Missouri. I was sensitive to cigarette smoke, but I put up with it around my smoking Italian friends just as I had toughed it out around my mentors in the smoke-filled *Columbia Daily Tribune* newsroom of the mid-1980s.

Matilde and I gained each other's trust on several social occasions. The first event occurred around the holidays in December 1996, when she invited me on an outing to the seaside town of Viareggio. A group of her friends had planned a dinner gathering at the vacation home of one of their parents. I was delighted to receive such an invitation, for I was craving the friendship and perspectives of a politically minded, intellectual young woman. As we drove to the coast, Matilde used me as a sounding board, openly complaining about the generational conflicts between her and her mother, Telsa, who would eventually make similar use of me. Matilde grumbled that her mother's generation demonstrated fastidious attention to the house. Her mother, she said, was obsessive about cleanliness to the point of being pathological. A vivid childhood memory of a chandelier that her mother kept so clean that it shone with magical brilliance had transformed into a haunting adult image that came to stand for her mother's enslavement to domestic chores.

At the seaside house, the men headed out to the patio to prepare the grill as the five women gathered around a table inside. Unwrapping a package of sausages that the men would grill, the women poured themselves some champagne and toasted their generation: "*A noi ganzissime donne*—To us very cool women—*perchè non si pensa sempre alla pulizia!*—because we don't always think about cleaning!"

I took great pleasure in this moment of explicit resistance to the dominant gender regime. I felt I had witnessed a secret moment of female bonding in which these young women collectively voiced their rejection of their mothers' generation's participation in old-style patriarchy through their service to the domestic realm.

My analysis, however, was fatally one-sided. I was soon to learn that Matilde's mother held a different perspective on the new generation, one that complicated my sense of contrast between the cohorts as oppressed versus liberated. An occasion in mid-February 1997 provided further insight into the conflicts confronting the generations. Matilde, who saw straight through to my weakness, invited me to go with her on a book-buying mission at Feltrinelli's, a breathtaking bookstore in Florence on the main drag between the train station and the Duomo. I arrived at Matilde's house shortly after lunch, and her mother offered me a coffee. I didn't dare deny her hospitality. As I sipped my espresso in the sparse and orderly living room, a scene broke out between mother and daughter.

Telsa ranted about the number of years Matilde had already devoted to studying at the university in Bologna. Telsa felt that her daughter had been at it far too long and that the time was ripe for the twenty-something-year-old to get serious about life: get a job and gain some independence. Better yet, it was high time she find a good man and get married. Matilde fumed. I couldn't help but feel implicated. I suspected that Telsa had intentionally lashed out at Matilde in front of me. She undoubtedly viewed me with mixed feelings: as an accomplice to Matilde's indulgence in intellectual pursuits and as a potential role model. I was, after all, an overeducated American spending years of my adult life—including years during motherhood—working toward a doctorate degree; however, I had also by comparison gotten on with my adult life, given that I was married, had a child, and had achieved some independence, as evidenced by my status as a funded researcher. I cringed as I listened to Telsa berate Matilde with questions: "Why this program of study? When are you supposed to start your thesis? What will you do when you're done?" And then what I dreaded: the criticism of our planned outing. "Why do you need to buy new books? Why can't you settle for used books?" Matilde's lips pursed with aggravation, her cheekbones protruded with tension, and her eyes squinted with anger. Telsa turned to me and explained her frustration.

"The day my daughter gets her degree will be the happiest day in my life," Telsa said, launching into an accounting of how much her daughter cost the family per month to stay at home and study.

I mentioned how much money families in the United States spend on their children's college educations, and Matilde's father, Nello, offered his view that the best system is one in which university education is open to everyone.

"Women nowadays study to have their independence," said Nello, a small, balding man who had worked his way out of peasantlike poverty to build a successful, specialized business painting luxury interiors, though he had always maintained his left-leaning politics that mirrored those of his daughter.

"What?" asked Telsa with a tone of outrage. "I was independent from the time I was fourteen. I was making my own income." She looked at me, then added, "It's hard to explain. It is different now, but I *was* independent. Not like these students today, who study, study, study and never work."[3]

These two incidents—the toasting young women and the mother-daughter conflict—drove home for me the challenges confronting a generation of women, particularly those born after 1970, determined to find fulfillment and identity in futures other than those narrowly defined by motherhood. Of course, the generation of women represented by Telsa—not to mention Emilia—did not narrowly think of themselves merely as mothers or "housewives"—unless "housewife" could be an expanded category to include women who, in industrializing areas such as Prato, frequently worked dual roles as mothers and artisans. Narrowly defined non-income-earning "housewives" were historically more of an ideological project of the state than a widespread experience of women.[4]

Categories aside, Matilde resented her mother's generation, and this feeling probably contributed to the skepticism she held toward my project. She was initially dubious about my coming all the way from the United States to talk to people she considered not well educated and perhaps even closed minded. I did not expect to win Matilde's approval but secretly yearned for it. When I confided in Matilde my need for someone to help me with transcribing interviews, she expressed interest. Her motive was clearly not financial, for my efforts to pay her were fruitless, and I was able to remunerate her only upon my departure, when I gave her a fine Murano glass lamp as well as some other household items that I had bought for my first apartment and that she had admired.

Some weeks after the interview with Emilia, Matilde sat in the farmhouse living room at a desk with a transcription machine whose foot pedal allowed her to stop the tape on a dime. She warned me that she could not type, but she made up for it by taking seriously her task of writing down the interviews verbatim. She filled pages and pages of my notebook with her stylized Italian script.

As Matilde transcribed the interview with Emilia, I sat across the room taking notes on an Italian text that I had bought at Feltrinelli's. At a certain point, she stopped writing, looked over at me wide-eyed, and exclaimed, "*Questo è proprio bellino*—This is really lovely," a smile of disbelief stretching across her face.

I sprang to my feet to see what she had just written down. It was the moment when Emilia's voice had softened to an intensified whisper as she told the story of her uncle-by-marriage fleeing the fascists because *he was a communist*. Matilde's reaction deeply moved me, particularly given what I knew about Matilde's own general disrespect for a generation of women whom she viewed as participants in their own oppression.

Matilde marveled at the way in which Emilia's story contained major aspects of twentieth-century Italy. Her reaction provided a link among three layers of translation: from rural dialect to standard Italian, from Italian to English, and from American academic views of social life to folk conceptions of local life and world history. A fleeting moment of popular memory spoke volumes to history. It was as if she had suddenly realized the point of my project: of studying people who are otherwise invisible to history, of trying to engage in the tension-rife task of combining erudite with subjugated forms of knowledge.

The task of merging elite knowledge with commonsense narratives presented formidable challenges. Matilde and I shared an admiration for Michel Foucault's work, and I explained the influence of his genealogical method on my project. At its core, the method aimed to counter the "tyranny" inherent in "totalizing discourses"—in other words, it sought to upend explanations of the world that by their very nature excluded less qualified versions of the truth. The method offered potential to emancipate significant yet hidden experiences and prevent the wholesale erasure of memory. Getting at this kind of knowledge, and making sense of it, however, was no simple endeavor. It relied on bringing into dialogue authorized and disqualified forms of knowledge, and knowledge that resides down low on the totem pole may seem naive, quaint, chaotic, or otherwise insufficient to the task. As Foucault foretold, the method would entail "a painstaking rediscovery of struggles together with the rude memory of their conflicts."[5] The prized anthropological method of participation and observation surely qualifies as a "painstaking" method for accessing struggles that common stories about reproductive trends elide. The memories of such conflicts may seem "rude" because they do not traffic in politeness or conform very well to the order of the day. But certain "rude" memories may very well have much more to say than their content might initially suggest.[6]

Matilde's reaction enlivened Emilia's words and led me to see them as a vivid case of subjugated knowledge that when examined closely was akin to William Blake's world in grain of sand. The narrative was remarkable for the way in which its author—a former straw weaver—wove together Italian fascism, political repression, family abandonment, kin networks, and the international hat market. At one point in the interview, Emilia explained how she had gone with four other girls to the town of Signa, just up river from Florence, to work in a factory that produced cloth and materials related to woven hats. About twelve minutes later, asked to clarify the work relations of plaiting, she explained the kin involved in consigning the straw material:

BETSY: But there was someone who would come give you the work?

EMILIA: Yes, there was his brother. He married this one, as I said. Her uncle worked as a dealer of hats and straw plaits, and she had the father who fled for reasons of fascism. In Genoa he boarded a ship and went to America. This little girl—Then afterwards his wife, the mother of her, she stayed here, understand?

BETSY: Right.

EMILIA: Then he wanted the factory to be in America, in Argentina. Her mother, he wanted her to come to America. And she went there during the period of fascism because of these hat dealers, and she brought with her the three sisters, and down there she had another, a boy and a girl. And he's been there. He's an engineer, you know, those that take these roads. And then he has land, a lot of animals, he made money, exactly how much I don't know, you'd need to ask my sister-in-law about it, but you know she's "lost it" a bit. She [the mother] went to America because of him. And her— her uncle, her mother's brother, he told her, "Leave me the—a girl," he told her, "at least—" And she left him this Germena, who would be the wife of his [Parigi's] brother, my sister-in-law.[7]

This piece of the narrative puzzled me, particularly in light of Matilde's reaction. Why had Emilia told me such a complicated story about a relative-by-marriage's abandonment when she knew I was interested in the demographic shift to small families? I wondered why she had emphasized how many children her sister-in-law's father had had and even why she had included these details. In the first part, she told me that the hat dealer had three children. In the second, some of the details contradicted one another. She said that the mother had brought three sisters with her—that three of the hat dealer's children and his wife had eventually joined him in Argentina. Across the Atlantic, they would have another daughter and a son. Inconsistencies aside, the important point is that the parents left one of the Italian-born children behind for good. As Emilia recalled the incident, I couldn't help but notice how her speech, which had been fluent in other sections of the narrative, became halting and hard to follow, even after I had listened to it closely numerous times.[8] I wondered what Emilia might have said had she finished that sentence ending with the uncle's command to leave him the girl, "at least—." Was she caught in a moral quandary? Had the relatives struck some kind of unspeakable deal? Why did the uncle ask the parents to leave him the girl, anyway? I wondered what lay beneath this story of family ruptures. Had I missed something? I set out on a genealogical research trail, seeking others who might interpret Emilia's truncated tale of a child who was given up and whose fate of being abandoned, I suspected, had settled deep into the town's collective memory.

FIFTEEN

Progress

By the return of spring, the couple had fallen for us, and Parigi sent signals that he wanted to be my accomplice. I was outside taking photos one February afternoon, my eyes following the visual dance of grapevines that dropped vertically down the hillside and rolled into the valley. The landscape looked different from every angle, from each slope, from each edge. Intimacy brings with it perception of the details, of the distinctions, that make a place what it is. Each terrace has its own history, its own distinct shape carved out from centuries of human labor. Each discrete curve calls forth another era, one of a different rhythm and time. "Six months of cold, six months of fear," the old peasants used to lament.[1] Once the cold season passed, and the threat of hail and frost, the peasants would begin to fear for the success of their crops. So much depended on the whims of the weather. The rest came down to the sharecroppers' hard work and the overseers' goodwill.

Figure 6.   Via La Volta from the road to Artimino, 1997. Photograph by Betsy Krause.

Parigi and a buddy his age appeared from nowhere, snapping me out of my reverie.

"Come along, we want to introduce you to some old folks," Parigi said with a commanding tone that suggested I had no choice in the matter. "You can take their picture."

The two white-haired men, on the verge of giggling, so proud they were of their secret intentions, refused to disclose any details about where we were going but simply insisted that I come along. They delighted in the mystery they had just created. Parigi's friend pulled out a piece of paper from his pocket. He had written a poem on it—a rhyme for every month—and he showed it to me. I held back judgment and gave him space to delight in his pride.

We headed up Via La Volta, and Parigi's older friend led us through a door to a narrow staircase. I waited with Parigi downstairs, my clunky, journalist-grade Nikon Nikkormat dangling from a leather strap around my neck. I felt like an ethnographic tourist in search of museum pieces. It was exactly the kind of salvage anthropology I did not want to be doing—a quest for the "folk"—or worse, museum-quality old folk. Boldly casting off my embarrassment, I cautiously began to delight in how much fun these two grown men were having. Parigi and I listened as his buddy knocked several times, each bang louder than the previous.

"They're in there, sure enough," he shouted down at us. "But they're in front of the television."

"Who's in there?" Parigi asked. My thoughts exactly.

"*They* are in there. I can't see them, though, so how can I tell you how many there are? I can't see them. They can't hear me. I'll go around to the other door."

Parigi looked at me, raised his eyebrows and chuckled as though to say, "Do you get it? They're *old* folks."

Before long the door opened and one of the residents invited us inside. I hesitated.

"I don't want to disturb anyone," I said.

"No, no, no! Quite the contrary," said the elderly woman, her face engraved with the wrinkles of time.

I walked on in, Parigi right behind me. Inside, through the narrow, tidy kitchen appeared two other women in floral housedresses.

"See what we brought you?" asked Parigi. "*Una bellezza della gioventù,* a beauty of youth. Ah, youth!"

Ah, their scheme was revealed, and the joke was on me. *I* was on display, not them!

The women teased the men. "Parigi, you don't have any wrinkles."

"I don't have any?" Parigi shot back. "*Bah!* You just can't see them. They're covered!"

The women burst out laughing. One buckled over. Their group hilarity revealed sexual innuendo. The old folks exploded like newly uncorked champagne bottles on the nuptial eve.

"*Hai visto com'è lei? Bellina?*" he asked them. "Have you seen how she is? Cute, huh?"

"Yes, yes, she's really cute. The *bambina,* too," they said, referring to my little girl.

"Well what do you expect?" asked Parigi. "The mamma is cute, so . . ."

A master at deflecting attention from myself, I quickly changed the topic and told them about my project on the family, a subject they might know something about. I might as well have put a match to a newspaper, my introduction got them talking so much. The biggest talker was also the eldest, a cousin of the two sisters. She was from a family of two and then had three children. Her husband, however, was one of eight siblings.

"In four years, I had had three *bambini*. Back then, *era un peccato non fare figli,* it was a sin to not have kids. But after I had had three babies in four years, *la mi suocera mi fece,* my mother-in-law told me, 'Oh, don't do what I did.' She was afraid I was going to have eight children the way she had done. Back then, we weren't well informed. There weren't all the modern methods like there are today. Is it true? You folks, you have methods, don't you?"

I nodded sheepishly.

The other two women, widowed sisters, chimed in. They were from a family of four children, and they themselves had had only one child each.

The excitement of the conversation eventually waned, and someone suggested I photograph the women. So I did. One of the women stood in front of a shrine she had made in memory of her late husband. The image was an old-world portrait of a generation whose numbers alarmed demographers and whose shifting values had proven powerful. The younger generations had clearly heeded warnings about having too many *bambini.*

Times had indeed changed, and they were reflected in incessant news reports. Italy had become famous for being one of the oldest countries in the world. Aging has been gradual but constant: in 1931, average life expectancy for Italians was only fifty-four years for men and fifty-six years for women; by 1961, it had risen to sixty-seven and seventy-two years respectively; by 2001, it had reached seventy-seven years for men and nearly eighty-three years for women. The aging ratio of old to young has been rising. In June 2008 the *International Herald Tribune* reported, in an article entitled "Italy Struggles with Immigration and Aging," that Istat, the Italian statistics agency, predicted that nearly 13.8 million Italians, or a quarter of the population, would be sixty-five or older in ten years. From

Figure 7.   Preparing *la minestra,* vegetable soup. Photograph by Betsy Krause.

my vantage point, each return to Italy brought stories from friends about the challenge of caring for aging parents. The task usually fell to daughters or daughters-in-law. Those with means sought help from immigrants.[2]

Several weeks later, in late February 2007, I stopped by Emilia and Parigi's house to request a recipe for a dish but left with a recipe for life. Perhaps the warmer season had instilled in them a self-reflective mood, for spring delivers possibilities for rebirth. I stood next to Emilia at the counter and looked over her shoulder as she pulled out a book of Florentine cuisine. The cover was stained, the pages yellowed. In the dim light I recognized some of the recipes; others were unfamiliar.

"Why don't you make those little *frittelle,* fried cakes, that my mother, bless her soul, used to make?" Parigi suggested from his seat at the table.

The recollection about a comfort food from his childhood must have triggered some old memories for the couple as they got to talking about how things used to be. Spirited memories shot back and forth.

"The wine isn't good like it used to be," Parigi began.

"The sheets aren't white like they used to be," Emilia added.

"Machines milk cows, the machines damage the udders," Parigi continued. "Machines take in the grain harvest, and you know how much they waste? Half. They only collect half, if that. We used to go hunting for every last sprig of wheat."

"You know how many sheets we washed for the *signorino?*" Emilia asked. "We used to have to do the laundry. My father had my mother do the count's sheets, plus he'd hire two other women. They'd take the sheets down to the *fontina,* the spring, where the water was clean and fresh. They'd soak the sheets first in *cenere,* ashes—but clean ashes—and then they'd wash them, soak them in laurel leaves, and boy, what a lovely smell they'd have when they were done. Now that was clean!

"Oh, and the *signorino,* the little count, he liked the crusts of bread. You know how many crusts he's eaten? One time I told him so. He'd come by while we were baking bread and he'd say, 'Oh, give me a bread crust,'" Emilia's voice rising to imitate the elderly count.

"What does that mean if someone eats a lot of bread crusts?" I asked, perplexed.

The two of them exchanged quizzical looks, then burst out laughing. The count's peculiar taste, I gathered, was beyond explanation.

Parigi stood up and walked over to the open front door and gazed out onto the field below, lamenting the state of agriculture. "A row of vines used to go from here down to the stream. Eight meters, then another row, and in between we seeded grain. *Farro.* Spelt. It helped the vines. And fruit trees interspersed. During the war, thanks be to God, that last summer when there was lots of hunger, we had a bumper harvest. The trees were just loaded with fruit. People from all over the town would come down into the field to eat pears and the like. We just let them: what could we do? *Avevano fame, morivano di fame.* They were hungry, they were starving to death. Now everything is a mess. All these vines. Vines, vines, and only vines. In three years, those vines will be finished. These young people, they don't know what they're doing. They don't know how to prune the vines. There's an art to it. Not every vine is the same. It's a craft. There were very few people even in our day who knew how to prune the grapevines. There was my father and my two brothers. That was it."

He walked back to his chair, sat down and rubbed his sore knee. "Grapevines are like us," he said, looking at me with utmost sincerity. "They have to be taken care of, otherwise they wither. In *parole povere*, in poor man's terms, it would be equivalent to someone who washed only the bottom half, or the top half, of their body and let the other half go. That's how they work this vineyard now. They take the tractor and push the dirt around in the middle, but they don't take care of the vines themselves. In a few more years, the vines will be finished.

"These workers, they get paid, go home. What do they care if the vines aren't healthy? We cared about the land because we lived off it. We had twelve hectares and worked it all by hand. When we were kids, we'd come home from school—I just did the fifth grade—and we'd eat, then go into the field. If we didn't do something right, our father would tell us, 'Go and do it again.' We grew up on *la practica*, on experience, working the land."

Emilia looked up at him, her expression forlorn. Her lips drooped as she voiced her misgivings about becoming modern: "*Il progresso ha portato il regresso*—Progress has brought us backwards."

For a moment, they agreed. "Someone ought to write a book about this," Parigi continued. "These are lost arts. We couldn't write it. We aren't able. But someone really should."[3]

SIXTEEN Singles' Sexuality

How Emilia and Parigi had avoided having a second child was a question that led me into a complex world of memories pertaining to the uprooting of rural life and the history of sexuality. Back in the intimacy of their kitchen, the daylight filtered its way into the room, they on one side of the table and I on the other. The couple was a contrast not only in perspectives but in physiques. Emilia appeared as fragile as a ceramic statue. Just looking at her made clear her fear of falling down, breaking a bone, and not being found. She steadfastly avoided taking walks alone except for the stretch of street up to her grown daughter's house. Parigi was a stocky man with a respectable belly. His weight took its toll on his knee. Talking to me eased their aches. For better or worse, my relative youth reminded them of their bygone days. They seemed surprised, in March 1997, when I told them I had just celebrated my thirty-fifth birthday. Why, I didn't look old enough to have a six-year-old child!

In reference to how the couple had avoided having another baby, Parigi began, "There were hardly the methods of today, so you had to suffer."

"I want to tell the truth," Emilia asserted. "As for me, I have never seen a condom."

"They were advertising them on TV the other night," Parigi interjected.

"I thought it was a chocolate, the war was on," Emilia said, recalling her first brush with modern contraception and the story of when a local guy had offered her and her girlfriend an "American chocolate."

This "American candy" pointed to a new world with new subjects who were able to engage in pleasurable sex without consequences. During the fascist years, contraceptives had been outlawed.

"Before, they didn't let folks see those things," Emilia recalled. "*Mamma* . *mia!*" She laughed at herself. "During the war, I thought it was a chocolate!"

Emilia was the butt of her own joke. She saw her younger self and her friend as ignorant. They were hardly modern. Qualifying as modern required sexual competence. You had to know about things. That's how you measured yourself.

Emilia and Parigi both associated the change to small families with being modern, being in control, being willing to "suffer"—to sacrifice one's sexual passions and exercise caution. They contrasted themselves with the big families of before, the patriarchal families.

Parigi shifted in his chair and showed me a poker face. "Now there was a problem, you know," he said, shaking his head.

My curiosity was piqued. I looked down at my tape recorder to make sure it was working properly. The reels were turning, and the little red volume lights were flashing as Parigi spoke, indicating that the microphone was capturing his speech. I glanced back up at Parigi as he explained that, normally, people's children would just come along.

"They didn't know at all if it went straight or crooked," he said, an obscure reference to some men's ignorance of sexual intercourse. "They had no clue."

"No!" I objected.

"No!" he returned, his confident tone and penetrating eyes proclaiming his veracity. "They didn't know. A lot of them remained old bachelors because they were afraid of women."

"Afraid of women?" I asked, incredulous.

"Ehh! Yet it is an unbelievable thing," he said.

"You're telling me," I agreed.

As Parigi spoke about the backward bachelors, each sentence that Emilia uttered offered a contrasting view of the past, as she steadfastly emphasized her grandparents' resourcefulness in seeing to her uncles' education. Parigi's and Emilia's versions of the past were at odds. Talking past one another, they revealed an ever-present tension between loving and loathing the olden days. Eventually, he seduced her into joining his version, but the seduction was short-lived.

"*S'era dimorto arretrati prima*—they were totally backward before," Parigi said in a rural cadence. "Normally, back then, they were afraid that women would bite them."

"*Che fa . . . ?*" Emilia objected. "What are you talking about?"

"That they would bite them, if they got together with a woman," he said.

"Really?" I asked.

"*Eh!* I used to say to my uncle, I knew him until 1940, 'Oh! Why, uncle?' I would use the *tu* form with him. 'Why, uncle, why haven't you got married?' And he would tell me, '*Va nini*'—they used to call us 'darling' back then—'*perchè quelle miliardarie le un m'hanno vorsuto, quelle brutte le un l'ho volute io . . . ,*' 'because the millionaires, they didn't want me, and those ugly ones, I didn't want them.' This was his response. But it was hardly true. Men like him were backward, I mean, really backward, they didn't even know what a woman was. I mean is it possible that a man—"

"And there are still men like this!" Emilia said, shaking her head and scowling at him. Her face was thin, and when she became emotional, her muscles tightened and highlighted her bony features.

"Those who would have ten or twelve, even fifteen kids, they'd have them because they weren't *al corrente dell'ambiente,* they weren't with the times," he persisted. "Even at Artimino there was this family. Remember the Bolognesi? They were about twenty all told."

"Well, there were two dads and two brothers," Emilia interjected, shaking her head, trying to undermine Parigi's exaggerations about the backwardness of peasants.

"Well even we were seven! *Bah!*" he said of his siblings.

"*Bah!* There were even one or two such *pigionali*," she said, using an old-timey term for the townsfolk who paid rent and referring to the exceptional townsfolk who had large families.

"*Eh!*" Parigi interrupted, ignoring Emilia's comment in order to push his point that in general townsfolk had smaller families. "Because the townsfolk were more experts," he reasoned, in what was probably a reference to coitus interruptus.

Emilia turned to me and gently explained, "*Pigionali* would mean those who were not peasants."

"The ones who didn't own or work the land," Parigi added. "There wasn't even one person who didn't know how to sign his name—what do you expect?"

"Well it wasn't like now, the families were more numerous," she said.

"Yeah, the families, they ate and drank and then they went to bed," Parigi said matter-of-factly.

"Forty years ago they were all more numerous, *bah!*" Emilia objected, challenging his stereotype of lustful country folk.

"Exactly," he said, "because they were not *al corrente degli affari,* they weren't up to date."

"All of these?" I tried to ask. "Because there was a tradition of—"

"The more children they had, the bigger they became so as to manage the land," Parigi acknowledged.

"Yes, especially the males. The females weren't worth much," Emilia said, a tinge of regret in her voice. I knew it wasn't that she didn't value women but that rural society didn't—except for women's reproductive capacity.

"That's right!" Parigi agreed. "The males. Yes, there was always a tendency to prefer males to enlarge the family so as to have a farm that rendered more."

"His brother got married and brought the daughter-in-law in the house, then there was another daughter-in-law, and we got to be too many women," Emilia recalled. "This one wanted to control that one, that one got in that one's business . . ."

The tendency for families to become smaller historically has varied with social class. Jane and Peter Schneider demonstrate in *Festival of the Poor* that in Sicily the gentry class began valuing and having small families at the turn of the last century, the early '1900s, just as they were losing their influence in international trade; the artisan class embraced a small-family ideology in the 1930s; and the peasant classes did so in the 1950s. They were all trying to realize the same thing—social "respectability"—but each of their economic realities made the shift from having between five and thirteen children before the transition to having "two or, at most, three" possible in different decades.[1]

The interview with Emilia and Parigi continued for some time until Parigi came back to his favorite subject of backward ancestors. "I'll bet that these uncles that died at seventy years old never knew what a woman was," Parigi said. "Even this uncle of mine that taught us lots of things, he was a skilled man; however, he didn't know what was a woman."

"They were virgins," Emilia added.

"Virgins." Parigi nodded, his hands folded on the table, as still as a stone.

"I say that they never stayed with a woman, these kind of men," she said, "but there are still men like that."

"One time this guy ran off because some guys took him to one of these 'houses of women' and he ran off!" Parigi remembered.

"Oh yes? This uncle?" I asked, confused.

"No, this *signore*," Emilia clarified.

"No, this *signore*," Parigi echoed. "They forced this guy there because he had never seen a woman. So, to see if they could teach him something, they took him there. When he realized that there were these women half-nude, he was like, 'Why are they practically nude?' And he ran off."

"Because he had a sickness, because otherwise there are also *accaniti* here. They were for women."

"What does *accaniti* mean?" I asked.

"*Accaniti* means men who chase after women," Emilia explained.

"Those who like that stuff, who are never satiated," Parigi explained.

"Now, on the other hand, you have the ones who call themselves trans-vestites, the ones who are a little homosexual," Emilia said. "Before there weren't people that way. They [the ones who ran away from women] were a little sick, they had some kind of defect."

"Maybe they were homosexuals?" I dared.

"Not even," Emilia said.

"If I—I don't know—can offer a hypothesis?" Parigi asked. "Let's say there's an apple and I don't eat it, so I have no idea if it's good or if it's not good. This is an hypothesis that's like saying these men, if they don't try this stuff, how can they know about it, somebody who *un s'accaniscano mica*, who doesn't even pursue it, *oh!*"

"Bah!" Emilia piped up. "But there are still those who never get mar-ried."

"Yes, yes, there are still!" I managed. "In Carmignano."[2]

Later, when my research assistant Matilde transcribed the tape for me, she buckled over with laughter at Parigi's reference to "straight or crooked." The humor, in part, led me to take Parigi's comment as a sexual metaphor that allowed him to talk about sexually incompetent males. The sexual in-competence pointed to a larger incompetence at being modern. People like Emilia and Parigi were new subjects, and they wanted to be mod-ern. They chastised the sexuality of their backward uncles. They teased their uncles for the way they talked. They teased them for their fear of women. They viewed these peasant men as old-fashioned. Their new ori-entation became clear as the couple took turns contrasting and comparing themselves against those who were more or less modern.

A new world order required that the masses be reeducated in the service of global economies. The British social critic Stuart Hall, in an influential essay, "Notes on Deconstructing the Popular," described the "moral education" inherent to a changing economic order. The couple's recollections revealed processes that oriented each of them to a changing capitalist context.[3] Consider the ironic education process: as people be-come modern, they have fewer children yet consume more goods. A world turned sideways permitted new crevices. Folks like Emilia and Pa-rigi perceived the world anew and in the process were remade anew.

The significance of the topic of backward sexuality was making its mark on me. Some weeks earlier, negative references to "singles" had come up during two separate meals over the holidays, one celebrating Santo Stefano with friends, the other marking New Year's Eve with acquaintances. The latter involved a marathon meal at the pizzeria 11 Giugno, the leftist Casa del Popolo in Carmignano named after the heroic act of resistance on the same date in 1944. On the wall next to the bar hung a portrait of the four local partisans who had died in the famous explosion of the Nazi train bound for Prato. Chris and I regularly volunteered there every third weekend, splitting the shift so that one of us worked Saturday and the other Sunday. We served a lot of Vin Ruspo, Tuscan antipasti, and oven-baked pizzas. Rather than put our names on the volunteer board, the coordinator simply wrote *gli americani,* the Americans. Some people initially suspected we were spies but then realized we were just a strange breed of Americans, not the kind they were used to seeing in the movies. Even my friends who swore they'd never set foot on U.S. soil until a Native American was in the White House took a liking to us. They invited us to join them in taking special mushroom and herb classes that involved gathering, preparing, then eating the fruits of nature as a way to raise funds for special projects: hospital beds to ship to Cuba or educational materials to send to the Amazon.

The holiday dinner got off to a good start. At 8:30 p.m. we took our seats at one of the long tables that filled the upstairs dining room of the club. Each accommodated eight or ten people. We had no idea what we were in for.

The eating began simply enough: an aperitif of pineapple and orange juice, chips and pretzels. Next came the antipasto, which involved three crostini, one each of liver pâté, salmon pâté, and mushroom pâté, a piece of salami, two pieces of prosciutto, and, of course, crusty Tuscan bread. When we arrived at the *primo,* or first course, we were in for a scrumptious surprise: two pasta dishes—an exquisite lasagna with local meat and white sauce and delicate farfalle with a creamy salmon sauce. As we drank our fill of water and local red and white wines, the conversation began to get interesting.

"Are things a lot different in the United States compared to Italy?" asked a man sitting across from me at the table who introduced himself as Giovanni. He was graying, and his bulky body showed the signs of middle age.

"Somewhat," I explained. "For Thanksgiving, we spend all day cooking and then in twenty minutes we've finished eating." When our Italian friends had accompanied us back to the United States in November 1996, they had experienced deep culture shock after participating in such rapid eating rituals at two Thanksgiving dinners in Missouri. Several recent nutrition studies that had received a lot of attention in the U.S. press came to mind. They pointed to the Mediterranean diet as the most healthy in the world: pasta, fresh vegetables, red wine, olive oil, and limited red meat. The shortcoming of such studies is that they look at what Italians eat but not *how* they eat.

"*A tavola, non si invecchia mai*—at the table, one never ages," said a woman across from me, about the same age as Giovanni. Both appeared to be closing in on the fifth decade of life. Her name was Paola.

The *secondo*, or second course, arrived: wild boar, cockerel, pork, peas, and mixed greens. We ate and talked some more. The couple revealed that they were singles.

Giovanni joked with Paola. "You always wanted to marry me."

"No I didn't," she objected. "I was born *libera*, free." She turned to me. "Besides, he's an *impiastro*, a nuisance." The adjective derived from the word *plaster* and was also used to refer to someone who has been close to you for a long time. "We've known each other for thirty years, but neither one of us has ever married."

"How did you meet?" I asked.

"We were young," Paola said, her memory tinged with nostalgia. "I was very young, about seventeen years old. I went to the Teatro Comunale in Florence. He was a friend of a friend's brother. He's an only child. Anyway, we met there, then saw each other later that evening at a bar where we were having a caffè. I had a lot of pimples, a bad case of acne, and he said to me, '*Quanti bollicini c'hai?*' 'How many zits do you have?' I was horrified. I was very self-conscious about my complexion at the time. But then after that he called me a lot; we'd go out and do things together. Meanwhile, he went with a lot of women, also foreigners: Americans, Germans, and the like. Then he got a job working for Michelin. He traveled a lot. The love of his life was Sardinian. They were engaged for seven years."

"And then?" I asked, looking at Giovanni.

"Then she left me," he said, as though he had seen it coming.

"She found out he was a *pazzarello,* a madcap," Paola added.

They both laughed. I was struck that even a single woman construed her single friend as a failure, as someone who didn't quite fit the norms of society.

The next course arrived in the form of a bounty of mandarins, walnuts, pistachios, and figs. Paola at a certain point admitted that despite her assertion that she was born to be free, "*mi è dispiaciuto che non ho avuto figli*—I've regretted that I didn't have children."

At midnight we uncorked a bottle of champagne and toasted, ever careful not to cross another person's arm during the toast for fear of bringing bad luck to ourselves and others. My daughter sprang up and headed outside to light sparklers and twirl them in the darkness. As others stood up from the table, the servers chastised them: "Come back! Come back! There's still dessert to come." A portable stereo blared accordion-driven ballroom music. I walked over to a table to look out the second-story window at Hollis swirling the glowing sparkler in a courtyard below, and I was surprised when an old fellow asked me to dance. Then another grabbed me for his turn. They were good guys whom I had befriended while volunteering at the pizzeria. My obligatory dances finished, I quickly walked, face flushed, back behind a table, against the wall. From my vantage point, I delighted in watching others dance. One agile dancer told me he had danced for fifteen years—until he had married a woman who didn't like to dance. Everyone watched as he effortlessly regained his footing. He found a partner in the large cook, and the two glided in perfect step across the floor. Her expression was priceless: stern and stoic. She kept her shoulders square and solid, her cigarette dangling between her fingers.

Eventually, the volunteer waiters delivered dessert: a layered cake and a shot of espresso along with liquor, whiskey, and some grappa for those who wanted it. Next to Chris sat a single man, retired from a textile factory. His parents had migrated to France, and he had lived there until he was five, but they had soon returned to Carmignano, where he lived the rest of his life. He had run with a lot of women; he was a *girellone,* in local parlance. He began to reflect on his life but soon changed the subject. He advised us to have another child. For our daughter to grow up alone would be sad for her, especially after we were gone. She'd be alone. We had heard this advice before, but it struck me as peculiar and profound coming from a single man who had never had children himself.[4]

A few days earlier, when we had gone to our dear friend's house for Santo Stefano, the day after Christmas, the same theme came up. Lorenzo and Daniela were robust and humble sweater makers. We had spent the first year of my fieldwork living in Daniela's mother's basement apartment. Over lunch, in the couple's kitchen adjacent to their workshop, we got to talking about single men, men who never married, men who stayed with their families well into their forties or fifties, men called *mammoni*, or mamma's boys.

I broached the subject of family, as I was admittedly missing my own. I regretted that my daughter did not have the chance to be around her cousins, aunts, or grandparents. The fact that my daughter had just celebrated her sixth birthday and that it was the holidays made me homesick. I mentioned my daughter's birthday party of the week before. One of her little Italian friends had not shown up because the girl had recently recovered from being sick. The girl was an only child, without any cousins, and was unaccustomed to having a lot of kids around. Her mother was afraid that all the excitement could cause a relapse.

Talk of childhood friends stirred up memories in Lorenzo, a man of few words but great insight. He was a tall, broad-shouldered man from rural Grosseto, near the area of Maremma, historically known for its marshes, cowboys, and cattle breeders. He had moved to Prato as a boy and had come of age in the 1960s, during the period of radical, leftist politics. He had a stoic demeanor but a teddy-bear presence that softened his understated humor. Soon conversation turned to a well-known older bachelor in the area.

"He has always been into hunting," Lorenzo said of the man. "Hunting *uccellini*, little birds." He chuckled, and his broad chest widened. Bird, or *uccellino*, was also a term of endearment for the male sexual organ. "I remember when I was young," Lorenzo continued. "My friends and I, we used to go around with older guys, partly because when we were seventeen we couldn't drive yet. They had cars. So we'd go in a group, and I remember there would be this other group of guys. We'd arrive there, at the locale—the dance club. We'd go on our way—" and he smiled a flirtatious smile that harkened back to his days as a young man on the lookout for women. "And they'd sort of stay there, by themselves, watching. But they'd never go with women.

"Some of us, we used to talk about this. We noticed that there was a group of guys who would never go with women. In fact, if there was a group of us, and someone wanted one of them to leave, it was enough to start talking about women. You know, first we'd talk about sports. Then we'd start talking about women, and then they, the guys who were known never to date women, they'd leave."

"That's wild," I said. "Who knows?" I suggested perhaps those men were gay, but he rejected the idea. He believed they simply were not interested in sex.

As we spoke, Daniela approached Lorenzo to serve him more of the special pork and pigeon shish kebabs she had made for dinner. A strand of her blond-highlighted hair dangled down from her sloppy bun, exposing her dark southern-Italian roots.

"You're not eating anything," she accused. "What are you eating?"

"*Non ne voglio più,*" he said, defensively. "I don't want anymore."

Daniela tossed one last piece on his plate and retreated to her seat, barely warm because she had been standing and serving for most of the meal. She had not eaten any pasta or meat but had instead opted for chunks from a dried fruit cake from Sienna. Yet looking right at me, she said, "*Io vivo per mangiare; te mangi per vivere*—I live to eat; you eat to live."

It was impossible for me to eat enough to satisfy her. I could almost imagine how Lorenzo felt after a lifetime of not satisfying her desire for him to eat more.

Lorenzo returned to our subject of single men. "Here in this town, there are lots and lots of *zitelli*, bachelors. Their families, they ruin them by overprotecting them. All the fear. Wanting them to stay close to the family. An exaggerated sense of overprotection."

I sensed he was reasoning that these men were never able to develop the necessary confidence to make the passage to manhood.

"Nora's son," Daniela said. "Look at him. He never goes out. He's content to stay at home with his mother. To hang up laundry. Something is not right with them. *Si rovina*. It's ruining him."

"It's their families who ruin them," Lorenzo asserted. "One thing for sure is that their families keep them at home too long."

"Oh, come on!" argued Daniela. "They don't keep them. The women complain, 'Oh, my son, he's still at home.' They don't like to continue doing their laundry, cooking for them, cleaning for them."

"Ah, but the women do it," I said. "In the States, it just doesn't happen. Or it happens rarely. In fact I remember when I was pregnant and my girlfriends would say, 'Wow, that's really a big responsibility to have a child. Eighteen years.' Meaning that there's the idea that for eighteen years they're yours, then they become independent."

"That's what I'm saying," said Lorenzo. "The families allow them to stay at home. They ruin them."[5]

Whether it was convenience, habit, financial motivation, or arrested sexuality, and whether the children or their parents were to blame, the trend reflected what the famous Italian demographer Massimo Livi-Bacci has called "too much family." That is, Italians retain strong family ties—in his view, excessively so—and care deeply about providing for their children. Young adults tend to wait to attain desirable personal, economic, and educational status before becoming parents themselves.[6] Istat noted in 2005 that Italian men on average are thirty-three years old when their first child is born, a statistic that distinguishes them as the world's oldest first-time fathers. The average age of first-time mothers in 2005 was estimated at 29.6 years.[7] The age at which young adults embark upon parenting is also an important link in the story of Italy's lowest-low fertility rates. Certainly secularism, feminism, consumerism, and a sluggish economy with increasingly precarious working conditions have all played a part.

Casual conversations and formal interviews during my years of fieldwork confirmed the view of a society that valued strong if small families. This characterization, however, overlooks the historical adjustments, at times traumatic, to the rigid pecking order of a patriarchal family in decline. The breakdown of a family hierarchy was deeply linked to economic shifts, and it necessitated a reworking of gendered subjects. Modern subjects were placed in new consumption and parenting contexts, which weighed heavily on mothers. The dominant stories that economists and demographers narrate, in which small families result from cost-benefit calculations such that children are increasingly expensive in terms of time and money to their parents, conceal a central dimension of the cultural origins of this transformation: the process and power of modern subject formation. There was a time when folks who seem old now and not up with the times were young and cared about being with it. Having few children was a symbol of being modern for both men and women. It signified that a person was rational and enjoyed a degree of autonomy over his or her life. For a woman in particular, having a say in her pregnancies represented control over her own body, still considered one of the most important measures of gender equality. Having very few children, therefore, meant adults could pursue their own desires and not just the agendas imposed upon them by those higher up in the patriarchal hierarchy—whether papa, *padrone*, or priest.

SEVENTEEN

Amazing Grace

At the end of our driveway stretched a clothesline that caught the wind and afforded a mesmerizing view of the valley while I hung the wet clothes. We shared the line with Emilia and Parigi as well as the neighbors who lived between us. Marika was a nurse from Hungary who had married Stefano, a leftist railroad man from Carmignano, and the couple lived with their two children and his mother in a house whose stucco walls butted up to Emilia and Parigi's place. Their patio, adorned with geraniums, jutted out just below the farmhouse. Their location between my protagonists and me made it inevitable that they would enter the story, but I could not have predicted the circumstances by which Marika and her family would come to play their part.

One afternoon in early January 1997 I warmed the farmhouse by making a light Tuscan lemon cake. A friend's recipe called for blending 250 grams of sugar with 300 grams of flour and three teaspoons of baking powder *(lievito per dolce)*, then separating the yolks of three eggs and beating the whites into fluffy peaks, adding the juice from three lemons along with the grated peel, pouring in 100 grams of melted butter, and throwing in a pinch of salt. After thoroughly mixing all the ingredients and pouring the batter into a pan, I opened the squeaky oven door and baked the cake for thirty-five minutes at low heat (about 350 degrees Fahrenheit). The top turned a perfect golden brown. I headed over to Marika and Stefano's house and invited them over for dessert later that evening. They insisted that we come to their house, so with the cake, husband, and daughter, we did just that. In company, we ate cake. The adults drank sparkling wine. Their twelve-year-old daughter, Giulia, found forgotten toys for Hollis, just half her age. We visited for several hours. Around ten o'clock, their son showed up from work. The twenty-two-year-old stopped in the kitchen just long enough to eat a piece of cake, then quickly left again to rendezvous with friends.

"It's not how I imagined it would be—parenthood," said Marika as she kissed a photo of her son from five years earlier. She was in her forties, and her auburn hair had a reddish sheen. Faint wrinkles lined her slightly ruddy skin. "I feel like a modern woman, I take interest in what my kids do, but they call me *antica*, old-fashioned. What a hopeless situation," she sighed, taking a smoke on her cigarette. "And the Italian mothers—"

"How do you view them?" I asked.

"Well, they are *brave persone*, good people, but they always talk about the house, their kids, food," she lamented. "All the culture and history here, in their *paese*, right here in Florence, they're just not that aware, they aren't very interested in it."

"Did you study?" I asked.

"Oh yes, I finished high school and then three years of university," she said.

"A lot of women around here probably only studied through elementary school," I said.

"It's true. Fifth grade. Go figure," she agreed. "They didn't even go to middle school."

She offered recollections about Hungary, mentioning frequent visits to Budapest. She and Stefano began to debate whether things had been better under communism. You could sense the tension in their relationship as she recounted how people would see a pregnant woman on the bus and get up to give her their seat.

"That's how it was in Florence maybe thirty years ago," Stefano said. "Now forget it. After capitalism took over, one person would see another with a Mercedes, and they'd say, 'Hey! What's that guy doing driving such a fancy car? I want one!' People became crazy competitive."

They compared the social landscape of pre-1989 Italy with the mid-1990s until, around 10:30, we made gestures to head home. Stefano would hear nothing of it and encouraged us to stay, saying he didn't go to bed until 3:00 a.m. Marika must have read the expression on my face and offered as explanation Stefano's refusal to give their son a house key.

"Tell them why," she said, looking toward Stefano with one of those expressions that wives cast at their husbands when they want them to 'fess up to a habit that they detest.

"I like my peace and quiet," he said. "I stretch out on the couch, watch a little TV, doze off and on, and wait until he comes home. There's no curfew. I started doing this when he first started going out, around sixteen or seventeen. By now it's an *abitudine*, a habit."[1]

I had heard stories, even read studies, about the autonomy that Italian youth enjoy in their parents' homes.[2] The parents hardly delighted in their kids' staying out well into the morning hours, but most of them accepted it—and continued to take care of them. They would lament, "*Questi giovani, sono vagabondi loro*—these youths, they're bums." But that was it. The adult children continued to live at home, commonly into their late twenties and thirties. Partly to blame was a rigid economy that offered uncertain, temporary jobs, combined with a shortage of affordable housing, but it was also a different mentality from what I had grown up with. Perhaps the culture of Catholicism, combined with a deep sense of responsibility to care for one's children and with the ideals that a style-driven consumer economy fostered, accounted in large part for the dynamic.

Even in a primarily politically "Red" area, one could sense the anticipation rise with the arrival of the annual benediction. A flyer announced the priest would be visiting our street in early March to bless each house. On the designated day, I hauled my trash to the dumpster as an excuse to go out and see what was going on. The dumpster overflowed with trash—evidence of collective deep cleaning. Along the lane, neighbors stood outside, sweeping, chatting, and waiting; Marika stood out on her patio, enjoying the sunny weather and dreaming of a trip to Hungary come summer.

"Come in! Come in!" Stefano said from the kitchen. Their son was eating. Stefano offered me a drink. His ninety-four-year-old mother, Asia, perked up as the conversation turned to the topic of the benediction.

Back outside, Emilia stood guard at her threshold.

"Go home!" she commanded, and then advised me how to address the priest when he came to my house. "*Reverendo* or *Signore priore.*"

"Ah, he comes every year so the house is good and blessed for a hundred years," joked Parigi.

"Go on now and get back home!" yelled Asia, from her porch. "The priest is about to come, and you're out here chatting away!"[3]

It felt good to get scolded. A willingness on their part to correct my behavior was a sign of affection. A year earlier, my landlady had described my social status as "*Non sei nè dentro, nè fuori*—you're neither inside nor outside."[4] Today, finally, I felt I had achieved insider status.

Asia asked me to accompany her to a special mass to mark the Festa della Donna, International Woman's Day. She walked with a cane, and we strolled arm in arm up the road to the private chapel, which was normally locked. It had belonged to an infamous noble family under whom Asia and her family had toiled as sharecroppers. We arrived to a packed house, about thirty people, mostly elderly women. Hand-chiseled marble slabs bore names of Lepri family members as well as their dates of birth and death. Was I wrong to sense that, in the United States in the 1990s, mortality was held at a distance? Moving from place to place, job to job, lover to lover, did we think we could outrun our fate?

The priest called upon us to remember the elderly, a clear case of preaching to the choir, and offered a moving story. Earlier that day, he had delivered bouquets of yellow mimosa to the women residents of the local nursing home, and they had been so thrilled, he said, that tears had filled their eyes. He confessed that his gesture had even brought tears to his eyes. Hearing the story, I felt tears, too.

Life felt heavier here in the Old World. History weighed on the present. Death lingered closer here than at home. Reminders of mortality pervaded village life.

"*C'hai furia?* Are you in a hurry?" Asia asked me.

"No, no, I'm not in a hurry," I answered.

She took me to a relative's house, an invalid, visited with him for a few minutes, and then turned to ask me again, "Are you in a hurry?"

"No," I reassured her, "I am not in a hurry."

She led me down a quiet side street to an old, stone farmhouse that sat at the bottom of a dip in the road. It was the *casa colonica,* or antique farmhouse, where she had lived back when her family had worked as sharecroppers. I wondered whether she knew that the owner was due to arrive, because before long he showed up. His key didn't work, though. He apologized, then explained to me he was an architect. He turned to Asia and began telling her about her old house.

"I'm returning it to how it was in 1300," he boasted. "I've taken stones from over there; they were the original stones. That's what I'm using to reconstruct the house. In the end it will be just like it was in the *trecento,* the 1300s."

"*Questo non ci credo*—This I don't believe," I asserted.

The man clenched his jaw in a gesture of defensive disbelief. "But I am an expert," he explained, taking care to detail his plans.

"Structurally, sure," I conceded. "But in the 1300s, they had animals in their house, didn't they? This will be a *casa di lusso,* a luxury home."

"No, no," he denied. "It will be rustic."

In my own mind, and I suspect in Asia's, too, I had made my point. Yes, it would have a rustic flair, but a very cultivated flavor. That was the new high style, the sort of rustic quality that very wealthy people could afford to buy. There was new prestige in the antique. Thirty years ago, when Asia and her family had left the house, it had been falling apart. *That* was rustic.[5] I sensed that Asia had gotten a charge out of my challenge to the expert, and as we walked home, I felt a newfound sense of closeness to her and her home.

Despite my growing insider status, villagers called me on my New World ways. One day a neighbor friend asked me, "You always laugh. Why?"

"No, I don't always laugh," I protested. The day before, the guy at the cinema concession had refused to serve me. Was it my accent? Did he hate foreigners? Americans? I encountered occasional anti-American hostility but also enjoyed a more privileged status as a white foreigner than most immigrants. When I got back to my seat, with neither biscotti nor orange sodas for the girls, awaiting *The Hunchback of Notre Dame*, my friend Gabriella asked what had happened. She saw how flustered I was. Her expression showed such deep compassion that I burst into tears. Even to my psychologist friend, how could I explain the rawness that accompanied getting close to people, all the while knowing full well the temporary quality of my bonds here?

April 1997

The test of my acceptance came one Sunday morning. Out my kitchen window a crowd gathered near an ambulance. Two pairs of jeans and a denim shirt hung from the clothesline. They blew eerily in the wind. Spotting Emilia and several other familiar faces, I put on my shoes. Hollis did the same. We left our cornflakes in their bowls and ran outside.

Marika lay unconscious at the bottom of the hill, beneath an olive tree, two pairs of muddy pants at her side.

"What happened?" I asked Emilia, whose face was drained of color.

A man walking his dog had come upon her lying at the bottom of the grassy slope. Marika had apparently been hanging out laundry when she fell down the slope. To think that only two days before she had been drinking coffee in my kitchen, sharing her Hungarian views on how restrictive she felt her life was; she had recounted the things she couldn't do here in Italy as a woman—even as a working nurse in her forties— because the obligations of a mother were so overwhelming.

Her daughter Giulia was crying. She feared the worst. The neighbors filed into the house to calm her like so many disciplined members of a brigade. One woman stayed outside to hang up the wet laundry that remained in a clothesbasket. Another rinsed off the two pair of pants that had ended up covered with mud.

"We are a pack of women," explained one, using the Italian term *branco*. Each woman did her best to calm the girl.

Hollis and I went back to the house to eat breakfast. She picked some flowers for Giulia, and when we returned gave them to her.

Asia sat in a chair holding a broom as though it were the staff of Moses. "I'm ninety-four years old," she said, shaking her head. "*Se era successo a me*—if only this had happened to me." She wiped tears away, but they kept coming.

I rubbed the old woman's shoulder. At a loss for words, I offered: "Let's hope she'll be okay, that it wasn't anything serious."

At 12:45 p.m., the kitchen table was empty, something unheard of for this time of day. Asia heated water in a pot on the stovetop. But the kids didn't want to eat. They wanted to wait until their mom returned home from the hospital.

I headed into the other room to find Hollis sitting in front of the TV with Giulia and her brother. Her six-year-old question was blunt: "Were you afraid that your mamma would die?" The girl fought back tears, then smiled, and shook her head. I left to go pick up Chris from the train station, only to return to an intensified scene.

Inside Stefano and Marika's house, Emilia and a relative were in the front room with Asia. She was carrying on about how Marika was the type to overwork herself.

"Why couldn't this have happened to me?" Asia repeated as she burst into tears.

"You don't have the health problems that Marika has," the female relative reasoned.

"Life is never all right," said Roberta, a middle-aged neighbor woman. "It's always something. That's just how life is. It doesn't help to cry. *Ha toccato Marika*. It was Marika's turn, not yours." She offered her spinach, explaining that she had cooked a lot of it. "I could have called my doctor friend. She'd come running. But then I saw the ambulance . . .

"There's already food prepared: a sauce, meat, a salad. The children don't want to eat. Their stomachs are in knots."

"Once I slipped down that steep embankment, but I slid on my feet and fanny, then stopped," said Emilia. "At least Marika wasn't driving when this happened. And that heart operation. She shouldn't smoke. Hopefully it's not so bad," she added, expressing the group sentiment. "She was probably just *impaurita*, frightened—the fear of her own body."

We all laughed for a minute. Nervous tension? The image of Emilia sliding down the hill on her fanny? The idea that Marika was scared of herself? The light moment was fleeting.

A car screeched to a halt. In walked Stefano, nervous, upset. *"Male! Male!"* he shouted to his mother, Asia. "Really bad!" He disappeared into the back room. *"Male!"* he shouted to the children. Giulia's voice shattered like a kitchen's worth of glasses crashing to the floor. "It's not possible!" Marika was in critical condition. They were going to have to operate. Chris and I exchanged glances. It was time to give the family some space.[6]

The next morning the women from the lane gathered above the spot where Marika had fallen. They said an aneurysm had knocked her down. The tall grass was still flattened, reminding everyone that it was the place where she had lain when the paramedics came to take her away on a stretcher.

"Is there any news?" I asked.

"Marika non c'è più—Marika is no longer with us," an older neighbor woman whispered. "But the children don't know. The sisters-in-law want to wait for her husband."

Roberta told me that her own father had died when her mother was pregnant with her. "So I never had much of a mother. She had to work, in the mines, in Sardinia."

"How tragic," I said, feeling my face flush.

"You see, this has also touched you," Roberta told me. "You've become part of this, too." The neighborhood was accustomed to foreigners who came to live in the farmhouse for brief periods, but most kept their distance. I felt privileged to be part of such an intimate community tragedy. This was my work, true. But it was also my heart.

The group began planning, and arguing about, a collection for flowers. I recounted how Marika had smelled lilacs on our walk. Of course, they would get white roses, only the best. I asked to be included.

Marika's sudden death had the whole neighborhood talking. "Children without a mother, what *disgraziati*, what wretches," one woman lamented.

"Senza babbo, si può fare, ma senza mamma no—kids can manage without a father, but without a mother, no way," said another.

Midweek, the town came to a halt. Bells tolled. By 9:30, well-dressed men and women, young and old, some in black, others in colors, headed down the streets, quickly and quietly, across the piazza, past the newspaper stand, and along the boutiques that lined the road to the Church of San Michele. Men packed the courtyard. I spotted Emilia, and she invited me to sit with her. Mostly women filled the church. Flowers fell off the sanctuary, there were so many of them. Candles burned the air dense and waxy.

"I was baptized in this church, had my first communion in this church, was married in this church, and I'll have my funeral in this church," Emilia said bluntly. I laughed through tears. I would never know such continuity with one place. Emilia's lifelong connection with the global economy seemed a gentle precursor to my surrender to dislocation.

The parishioners rose as the casket rolled in. The daughter's cries echoed through the nave. *Amazing Grace, how sweet the sound / That saved a wretch like me / I once was lost but now am found / Was blind, but now, I see.* The song "Amazing Grace" delivered depth and hope. The priest remembered the wife and the mother. He delivered the mass, and some partook in communion. I exchanged a handshake of peace with Emilia and others in nearby pews. The priest promised Marika's passage to the other side and her arrival to the afterlife. The bells droned with mournful dissonance. No one was ready to accept this journey for a woman in her prime even if they were believers. The pallbearers carried the casket out. The daughter wailed. The villagers slowly exited. Giulia's screams echoed sorrow that touched everyone. I rubbed my tear-smudged cheeks and licked my salty lips.

Outside, a procession of villagers clogged the street from side to side and extended for blocks as it moved through the narrow streets. Giulia stayed behind. The mass of mourners walked past an Etruscan tomb, where the field rose above the road and the eyes of the living met a blanket of yellow flowers. The townsfolk entered the cemetery gate, encircled the plot, and stood in silence as the casket was lowered. A small backhoe pushed dirt into the hole. The closure seemed too sudden. Several men used shovels to square off the mound, finishing the gravesite with a temporary wooden cross and a mound of flowers. One by one, people greeted and kissed the widower and his twenty-one-year-old son, then returned to their jobs, their families, their gossip, their cooking, their laundry.

The neighbor women's words echoed through my mind: "Motherless children, what wretches"; "Kids can manage without a father, but without a mother, no way." These statements spoke volumes about Italy's "culture of responsibility": the intense expectation for parents to raise and nurture their children rested primarily on mothers. As my social and emotional roots took hold, so too did my empathetic understanding of the world in which Emilia had come of age.

EIGHTEEN A Burning Question

A friend lent me back the old Fiat 127, which was well into its second decade of motoring when we returned in fall 2002. A cold and determined
November rain beat down upon the hilly Tuscan countryside, making the
narrow roads slick. Chris drove, taking the curves slow. It was still pouring
when we parked at the dead-end street beneath the farmhouse. The four of
us sat in the little car. Packed in the back were preteen Hollis, eleven, and
her brother, Luca, a two-year-old dynamo. The windows fogged up as we
debated how long we should sit and wait it out. Rain gushed on the wind-
shield like a carwash. Patience depleted, we opened the doors and ran for
the nearest cover—Stefano's porch.

That wind-catching spot had never been the same since Marika's death,
and Stefano had never quite regained his sense of humor. Sitting on the
long wooden bench in his kitchen brought back vivid memories, which

none of us talked about. I had returned to Italy raw. Just a month before, in October 2002, I had lost my four-year-old niece in a freak bathtub accident. My little sister was devastated. My parents were devastated. The girl had drowned one night while in the care of her paternal grandmother, an able-bodied woman in her mid-forties who lived in a modest mobile home. She had stepped out of the bathroom and walked to the kitchen to prepare her drip coffeemaker for the morning. A few minutes later, she went to check on the girl, only to find her motionless in the water. No one could revive her. "Two minutes is too long," an emergency room doctor friend told me of death by drowning. I had never known such grief as that day when I sat with my parents and three sisters on a rural Alabama hillside. Watching my niece's ashes drift into the wind turned my universe upside down. Hearing my sister bid her child a final farewell felt terribly out of order. The death was a tragedy so deep and so profound that it made me sense the trauma of losing a loved one, particularly a child, in a way I had never before felt. Life felt particularly fragile. My can-do American outlook on the world had been shattered between visits to Italy. I could relate to Old World fear and loss in a way I had never known before.[1]

Leaving Chris to graciously indulge in Stefano's hospitality, which included the standard but much-appreciated fare of local red wine, I excused the kids and myself, stepped out into the wind and rain, and headed next door.

The shutters blocked as much light as they did cold. Hearing my knocks, Emilia slowly shuffled across the floor. She frowned at the strangers standing at her door. Within seconds, the wrinkles around her lips and eyes softened with recognition, and she invited us in. Parigi sat at the table, wearing days' worth of white stubble. Stale air lingered like the coming of death. They had aged since my last visit three years before. They would have been eighty-two by then. I had come to give the couple a photograph as well as a paper I had written for an anthropology conference. Several colleagues had encouraged me to return and ask Emilia some follow-up questions. Was there more to the tale of her abandoned sister-in-law than she had told me? What had she meant by that fleeting "at least—"? Their excitement was the oxygen that fueled a burning question.

My timing was off. The couple was in a state of confusion, particularly Parigi. He had lost his glasses and was disoriented, to say the least. Emilia was not much help. Her heart was giving her trouble, she was not feeling well, and she found it a chore to eat. Her housedress with its small blue floral print sagged like an empty burlap sack. She was reduced to a nervous state that marked the brutal side of aging. The couple did their best to welcome me, as they always had. I reintroduced my daughter and introduced my son, thinking Emilia and Parigi would enjoy some youthful company. Hollis covered up her discomfort with politeness while Luca squirmed in his seat, so I sent them back to their dad next door. The air and the mood challenged the senses to a degree that would have been unfair to expect them to bear.

I placed the manila file folder on the table and explained its contents, which included my university business card, and then gave them a copy of the photo: the two of them aglow in a late afternoon light, standing in front of those same shutters three years earlier, the wood a little less weathered than it had become. Parigi mumbled something about an *extra-comunitari*, a non-European. At first I thought he was accusing an African man of running off with his glasses; then I realized that the immigrant was a friend of his and that the old fellow thought he himself might have left his glasses on the guy's truck. Parigi held a scrap of paper. I offered to help. I lifted the heavy black receiver and dialed the vendor's number. A voice spoke. *"Il cliente non è raggiungibile."*

"It's an answering machine," I said regretfully.

Parigi looked at me, like a child looking at an adult, and asked if I might go check at the Superàl in Poggio, the supermarket where the vendor had parked his truck. He gave me his name. I assured him I would do this favor.

A couple of vendors' trucks were parked in the lot. Normally when these men approached they aggressively sought to make a sale, so I was on guard. But when I advanced toward them with my urgent request, they seemed not eager hawkers but empathetic acquaintances. Did they know Parigi's vendor friend? They did, but they hadn't seen him that afternoon.

My three-week visit to the country was quickly coming to an end, and I had abundant social obligations to fulfill before my departure. I had to make peace with the fact that there was little hope that between now and the time when I could next return my aging guides would regain the zest for life they had shown when I had lived on the lane back in 1997.

Historians and scholars who work with documents often envy anthropologists who work with people. They sometimes assume we can simply go back to the source and ask them to explain what they meant. The reality is, memories can be as fragmentary and partial as archival documents. They are certainly more fleeting. Yet what is life without memory? So much of social life involves telling stories of what happened, and, in turn, so much of what happens is shaped by deeply ingrained memories.

For the time being, I had little more than a fragment. One side of me reasoned that if only I had allowed more time to renew my relationship with Emilia and Parigi, they would have been interested in revisiting their past. The other side of me responded that they simply were no longer interested in those old stories. They were dealing with another crisis—one that involved aging and losing control. It would not have been fair to insist on their attention when they were not feeling up to the task. Such insistence would have violated an unspoken pact I had with them—that I never forced them to speak. I listened willingly, and they took great joy in my curiosity. Ultimately, I knew I had done the right thing: I had let it go and helped them with their pressing need of the misplaced eyeglasses.

NINETEEN

Generation Gap

In a photograph taken in Carmignano in 1930, strands of straw dangle from the fingers and plaits drape over the arms of five women seated in straight-backed chairs. The young women sport stylish bobs and wear leather sandals. Their beaded necklaces suggest they are dressed in their Sunday best. At either side of the lineup are seated two barefoot children, probably four or five years old, clutching a bunch of grapes. A third child, a little older, stands with her fingers together holding a piece of straw. The photograph was taken along with hundreds of others as part of a linguistic and ethnographic atlas on Italy and Switzerland for the University of Bern between 1919 and 1925 and again from 1930 to 1935. The ethnologist Paul Scheuermeier sought to document peasant life, and Carmignano was one of several territories where he carried out the project. Nearly eight decades later, the photograph would become not only

Figure 8.   Women weaving straw plaits in Carmignano, 1930. Photograph by Paul Scheuermeier. AIS Archive, Institutes of Romance Linguistics and Literatures and Jaberg Library, University of Bern. Reprinted with permission.

an artifact but also a tool for reconstructing social life and transformative experiences.

I came across the image of the weavers one day in November 1995 in a photographic archive that shared the building with the Università Popolare. The "people's university," geared to adult learners, was located in Via Giuseppe Mazzoni in the historic center of Prato, where I was enrolled in an Italian language course. A wooden door large enough for a horse marked the entrance. A dimly lit stone stairway led to the main floor. Inside, the Archivio Fotografico Toscano was a treasure trove of visual history of twentieth-century social and economic life, both rural and urban. The archive housed volumes of well-organized photographs from the region. Upon hearing of my interest in the cultural roots of family transformation, the staff had suggested that I look at the Scheuermeier photographs, which were held in the archive's permanent collection. Sliding tight rubber gloves onto my hands, I handled images contained in several boxes of Scheuermeier's photographs: women weaving straw, men sitting in olive trees, women sewing, men carrying baskets filled with grapes over their shoulders, chickens brooding in woven cages, a peasant family sitting for a portrait, figs drying on racks before a panorama of the countryside, men planting seed, the face of Mussolini looming from a wall. Another image of the weavers, taken the same year, shows bedraggled women with hair pulled back in buns, wearing sacklike dresses of rough homespun fabric, barefoot or in soiled house slippers, expressionless, with gazes cast downward. An article about the images appeared in the archive's journal, *AFT: Rivista di Storia e Fotografia*, in 1993, and the author, Giovanni Contini, visual historian and native son of Carmignano, described the images as conveying a sense of poverty and subalternity. The exception was the photo of the seated weavers, who smile as they look directly into the camera lens. They seem more like *cittadini*, townspeople, than *contadini*, countryfolk. The image stands as a harbinger of what was to come.[1]

I took this issue of the photography journal back to Italy in February 2004 with the intention of using the images to elicit memories. Photographs may be worth a thousand words, but words may be worth more than a thousand photographs. The photos had the potential to reawaken consciousness related to the structures of a bygone era when the cultural roots of the demographic transition were taking hold.

I had little hope of being able to share the images with Emilia and Parigi. Shortly after my arrival, several friends confirmed my doubts in the worst possible way. Emilia and Parigi had recently passed away. The news had an ethereal quality; its earthly significance took time to settle in. An only daughter, a son-in-law, and two grandsons survived the couple. I did not know their daughter well enough to seek her out on my own, and I was hesitant to contact her, yet I felt an obligation to do so. Friends' offer of help came as the telltale sign of how to proceed.

As local people rely on their social networks, so too do anthropologists, and in my small world there was the late Nicoletta, my landlady during my first year of fieldwork. Nicoletta, amazingly enough, was the first cousin to Emilia's son-in-law, and although she too had passed away, in April 2000 her daughter, Daniela, and son-in-law, Lorenzo, were dear friends of mine and among the first to break the news to me. They recognized that the couple's passing marked a sort of concluding chapter to my work. I shared with them the abandonment narrative as transcribed into text and hinted that I would very much like to at least give a copy of the paper to Emilia's daughter, Patrizia. As it turned out, my sweater-making friends had a favor to ask of Patrizia's husband, Guido. Like Nicoletta, Guido was a southerner from Calabria who had migrated north to Prato during the postwar boom and had made good in a small industry that manufactured residential and commercial lighting.

Daniela and I arrived at his workplace, and Guido gave us a tour of his lighting factory. He beamed with pride and shone as brightly as the small, shiny disk-shaped metal parts that dangled like so many Christmas tree ornaments. He and Daniela posed for a photo. There was a family resemblance between them: he had the stocky male version of Daniela's robust body type, and smiling came easily to both of them. He spoke from the heart as he explained how hard his wife had taken the loss of her parents, his in-laws, and he described what had occurred.

Parigi had gone into the hospital and stayed for three months. He was a terrible patient, resentful of any help or care that people offered him. He made the situation really hard for everyone. The night he died, Emilia had a heart attack. She spent her last nineteen days in the hospital. Since both were born in 1920, they had lived full lives, both having completed their eighty-third birthdays. Age, though, does not lessen the weight of losing both parents in one blow. Guido assured me that his wife would like to see me and offered to let her know I would be stopping by at the acceptable afternoon hour of three o'clock.

Pulling up to her house, at the opposite end of the lane where her parents had spent their lives and where I had spent my farmhouse year, I caught a glimpse of a woman sitting in her garden. Her head hung down. She cast a depressed shadow. I had rarely if ever seen an Italian woman in these parts just sitting, relaxing. They were always busy. Then it dawned on me: she *was* busy—busy mourning.

As an only child, Patrizia had taken her parents' deaths particularly hard. I knew she and her mother had had a close relationship. Most days

Emilia would walk up the road to her daughter's house. She didn't dare go much farther for fear of falling in a field and not being found. The mother and daughter checked in with each other at least once a day. Emilia did not let Patrizia do much for her, but she insisted on doing things on a daily basis for her daughter, such as preparing a nice brew of *malva*.[2]

I stood on the other side of a giant iron gate from a formidable Doberman that barked ferociously.

"Igor!" shouted a woman's voice.

A buzzer unlocked the gate. I dared not proceed but waited patiently until a petite, pale woman welcomed me into the dog's territory. Once I was inside, the dog changed from vicious beast to needy juvenile. I explained who I was and expressed sympathy for the loss of her parents. There was no hiding her pain. She invited me to sit down in the garden and offered me a coffee. I declined. She explained that she was still suffering but not as badly as a few months ago. She had heard of me. I told her I was preparing a book that included her mother. She welcomed me to return another time. The shadow of death made me hesitate. I wanted to be careful not to stir up too much sadness. I planned to bring the journal with the historic photos to give us something to talk about.

Igor greeted me in the same way when I returned, only this time managed to interrupt our discussion with effusive affection in the form of slobbery licks as close to my mouth as he could reach. "Sit down! Be good!" Patrizia shouted each time the dog approached me, tongue and all. I laughed uncomfortably. The dog was vying to be the center of attention; there was no doubt about it. Patrizia offered me something to drink, and I accepted espresso.

Patrizia had indeed suffered greatly over her parents' deaths. She took their loss particularly hard because she was alone, she explained, without any siblings to lean on. At least, she reasoned, she had her two sons to give her a sense that life was worth living. I expressed deep empathy for her and even shared with her my own loss, that of my niece—somehow without crying.

Her mother had aged a lot in the end. She had become skinnier than ever. "*Mangia, mangia, mangia,*" Patrizia recalled telling her, trying to encourage her to eat. "She'd become a little anorexic."

From my computer bag I took out the issue of *AFT* with the historic photographs of straw weavers and peasant cultivators from Carmignano and set it on the kitchen table in front of Patrizia. She admired the photographs, especially the ones of the women working the straw plaiting. "I really like these kinds of things," she said. "Back then, *mamma mia*, it seems impossible: to think that these were the days when Mamma lived." She recalled that her mother had earned a little money from her weaving and that it had been important for the family.

Had she ever heard of the hat dealer who had abandoned his daughter, Germena? Of course she had. Why did she think they left her behind? She explained how the family had left their daughter with this uncle. The father had been constrained to leave for political reasons. The uncle didn't have any children. She wasn't sure of their motives, but she imagined that, in part, they figured the girl could give the uncle a hand. He was alone. He had a nice house. He was pretty well off for those days, so they were leaving her in good hands, so to speak.

"Do you think it was traumatic for her?" I asked.

"I think so," Patrizia said. "Germena always wanted to be the center of attention, she always wanted to feel that she was better than everyone else. It was obvious that something had happened to her. . . . Then in the end she got married and had a son." Yet Patrizia recalled with admiration what Germena had done in terms of innovating sample hat designs. Her uncle then would ship the goods to his relatives in America.

I offered to play for her a recording of Emilia's narrative about the hat dealer's escape and the abandonment. She said she would love to hear it. As I prepared the computer to play the CD, Patrizia marveled over all my equipment. She asked if I liked my work. I had asked her whether she missed her work. And she had said that she did, that it wasn't like before, that there wasn't really much work for women like herself, that there was no sweater work or Italians, and that many firms had to rent or sell to Chinese, whom she said had taken over sweater making and production in the ready-made fashion sector because they would work for lower pay. She harbored some resentment toward the immigrants in the area and blamed the global economy for her now being so idle—reduced to just a housewife. "*Non è considerato come una che lavora*—It's not regarded like someone who works," she explained. I described to her the challenges of my work—not so much the challenges of speaking with people but of taking their memories from one context and placing them in another. The problems of translation were not merely the nuances in people's utterances but also the problems of connecting people's experiences with the broader world and not losing the meaning in the motion.

I put the CD into my laptop and clicked on the play arrow. The sound made her eyes well up. I followed suit. Then we both laughed. Laughed and wiped our watery eyes. "Così," she said, "It's like this," meaning that they weren't tears of pain so much as tears of remembrance.

Patrizia loved hearing her mother's voice. She asked when I had made the recording, and I recalled that it had been 1996, hence eight years earlier. "Listen to how she sounds," she said, her mother's vibrant voice transporting her to another period of her life. "She was doing well."

She invited me on a walk. We left Igor behind and followed the road down to La Fontana, a creek with a spring, where we came upon boys fishing and splashing around. Here, in Emilia's day, peasants had done laundry for the property owners about once a month. We headed up a path that skirted the creek. Deep and wide tracts of black mud made the trail difficult to traverse.

"Look at me!" Patrizia lamented, looking down at her feet. "I'm wearing house slippers." I smiled, remembering that day when Emilia had come to the farmhouse in her slippers and walked down the muddy driveway with the *malva* leaves for her daughter. We walked for a long way through the woods, and I admired her stamina even as she told me about her postmenopausal health issues. The trail emptied onto a narrow road with a view of the Medici villa of Artimino. We climbed the road, careful to avoid cars that sped around the curves. We passed a group of five elderly folks taking their afternoon *passeggiata*. "There are so many *anziani* now," she said. "All old folks."

I remembered Parigi sitting on that concrete ledge, nursing his knee.

"*La vecchiaia gli' è brutta. La vita gli' è una*—Old age is ugly, and you only live once," he used to say.

Red poppies dotted the tall grasses lining the road. A man on a motorcycle stopped us to ask if we knew anything about an old stone farmhouse before us. Patrizia volunteered minimal information, saying that people asked about that place all the time. The owner wasn't interested in selling, as far as she knew. An hour and a half after we had left, we were back at her house. "If only my mother could have lived a little longer," she said.

Our time together finished for now, I packed up my equipment, thanked her, and went on my way.

Initially afterward, I viewed the interview as just short of disaster: the dog had deluged me, Patrizia had sobbed, I had joined in, and I discovered that my tape recorder had shut off midway through. That had never happened before. I came to conclude that the malfunctioning recorder was the result of either the dog or the ghost of Emilia or my state of emotional involvement. In retrospect, I reasoned that I had been flustered and hence had been distracted from monitoring the equipment, but I also realized that I had been focused on what she was telling me, and on her feelings, and that I had felt bad for having made her cry. In listening to the tape months later, I was struck by the interview's layers of history. I resisted having regrets. Patrizia seemed sincerely happy that I had come back to talk to her and that we could share these memories of her parents. I was delighted to hear her describe her mother as *una protagonista,* a protagonist.

TWENTY

"Wet" and Hidden Economies

Serendipity finally seemed in my favor, and it rekindled my interest in Emilia's truncated tale. On April 2, 2004, we were guests at a pizza party, thanks to our dear friends Marco and Gabriella. Back when we were moving into the old farmhouse, they had introduced us to a generous couple, Riccardo and Fabiana, who lived around the corner on the lower portion of Via La Volta. She was a talented seamstress, and he was a sought-after appliance repairman and a lover of things cowboy, western, and retro. Both were precise in their work and appearance. They were a family of three, the third member being his mother. Since we had a history with them, we showed up unannounced at an appropriate hour— just after lunch, before the stores reopened—and received nothing less than bear hugs and reminiscences. Riccardo was quick to remind me how he had comforted me when I was in a funk of homesickness and project confusion, secretly longing for my days in the newsroom when the results of reportage were immediate. Sometimes it is better not to know what people remember about you.

Upon hearing that we were back in the area for four months, Riccardo and Fabiana invited us to a Saturday night gathering in her parents' retired textile workshop. In the boom years following the war, textiles had been the rage, and many people had acquired a mechanized loom or two. Knitwear was particularly big. As a faster globalized economy moved work elsewhere, however, the workspace came to serve other purposes, such as family gatherings.

Beneath fluorescent lights, twenty guests sat at one long vinyl-covered table and drank wine, orange soda, or water. Half of them were retired. Only four children were among us: my two and the two of Marco and Gabriella. Across the room, next to the glowing wood-burning oven, Fabiana and Riccardo made pizzas to order. They had accumulated years of practice churning out custom pizzas for extended family and friends. The couple worked atop a large rectangular marble slab. At the back edge of the slab, they had neatly arranged precut vegetable and meat toppings on paper plates. Riccardo rolled out dough balls into perfectly thin, round crusts, and Fabiana finished each pie as requested. Her brother-in-law used a six-foot-long metal pole connected to a large, pizza-shaped spatula to place them into the oven. I snapped a few photos and couldn't help but notice that the couple looked more chic than ever. They wore stylish jeans with black shirts—hers long-sleeved, his short-sleeved—gold chains with pendants, and white aprons pulled taut around their slender waists. They seemed to fend off aging even as their hair was graying; their haircuts were textured and current. I wondered if their nephew who worked for the Florentine designer Roberto Cavalli had had an influence. Or was the source of their hipness some middle-aged sexual renewal that derived from not having children?

I struck up a conversation with Riccardo's mother. Well into her eighties and wickedly sharp, Natalina perked up as I asked her about Germena, the abandoned girl turned transnational hat dealer. Natalina knew her well. In fact, in decades past she had moved in the circle of women who had worked for Germena. I was excited about the possibility of having

Figure 9.   Riccardo and Fabiana making pizza, 2004. Photograph by Betsy Krause.

another perspective on the story with the unfinished ending. Besides, Natalina was interesting in her own right. Like Emilia, she had worked as a *trecciaiola,* a straw weaver, in the global hat industry since she was a young girl. Also like Emilia, Natalina came from a large family of seven siblings, and she herself had an only child. Unlike Emilia, however, she had no grandchildren, since Riccardo and Fabiana had not had children. I asked her if she would be willing to speak with me further. She agreed. Come Monday, I phoned Natalina and set up an interview at her convenience.

Natalina and Fabiana, her daughter-in-law, sat in the orderly yet well-used kitchen around a large square wooden table, rich from use and from care and regularly refinished with oil. A refurbished retro refrigerator stood across the room. I took out my trusty tape recorder and the *AFT* magazine with the historic photos of peasant life in Carmignano and began the interview with some questions about Natalina's work history. My use of the respectful *lei* form of address was not well received.

"Io voglio del tu, eh!" Natalina said, insisting on the informal form. I was relieved because the *lei* form confused me, since it simultaneously can mean "you" or "she," depending on the context. Natalina's family, like many former peasant families from the area, rejected the social distance that the formal pronoun created and instead embraced the intimacy conveyed in the informal usage. Later, as I learned about Natalina's father, her insistence made sense.

I would eventually play for the two women Emilia's narrative, but first I wanted to hear Natalina's version of the abandonment story. I could not simply go and ask Germena. She had passed away some three years ago.

Germena was remembered as having a tough character. She had gotten along well with her aunt but had had a strained relationship with her mother.

"Her mamma came, you know, for a visit, as people do," Natalina recalled of her trip back from Argentina. "The people who lived next door used to say that the two of them were always fighting—well, they never actually hit each other." She laughed.

"I mean," Fabiana added, "there wouldn't have been a good relationship between the mother and her daughter."

"Well, my God, I know, but in short, you know, if your mamma, she would come for a few days, I mean—" Natalina added.

"So she felt a little abandoned?" I asked of the girl.

"Bah, oh!" Natalina exclaimed, as if I had just asked the dumbest question ever uttered this side of Florence.

Thick-skinned, I pressed on about Germena. What type of person was she?

"She was a little, a little *crostino,* as we say in Italy," Natalina said.

"Crostino—hard?" I asked.

"You know, she was a little, *di garbar come andavi,* she liked it her way, also with the women, you know, if something, if something wasn't returned to her on time, she'd have a fit. Not to me, however, but with those who worked for her she'd do it. But her husband, no, poor thing. He was calm, he was."

"Oh really?" I asked.

"Yeah. But she, she was a little, a little of a *comandera,* a drill sergeant, let's just say it," Natalina said.

"Was she the *padrona,* the boss?" asked Fabiana.

"She was the boss because when her husband married her she had money and he was a peasant," added Natalina.

Germena and her uncle had consigned the raw materials to the rural women to weave. The consigners had actually worked for others, a factory in Florence, where they would deliver the completed plaits. It was their job to oversee the diffuse domicile production, which took place in homes throughout the hilly countryside. And they'd come round and say, "For to-morrow I need so many hats, so many shoes." There were strict and fierce deadlines to be met.

"When the work was finished," Natalina said, "they would go to Florence and bring these hats, and then they would give them material to make hats, shoes, and purses once again; in short, that's how it worked back in those days."

Straw weaving figured centrally in the regional economy. The Italian historians Alessandra Pescarolo and Gian Bruno Ravenni state in *The Invisible Proletariat* that the activity of the straw weavers, or *trecciaiole,* represented the principal sector of industrialization in the countryside of nineteenth-century Tuscany. Middlemen called *fattorini* acquired the raw material at local markets in Prato, Empoli, and Florence and dispersed it throughout the surrounding hamlets to women weavers, who worked in their homes—often in groups. They laboriously wove the consigned straw into long plaits, which were then fashioned into hats before being sent to consumers in France, England, Germany, North and South America, and, later, Mexico as well as Egypt. The weavers were paid by the piece. Lamenting the difficulty of counting the precise number of women workers in Prato, the author of a report in 1896 noted, "In this commune nearly all of the women and some of the men weave braids for hats."[1] To gauge the importance of this activity to capitalist growth, it is noteworthy that in central Italy the most extensive strikes of the nineteenth century erupted that same year and involved these nonurban weavers. Few expected the strikers to reach some forty thousand workers in the towns and rural hamlets that lined the banks of the Arno River and extended along its tributaries.

Figure 10. Natalina Rossi with straw plaiting, 2008. Photograph by Betsy Krause.

I asked Natalina how she had gotten into this line of work.

"That's all there was," she explained. "The straw hat is a Florentine thing. So you see, women worked at that."

"But how did Germena get into it?" I pressed.

"It's as she told you," she said, referring to Emilia. "You see, her daddy and mamma—now if they are living I don't know—they had to flee from the fascists, no? Her mamma and daddy had to go to America, you see. They took off. And Germena, she stayed back with this uncle and with this uncle's sister. And her folks decided to go there. They told her daddy and her mamma, 'Don't take her away, leave her with us.' So you see, she grew up with this uncle and aunt until the end. She died before her uncle. They kept her like their own daughter, you understand? Then she got married, and her husband, he came to live with her, and they had a son. It's like this. And they always worked in this sector."

She explained the kinship between Emilia's husband, Parigi, and Germena's husband—the two were brothers. I let on that I knew the story of how Germena had worked with her uncle to export hats to America, where the girl's dad had moved.

"This aunt and uncle, they wanted her, they're like, 'You leave her with us,' they go," Natalina recalled. "Anyway, her folks had the hope of coming back. Instead, they never came back to Italy."

Her version was so similar to Emilia's, even in the way that she emphasized the uncle's insistence that they leave him the girl. The townsfolk had woven the memory of the abandoned girl's family history tightly into the fabric of their social life. The number of people who knew the girl's history suggested it was a meaningful story worth telling and retelling. Remembering the past had a bearing on the present. This memory work certainly shaped how people viewed themselves and their families.

I pulled out the transcript of Emilia's narrative and slid it across the table toward Natalina. I stood up beside where she sat, leaned over, and began to read it. As I got to the detail of Emilia's sister-in-law's father fleeing to America in a crate of straw hats, Natalina laughed.

"Hats? Eh, in fact," she quipped.

As I read on, unable to sound anything like Emilia, I suggested one of them read the text. They declined. My accent botched her words. I pleaded with them to read it aloud, like a script.

Fabiana took the lead, then stopped herself, objecting: "But it's written as she would have spoken it."

That a local woman would object to my diligent attention to accuracy surprised me. Granted, I was accustomed to local people telling me what an "ugly" dialect they spoke. But I was aiming to "give voice" to local experiences of transnational histories, and I wanted to get it right. My background in linguistic anthropology had trained me to transcribe interviews word for word. This meant leaving dialectal renderings in their original form—not "cleaning up" the language to standard Italian conventions. I tried to clarify my intention to revalue the local talk, not mock it. That was a fine line to walk, especially for a foreigner.

I read Emilia's recollection about how after World War II the straw weaving began to disappear and women began to go work in factories.

Natalina interjected, "Ah yes, then they began to work in the factories."

"And you too?" I asked.

"No, no, me, no. I always worked hats," Natalina said.

"Okay. Read this, read it, read it," I begged, pointing to the transcript, then laughed. "Come on! Please?"

Natalina refused, but the younger Fabiana took it upon herself to voice the narrative. "Leave me the girl. *Almeno*, at least—and they left this Germena to them, who would be his brother's wife."

Natalina chuckled. "In fact, it's the truth."

I had never doubted that the story was not the truth. But with Emilia always emphasizing her story was true and then Natalina also doing the same, I came to wonder where the untruth might lie. So I decided to ask point-blank the question I had wanted to ask from the moment of my conversation with Natalina at the pizza party but had never found the proper context for asking.

"But I always ask myself, why, when Emilia mentioned that they left the girl, why did she say '*at least*—'?"

"So, they went to America," Fabiana said, "but even people here, they'd give babies to wet nurses. My mother, who was a twin, her grandma gave her to a wet nurse. Her mother kept one, and my mamma, she was sent away to a wet nurse, an aunt, until she was fourteen years old."

I was perplexed that she would respond to my question about Emilia's dangling "*at least*" with an answer about the historic practice of giving infants to wet nurses. At times, the answers to my questions were so un-expected that I felt I had been asking the wrong question all along.

"My mother also took one in," Natalina said.

"For a year?" asked Fabiana, directing the question to her mother-in-law.

"A year, and then some," Natalina recalled of her mother, Enza. "My mamma, poor woman—back in those days, a woman would have a child, you see, and money was scarce, and if she had milk she would take in an-other baby for a period, up to a year, and they'd give her a stipend for a year. And it amounted to something."

Enza had been born in 1889 and had had her first child when she was twenty, in 1909. She had named the girl Teresa. As she was preparing to wean the girl, at around twelve months, she learned of the opportunity to take in a baby from the Hospital of the Innocents in Florence. Money was short, the farm wasn't rendering, and she knew that she still had milk, a valuable substance in those days. Hospital administrators needed wet nurses for the babies who had been abandoned. They offered a stipend to lactating women willing to take in the newborns. As the anthropologist David Kertzer has argued, artificial feeding was frequently no more than a death brew for newborns. Babies given animal milk would often develop diarrhea, which dehydrated them. Their weakened condition made them vulnerable to pneumonia and other life-threatening diseases. A Bologna foundling home established an artificial feeding ward in 1895 to avert the spread of syphilis from wet nurses to infants and vice versa. The experiment failed. Kertzer documents the virtual slaughter of the bottle-fed babies. Some 128 were sent to the ward, and after ten months ninety-five had died—almost 75 percent—most within their first two months in the ward. The survivors were pale, small, and disease prone as compared with the breast-fed infants. An institution's ability to recruit wet nurses represented babies' best chance of living beyond their first birthdays. He writes: "And so it was that wherever there were foundling homes, from Portugal to Russia, Italy to Ireland, foundling home officials devoted much of their energies to recruiting lactating women to nurse their little wards."[2] Many of those recruits lived in the countryside, and for a variety of reasons the officials preferred to place infants outside the institution in the homes of the nursing caretakers.

For rural women, some extra cash could mean the difference between surviving or starving. With some trepidation, Enza had agreed. One foggy morning she set out to the city to pick up the abandoned baby and to register as a wet nurse. She probably would have carried a medical certificate from a doctor that certified her good health as well as her husband's and that confirmed her baby was at least twelve months old. She may also have had a notarized document from the town office that certified her good morals. As long as the foundling home deemed she had milk, she could expect a monthly stipend for up to a year.[3]

She would have arrived in the supersanctified Piazza Santissima Annunziata and approached the renowned hospital that the famous architect Filippo Brunelleschi had designed. Since the fifteenth century, terra-cotta babies have gazed down from above the nine arches that form the foundling home's facade, their legs and torsos swaddled with sculpted strips of cloth. The structure's Renaissance rationalism contrasts with a tragedy that is not even mentioned in the most classic of art history texts on the Italian Renaissance: hundreds and thousands of abandoned infants crossed the hospital's threshold, and countless infants did not live to walk back across it. Desperate parents, typically said to be shamed mothers, left their babies outside on the wheel, pulled a bell string, and ran away. An attendant on the other side rotated the wheel, allowing the little innocents passage to their destiny.

The wheel in Florence was dismantled in 1875, so it would not have been in operation when Enza arrived to take her charge. Today, tucked away in a nearly hidden wall of the loggia, beside a barred window, is an inscription carved into a slab of stone:

Questa fu per quattro secoli	This was for four centuries
Fino al 1875	Until 1875
La ruota degli Innocenti	The wheel of the Innocents
Segreto rifugio di miserie e di colpe	Secret refuge from poverty and guilt
Alle quali perpetua soccorre	For those to whom charity
Quella carità che non serra porte	Never closed its door.[4]

The abandonment of infants became popular in Florence during the mid–nineteenth century not only among unwed mothers, who faced severe social stigma from their communities, as well as surveillance and control on the parts of the state and the Church, but also among married women. In his book *Sacrificed for Honor* Kertzer offers the profound statistic that during the 1830s some 43 percent of all children baptized in the city were abandoned at foundling homes, where many died within a year. There is intriguing evidence that married couples in Tuscany began trying to control conception just as foundling homes began to close to their doors to unwanted "legitimate" children.[5] Sanctioned couples' practice of giving up their baptized infants points to an emerging desire to have smaller families. Kertzer has described infant abandonment as a precursor to fertility decline. The widespread practice of wet nursing, together with its benefits and traumas, may have also figured into people's changing attitudes toward families, if Natalina's recollection of her mother's experience is any indicator.

Time passed and the twelve months that Enza nursed the baby neared an end. Nobody came for the baby. From time to time the *carabinieri*, state police, would come round and check the baby's condition. They would make sure Enza still wanted him in her care. Each month a bank note arrived. She came to realize that the boy's mother must have been sending this extra money, although she had not had any contact with his parents.

Her daughter, Teresa, and the baby boy grew closer. The boy was like a brother to Teresa. They grew up together. They were *fratelli di latte,* milk siblings. Enza came to treat the boy like her own son. In 1912, when he was two, she bore a second son, who died at birth. In 1914, she gave birth to a girl, who died at twenty-eight months. Childhood illnesses were life-and-death matters back then, and many little ones ended up in cemetery plots reserved for the little "angels." It was a rough time for losses. One day, when the boy Enza had nursed from infancy was almost six, the police arrived to take him away, to put him in school.

"My mamma, poor thing, she used to say, 'But by then he was old'— poor woman—'old' so to speak. But this baby, him, for my mamma and daddy—he knew them as his daddy and mamma. He had been with them, taken in from when he was little, you know. And she'd say how he was, how the baby suffered, and so did my parents because they say it was a really awful parting. So she used to go, she'd say, 'No, no even if I starve to death,' she'd go, 'I'm not doing these things any more.' You see, when she went to get the baby, when they picked him up, they got him and that was that. But when she went to bring him back, his mamma was there to take him. So she met his mamma. My mamma met the boy's mamma. Hmm. But he told her, 'No! My mamma! My mamma!' But that was his. In short, it was awful, she used to always say, it was just an awful scene."

Enza gave birth to Natalina the following year, in 1917. In 1921, a son came along but died after fifteen days. A baby girl, Milena, was born in 1922. And then she bore three sons, Enzo in 1924, Marino in 1924, and Natalino in 1929. The last was born in Carmignano, where they had moved in 1927 because of orders from their *padrone,* who decided he needed them on a farm he had down south. The family joined the parish of Santa Cristina a Mezzana until 1935, when they moved to the other side of the commune and became members of Saint Michele.

All told, Natalina counted her mother as having given birth nine times and included herself as one of seven children who had survived long enough to be considered part of the family. Plus there was the milk brother. "She had him, she thought for a year," emphasized Natalina of her mother. "But then she ended up having him for five or six years."

The historic archive of Carmignano was more of a disorganized storage room than an orderly collection of documents when I first worked there in 1996, but among the dust lay another piece of evidence that was beginning to call for its place in my search for the cultural roots of demographic change. A biology teacher turned local historian who was also conducting research in the archive suggested I take a look at a turn-of-the-last-century ledger. The word *Baliatici* was scripted in pen across the cover. Translation: Wet Nurse Registries. The brown string ties along the side were rigid from nonuse. Despite efforts to carefully untie them, they loosened abruptly as though I had just picked at a crusty scab. Inside, the registry recorded subsidies paid to poor mothers whom doctors had "certified" as lacking in milk. As such, these women were eligible to receive state money to hire a wet nurse to care for and nurse their infant.

Historically, there were three major types of wet nurses in western Europe: those who worked for the rich, those who worked for foundling institutes, and those who worked for the poor. The most widely documented are the wet nurses who worked for wealthy families. Luigi Pirandello's novella *La balia* inspired the Italian filmmaker Marco Bellocchio in 1999 to produce a film of the same name, (translated as *The Nanny* in the version distributed in the United States and as *The Wet-Nurse* for the Canadian release).[6] Set in Rome during a turbulent period of the early twentieth century, the story follows the wealthy psychiatrist Mori and his depressed wife, Vittoria, who has just had a baby that allegedly refuses his mother's milk. Mori deems an illiterate yet subversive country girl, Annetta, to be in good health and, after making a contract with her to abandon her own baby boy, hires her to feed and care for his child. Against a backdrop of class conflict, the wet nurse bonds with the baby and develops a friendship with Mori, who teaches her to read. Annetta's presence threatens the stability of the family, sending Vittoria into a state of desperation. The film sheds light on the uneasy relationships connected to the practice of wet nursing.

In *Peasant Women and Politics in Fascist Italy*, Perry Willson assesses the experience of peasants in Tuscany and Friuli who moved to the homes of the wealthy to nurse and care for babies: "This . . . form of temporary migration could be very traumatic, uprooting women from their families and their own children, but it offered excellent wages." The researcher Adriana Dadà collected memories from the Commune of Ponte Buggianese, in the province of Pistoia, where as many as 20 percent of the women migrated from their towns to work temporarily as wet nurses for wealthy families between the 1880s and 1940s. Memories were not always free flowing or forthcoming, but a number of traumatic stories emerged from the interviews, in which women or their descendents told of feelings of having abandoned children. Common were sentiments of remorse and pain. The migrants had sacrificed happiness and bonds with their own children to improve the economic well-being of their families. Many spoke hesitantly. The daughter of one woman who had worked as a wet nurse, however, offered an elaborated account of her mother's experiences. Her mother had worked several wet nurse jobs, and while she had been away her eight-year-old son drowned in a ditch. The loss of her son left painful traces. As an old woman, the daughter recalled, she would constantly cry out deliriously for her dead son, wanting him next to her. One evening, an acquaintance came to visit her and she mistook her child for her own son, insisting on keeping him for hours near her bed and refusing to let him leave.[7]

As part of a video archive project in Carmignano the visual and oral historian Giovanni Contini conducted two interviews in 1991 with Iolanda

Drovandi, born in 1906, who told of being coerced into working as a wet nurse. Iolanda described herself as a "sold woman," recounting how her family had convinced her to become a wet nurse in the early 1930s after her midwife told her, "The baby was born dead. She's missing all her nails." Iolanda, shocked and overcome with fear, succumbed to her mother-in-law's pressure. The wealthy man whose baby she nursed scolded her when she went into the fields because of a belief that physical labor made woman sweat and could make the baby sick. "You have a pension and I pay you," he'd say. "You're a sold woman." As the interviewer, Contini asked her whether the money she had earned had been important to the household, whether it had made a big difference. She responded: "The difference was this: that when he paid me each month my mother-in-law took it." Iolanda never saw a lira in the thirteen months she nursed the child. "It seems like a song, but it's actually a true story." And when the child had to go back to its mother, the separation was painful. Women of her generation were subordinate to the senior members of the household and accepted their place in the hierarchy. In retrospect, she described herself as *grulla,* or stupid. As she matured, she drew the line. Smaller families would pave the way for a peasant protest and render those hierarchies less rigid.

Wet nurses who worked for other poor women also had to deal with the emotional traumas that followed from this trade. This variety of wet nurses fell into two subcategories. First, there were village wet nurses who tended the children of emigrating wet nurses who had left home to work for elite women elsewhere. Second, there were the least-known type of wet nurses, those who worked for women certified as lacking milk and were paid by state subsidies.[8] Those who served other poor women are all but forgotten—even though this relationship was crucial to the development of a global economy and probably impinged on reproductive trends.

Another rare recollection emerged during an interview with a couple who were descendents of a peasant family featured in Contini's *AFT* article with photographs from the Scheuermeier archive. My well-connected friends Marco and Gabriella also introduced me to this couple and their wonderful hospitality, which included a dinner of freshly made *gnocchi.* I came back later with the images. They prompted memories in Piero and Amadea, both in their sixties, about how people endured poverty and loss. Looking at a portrait of the large family, Piero pointed to his grandfather and an aunt. He could not identify everyone. The photo had been taken at the beach, and the individuals wore their Sunday best. Some were barefoot.

"But because they didn't have shoes or because . . . ?" I asked.

"*C'era anche la miseria,* there was poverty. It's not that. . . ."

"They had to save their shoes, oh!" interjected Amadea. "They had to save them for winter, so they'd go barefoot."

"Oh, I see, of course," I said.

"It's not like now, *se garbano delle scarpe, si comprano,* if you like some shoes, you buy them!" she explained.

Comparison continued of the material conditions before and after the economic boom of the 1960s. Piero noted that his father's family was large: "*Gl'eran tanti, tanti, tanti.*" He counted off the uncles, and then added them up, getting corrected by his wife, who included the women in her count, and arriving at ten.

"But how many children?" I asked.

"*Povere donne,* poor women . . . ," Amadea said.

"Then, to earn a little something, they would take, my aunt to earn a little, to make ends meet, with so many children, *gliene pigliava uno a balia.* She would take in one as a wet nurse. . . . She gave them milk. But she didn't just take one, she took a number of them, *n'avea presi diversi, diversi, diversi.*" Amadea added that her grandmother had taken in an orphan to nurse. Piero repeated, "There was poverty back then."

Amadea offered her analysis of the repercussions: "I'd say they had more than trauma because when there's poverty . . ."

"More than trauma, in fact," I echoed.

"You might say people had to let things be—*Sara' anche lasciare un po' fare.*"

Striking about the registries in the Commune of Carmignano is the occupation of the recipients of the subsidies. Some 390 women, or 96.3 percent, were listed as *trecciaiole,* or straw weavers, among the 405 cases that the Charity Board in Carmignano reviewed from 1883 to 1902. Only

15 cases, or 3.7 percent, had no occupation listed, and four of those were without a mother, probably because of death during childbirth. Therefore, the overwhelming presence of weavers in these wet nurse ledgers suggests two possible explanations.[9] The official version is that these women were among the poorest strata of society and that because of meager living conditions malnourishment prevented their bodies from producing milk. I came across numerous notes from doctors who certified that women were *"tutto priva di latte,"* completely without milk. The records did not indicate how the physicians determined this lactation lack; however, it is unlikely that so many women would be biologically unable to nurse. In the Commune of Prato in 1886, the Casa Pia dei Ceppi recorded 316 cases of milk subsidies paid to mothers defined as *"impotenti ad allattare la propria prole*—impotent to nurse their own offspring"—or 22.5 percent of the 1,404 annual births.[10]

Milk volume appears unrelated to nutritional status except in extreme cases of malnourishment. The biological anthropologist Meredith Small observes in her *Our Babies, Ourselves* that insufficient milk syndrome across cultures results far more from cultural practices related to breastfeeding than from biological predisposition or nutritional status. The amount of skin-to-skin contact that a lactating woman has with an infant, including whether she sleeps with the infant, the frequency as well as length of lactation, and the extent of the social as well as emotional support and hence serenity that she enjoys all figure into producing levels of milk that satisfy the infant's demand.[11]

A more plausible scenario is that the weavers felt pressed to continue working and motivated to take advantage of state charity. Nearly every household of Poggio a Caiano, at the time under the jurisdiction of Carmignano, listed at least one *trecciaiola*, or weaver, in the 1901 census when its bustling township was 2,784 strong.[12] A few years earlier, in 1893, a report on women's work in the commune noted that female labor was "limited to the fabrication of straw plaits for hats," detailing that the women often worked fourteen- to sixteen-hour days, earning income that was significant to the household economy. The author concluded of women: "They are viewed as not very useful by the men."

Despite this astute insight into the gender relations of the day, the report did not make note of the underground economy linking weavers and wet nurses. Probably these women's time spent weaving was so critical to the family economy that they could not afford to lose work by tending to an infant. Nursing and caring for a baby took a good deal of time and energy. Hence they applied for the state subsidies and sent their newborn to a wet nurse, even though the practice clearly was against the moral order of the day and even though, according to a letter from the Hospital of the Innocents in Florence to the Commune of Carmignano, handing a baby over to a wet nurse increased the risk of infant death.[13]

Archival records testify to an embodied aspect of the history of global capitalism and demographic shift that is rarely considered. The weaver–wet nurse connection complicates the conventional split between production and reproduction: that is, between those who work for pay and those who work for nurture. Furthermore, the state's proclamation of moral standards reveals how ideas about gender underwrote conventions of motherhood.

Various forms of stigma were associated with wet nurses. These along with the haunting memories of those who sold their milk may in part explain Natalina's interpretation of Emilia's unfinished thought. Even as state officials funded this system of subsidies, they simultaneously condemned it.

The frontispiece of the *Baliatici,* provided to the commune from the state, delineated *avvertenze normali,* or standard instructions, for carrying out the subsidy program. The subsidies were for poor parents of "legitimate" children, meaning those born to married couples. The "valid" reasons for a woman to receive the subsidies were limited to inability to breastfeed due to physical impotence or insufficient nutrition. An infant's mother's death was also considered valid. The guidelines included sections on maternal nursing, the hygienic necessity of nursing, dangers eliminated from maternal nursing, and wet nurses. The guidelines dissuaded local officials from supporting women who would give up their infants to wet nurses "without just cause." Such women were portrayed as lower than the most bestial of animals:

By law of nature, and by sentiment of love, the mother is called to suckle her children, unless the woman, who is the most beautiful and gentle part of the human species, would want to place herself below other brutish female animals, which provide her with an example not only by nursing their own offspring but also by refusing themselves to be milked when they do not have offspring present. In fact, mother's milk is food, the most valuable for the neonate; and the mother who denies it to the child must fear that her refusal of this saintly responsibility of nature exposes her creature to dangers that can not only compromise her beauty but, even worse, threaten her health. (*Baliatici* 1883, my translation)

Nowhere in the registry is there any acknowledgment of women who might have been motivated to apply for the subsidies so as to continue working in the regional-global markets.

Instead, the instructions established the superior moral value of breastfeeding and provided evidence for the health benefits of nursing, concluding that the postpartum death rate increased among women who did not breastfeed. Maternal breastfeeding was good for mothers and infants as well as the nation, and those who refused their calling were "evil": "Observing the law of nature that obliges mothers to nurse their own children not only has salutary effects for themselves, for their children, and for the nation but eliminates danger as well as doubts about exchanging newborns, as in the case of Nourishers—evil women who unscrupulously will replace their care for their own child with someone else's—and to safeguard the infants from the syphilis virus, that with such facility transmits itself from the wet nurse to the newborn, with damage to the family and to the population." Syphilis had become a major public health concern and could be transmitted from infected infant to healthy wet nurse or vice versa. Mention of the benefits of maternal lactation to the nation reveals that the health of the population had become a national concern. The standards specified ideal characteristics of wet nurses when it was absolutely necessary that they be used. Preference should be given to "those women who offer the greatest guarantee to be good caretakers, to keep the infants' limbs straight without using *fasce e legature*, wraps and bindings, and to accustom them to every food; must be between twenty-five and thirty-five years old, have good milk, abundant and perfect, and *il primo fuoco concupiscibile è spento*, the initial lustful fire is put out—that she enjoys good health, is a conformist, of tranquil character and of upstanding moral quality, casting out those who are devoted to wine because such a vice predisposes the infant to convulsions, epilepsy, and anxiety." That sexually active or "lustful" women were regarded as unqualified is not surprising. Obviously, given the fear of syphilis, there was a pragmatic health reason for this, but the language used, "the initial lustful fire is put out," resonates with moral overtones. The state was administering not only subsidies but also morality of a type aimed at women and their sexual as well as bodily comportment.

The proceedings of the Carmignano Charity Board reveal that local government was also in the business of monitoring the morality of its citizenry. On October 28, 1901, an anonymous mother was so ashamed of having birthed a child out of wedlock that she sent the midwife to the city hall to register her child's birth. The record indicates that the mother did not want to be recognized. Less than three weeks later, however, Erminda Pagni changed her mind. She went to the civil office to declare herself the natural mother of her son and request that his last name be changed.[14] But when Signora Pagni turned to the state for assistance, officials refused her. The board rejected Pagni's request to receive a milk subsidy to pay a wet nurse to suckle her natural son. An investigation by the Municipal Guard, a policing arm of the state sent out to check on the families who requested subsidies, noted that Pagni had failed to "follow correct conduct, having brought into the light a son without being united with someone in marriage." The so-called Charity Committee unanimously rejected her request. Being denied for her failure to display "correct conduct" was probably a heavy blow to Pagni, who was a widow.

Moral commentary extended to men. In the case of a man by the name of Berti, the guard noted that he worked only several months in the summer as a *barrocciaio*, bringing fruit down from the mountains, and that his wife was a weaver. A medical certificate indicated that she was without milk. The report observed that the couple had four children in their *carico*, or load. "Thus their financial situation must be wretched, but there is evidence that Berti is always gambling, and hence this would indicate the contrary," reads the report. The Municipal Guard concluded, "Thus we cannot conscientiously make a judgment about the situation." In other words, the guard did not offer a recommendation to the decision-making body as it typically did. A man's gambling, however, was evidently not as great a sin as a woman's bearing a child out of wedlock; the charity board eventually approved Berti's request for a wet nurse subsidy.[15]

Although many people I spoke with offered memories of relatives who had worked as wet nurses or straw weavers, no one had ever heard of the wet nurse subsidies. The only exception was the biology teacher who had seen the *Baliatici* as important to my project.[16] As archival fragments, the wet nurse registries provide rich if messy evidence of a state project that used moral proclamations to conceal the economic motivations behind the subsidies, which intimately linked wet nurses and weavers, their work and their children, to a transnational market. The wet nurse ledgers from the late nineteenth and early twentieth centuries reveal that although the state underwrote vital economic connections between weavers and wet nurses, it did not openly acknowledge its actions. The wet nurse subsidies in Carmignano served to free up women so that they could continue weaving; but rather than focus on the economic realities facing these women, the state opted for moralizing discourses rooted in gender ideologies. This strategy served to turn women's work into a moral project and thereby to discount it as productive work.

Giving birth back then was not just about giving birth. It was also about the negotiation of labor and capital accumulation. Giving birth affected possibilities for the accumulation of capital, not only in terms of labor for the farm, but in terms of a potential "wet" resource for a struggling household. In fact, as the wet nurse–weaver connection demonstrates, the work of giving birth could translate into paid labor. Women in central Italy brought capital and cash into the household through several types of work: agricultural labor, weaving, and wet nursing. To be a paid wet nurse, one had to first give birth to one's own child as a way to stimulate milk production. One's milk could then be "sold." It became a commodity.[17]

I intend the term *wet* to draw attention to the way in which bodily substances saturated economic activity in the environs of Florence.

Submersed beneath all of that "dry" mercantile activity of straw was a "wet" movement in lactating women. The dominant economy would have withered had it not been for the wet aspect that kept things flowing. The weavers would not have been able to keep weaving if it weren't for the wet nurses, their milk, and the subsidies. The hidden traffic in milk moistened—even lubricated—the economy and kept it "flexible." Here, *flexible* meant that labor was cheap and available on demand. This equilibrium, however, ultimately could not be sustained. Women's milk forged and broke social relations and left its mark. A resonance of trauma resulted from this traffic in human substances.

Emilia's tale of the abandoned sister-in-law and the other memories it provoked, together with archival evidence about wet nurses, paint a vivid picture of the multifaceted and painful ways in which so many women were linked to the global market, not through formal business relations, but through informal and intimate kin relations. Kinship is typically associated with the monetarily unproductive domestic sphere. Conventional approaches to studying markets have erased the significance of domicile work to global economies—let alone transformations in family making.

The history of fertility decline is deeply entwined with the formation of a transnational system that sprang from a regional economy founded on subjects who were sandwiched between capitalist, kin-ordered, and tributary modes of production. Such arrangements exacted costs on certain individuals. Women's particular devalued location beneath industrialists and mercantile go-betweens, husbands and mothers-in-law, and counts and countesses meant that their contributions, and even arrangements, were not fully recognized, in no small part because of gender ideologies deeply rooted in the hierarchies of the patriarchal family. Further, the home-based location of work metaphorically placed women behind a curtain, concealing their significance and their sacrifices.[18]

Eventually, mounting tensions pushed daughters and wives, but also sons, to challenge the patriarchal family form. Indeed, the economist Giacomo Becattini suggests that these tensions led to a "peasant protest, particularly by women and youth, not so much against the countryside itself as against the rigidity of the pecking-order in the family and against their close economic dependence on its older male members." People began rejecting sharecropping and embracing industry. Under the *mez-zadria* system, the powers of decision making and the availability of income were inconsistent with the distribution of workload, capabilities, and responsibilities. The interwar generation in particular began objecting to a structure and ideology that permitted, even necessitated, an unfair distribution of duties and rights. They sought autonomy, especially in monetary affairs.[19] The unraveling of the patriarchal family and landholding system forced new adjustments that had deep and lasting repercussions for families in terms of size and dynamics. Families' size became smaller and their dynamics less hierarchical.

Forgotten memories about arrangements such as the wet nurse–weaver connection conveniently allow space for more palatable explanations to dominate in academic and popular contexts, such as half-baked assertions that "before" women did not work and now they do, to explain the quiet revolution that resulted in small families. If women's contributions to the household historically entailed such painful choices and exploitative arrangements, it is no surprise these histories have been silenced, for they required sacrificing bonds of affection that have come to be seen as "natural." Bringing these memories and the scaffolding on which they were formed into public light may dispel that social amnesia.

As a little girl in the Apennine watershed of the Mugello, Natalina learned the arts of crochet and sweater knitting, the common forms of domicile economic production in her day in that mountainous region of north-central Tuscany. As soon as her family moved southeast to Carmignano, Natalina began weaving straw for the market. Several of the older townswomen took her aside and taught her the tricks of the trade. They recognized her agile fingers right off. She was pleased. She liked the work. It made her feel important, like a grown-up.

At thirteen, she began "commuting." This meant walking a good piece of road to get from the farm in the countryside to the town some seven kilometers away, where groups of girls and women gathered in houses to weave and where the consigners delivered the raw materials. The weaving was a little more complex than what she had been doing before, and the deadlines were stiffer as well. They earned a little more, too, upwards of ten lire, a good amount for those days.

Whereas some of the girls were easily confused by new jobs, Natalina savored each challenge. The more novel the design, the more she enjoyed it. At times, the *datore di lavoro*, the bosslike giver of work, recruited her to do the "closed jobs"—jobs that you had to do alone so that no one could see the new design.

One day, a woman named Leontina came to her house to consign some straw. She took her aside. "Look, Natalina," Leontina said, "if I give this to you at the house, then you go into the field and stay there. Down there, nobody will see you."

Natalina felt strange going into the field by herself. These were times when mostly men went into the fields to care for the grapevines or the olive trees. The exceptions were the fall harvests of wheat, grapes, and olives. Nevertheless, Natalina agreed. Leontina instructed her to finish the job that evening after dinner and bring it back to her the following morning. For this more complicated, secretive, and quick-turnaround job she would earn extra.

Natalina made sure no one was looking as she headed down the hill into the vineyard and sat beneath a fig tree. She wove all day. There was something exciting about being the keeper of a secret. Understand, the consigner risked losing her *campione*, sample, if somebody caught a glimpse of the new design. Such secrets were closely guarded. Copying other people's designs was a given of the market, but if you were clever enough to keep new designs out of sight at least until the orders came in and production got going, you had a chance of getting a step ahead.

Exposure to such secrets had its effects on Natalina. She came to view herself as not merely a weaver but a guarder of secrets and a creator of new things. Working the straw converted energy into economic capital, but it also manifested a sort of symbolic capital of novelty. As the market changed, her work changed, and so did she.

Natalina married relatively "late," in 1950, at age thirty-three. A year later she gave birth to her only child, a son. In one generation, there was a tremendous change, from her mother having seven children—or ten, depending on how you count them—to Natalina herself having only one.

Asking the "why" question struck me as risky. Would she take it as too personal? I had known her, Fabiana, and Riccardo for a long time, some eight years by then, and they knew my interests, so I took the chance.

"So why in your view did you only have one?" I asked.

"Well, you see, that's the only one there was," said Natalina, and then she laughed.

"Well, that happens too," I said, laughing with her. The anthropologist knew that such quips were unrepresentative of the whole story if there ever were such a thing.

Natalina laughed again. Initially, I heard this as the laughter of privacy. Upon second listening, I heard it as the laughter of being so inside a revolutionary trend that you cannot quite explain what force just took you with it.

I pressed on, gently. "However, different people make different choices."

"Oh and how, yes, you bet," she said, then deflected attention from herself and referred to an aunt who had had ten children.

We cannot chalk up momentous changes in fertility trends to individual circumstance or "choice." Sure, choice plays a role, but it is small compared with shifts in the outlooks, or ideological fields, that shape people's sense of who they are, of their subjectivities.

"Maybe these kinds of traumas have something to do with it, what do you think?" I asked.

"That too," she said. There was a lot of *miseria*, a lot of poverty. "There were a lot of people who did it before, eh," she said of women who agreed to serve as wet nurses in exchange for some cash. "*A' voglia*, you bet."

Indeed, the practice was so widespread and the memory so persistent that there is a saying in these parts: if you don't see someone for a while and somebody asks about his or her whereabouts, you might say in jest, "*Eh, l'ho dato a balia*—oh, I gave him to a wet nurse!" Finding dignity in such a tight spot required finesse.

The birth name of Natalina's father's was Angelo, but they called him Nebbia, or Fog. The inspiration for his nickname had long been forgotten, but one could imagine that it had to do with his penchant for nebulous and lighthearted interactions with his social superiors. Fog could get away with a lot. He got away with things that most men of his social standing dared not dream of. He was a peasant, the head of a sharecropping family who worked under a countess called La Lepri. She had no brothers and no sisters and no children of her own. She grew up to become a sharp attorney who married late in life. The word on the street was, "*Se tu vo' vincere bisogna che ti pigli la Lepri*—If you want to win you'd best hire Lepri." She was a keen manager of real estate. She oversaw seventeen farms in the county and owned acreage in the nearby towns of Campi and Castelnovo, villas in Empoli and Arezzo, and forests hither and yon; Florence was said to be half hers.

Her status made no difference to Fog. He was upbeat. One day he was threshing wheat and she turned up. "Well, what do you think you're doing in this sun, under this dust?" he teased. "Go back home, you'll be better off there." Everyone knew landowners had a habit of showing up during harvest time to make sure they were getting their fair share, their half. But he liked to joke. And she would joke back with him. Just him. With the other peasants, she kept her distance.

Fog lived with his wife, Enza, and their seven-plus children between 1935 and 1950 in a farmhouse on a hill that overlooked the town. From up there, you could see the whole world. One day, not long after Natalina had culminated a fifteen-year engagement by marrying her husband, she was up at the house eavesdropping on her dad and a *signorone*, a wealthy man. It was just a few years after World War II, and the textile industries of Prato were beginning to boom. The visitor wanted to buy the house where Fog and his kin were living. The man asked if the family was still under *la contessa*, La Lepri. He was trying to be sly, for he surely knew they'd been sharecropping the same ridges for some fifteen years.

"No, there's no price," Fog said. "She won't sell a thing. If she finds something to buy, she'll buy it, but as for selling, forget it."

The man returned a couple of times. And Fog repeated, "If she doesn't sell, she doesn't sell." But one day the man pressed. "Look, if she sells it, you folks will be better off, too." Many of the roads were rough and unpaved back then. "I'll pave the street all the way from down there to up here; just think of it, the whole road paved with asphalt," he promised.

And like a mantra, Fog repeated: "So what, if that woman doesn't sell?"

Fog had a one-of-a-kind rapport with Lepri. He knew her ways. One day he asked her in his teasing yet forthright manner, "Why don't you marry yourself a husband and get out of here?"

"Fog, I'll get married when I can't have children any more." That's what she always said, and in fact that's what she did. She married late in life, and she never had children of her own. Perhaps she thought she could retain her power by avoiding the female call to reproduce. Instead, she adopted her husband's niece and nephew. Natalina's brothers bore witness; they went to the town hall and put their signatures to the adoption paperwork. When La Lepri died, her adopted niece and nephew inherited everything. They had no idea of the extent of her estate. But they dealt with it like sheep come early morning to pasture. No fretting. Fast and clean.

For the most part, well-to-do Pratese bought the old farmhouses, restored them, and converted them into villas or agri-tourism destinations. Even Natalina's family's old house was among those sold. Word is, the place is just lovely now—but the land, nobody works it.

In calling forth this lost but not forgotten world, Natalina revealed an old economic system replete with fissures between the haves and the have-nots. The tribute-paying peasants ended up with only memories, whereas the wealth-receiving niece and nephew by marriage who had no memories of place and no connection to its land walked away with the goods. Unlike their conservative adopted "mother," who had prided herself in accumulating jewels and real estate, the heirs unloaded the possessions with no regrets. Let us not forget that behind the lush estate was the labor of the grown-ups and all the children of couples like Fog and Enza, couples who in order to reinforce the domestic economy nursed other people's children in exchange for some cash and then some heartache and who watched their own children, such as Natalina, complete only the third grade so as to work as a straw weaver in a transnational rural economy. Ultimately, the end of the countess's legacy served as a symbol of injustice for the peasants turned townsfolk who had worked her land and rented her houses for so many years. It was also a story about the unraveling of old obligations and the creation of new worlds—worlds in which having fewer, well-nurtured children made perfect sense.

Epilogue

Patrizia received in the mail a copy of the sheet of paper, n. 156 of the Foglio di Famiglia, that contains the 1931 census record of Emilio Raugei's household. I sent it to her so that she would have a chance to mull it over prior to my visit. On July 6, 2006, we sat at the table in her summer kitchen. Located on the ground floor of her three-story house, it provided relief from the sweltering midsummer heat. She offered me an espresso and water as she fended off Igor, the persistently affectionate Doberman obsessed with giving me dog kisses with his floppy tongue. I elbowed him away and pulled out my copy of the paper from the archive. We went through each family member's entry. How odd, Patrizia said, that her grandmother Giovanna was not listed as her mother's mother.

One by one, she told me how many children each of Emilia's siblings had had: Sergio, two; Maria, two; Matilde, two; Hamidie, one; Osvaldo, two; Carlo, one. The numbers were a mirror image of Italy's reproductive trends. The National Statistics Institute, Istat, in its *Italy in Figures,* reported that as of 2001 Italian women had on average 1.25 children. The average household consisted of 2.6 members.

The story of Germena came up again, and Patrizia remarked on her history. "*Da questo trauma, è diventata un pò aggressiva*—From this trauma, she became a little aggressive," Patrizia said. "She always wanted to be first. You always saw some trauma."

She opened up to me during the interview, filling in gaps in the story in terms of (1) Carlo, the brother who had been a partisan and was still living nearby; (2) another brother who had been captured and as a prisoner had been forced to fight against the Russians in World War II; and (3) the household composition in Artimino when Patrizia was born and details from after the war, when they had lived on Via La Volta.

At the end of our conversation, she promised to try to get down to her parents' house and look for photographs and letters that Emilia and Parigi had exchanged. More than two years had passed, and she apologized. She just hadn't been very motivated to clean out their house. It was an overwhelming task. Could I help? She would consider it.

The following week, I returned as arranged, and at ten o'clock in the morning on Wednesday, July 11, we walked down Via La Volta to the old house. The weathered wood of the shutters was exposed as though someone had scraped off the paint. Inside, the air in the kitchen was heavy. The emptied contents of the drawers and cupboards crowded the countertops: bottles, papers, stuff. Patrizia's eyes glazed over as she scanned her parents' old belongings, their lives reduced to piles of unmanageable clutter. Patrizia apologized, again, that she just had not been able to get things in order.

I didn't dare touch a thing. Patrizia led the way. We bypassed the kitchen and climbed the narrow staircase to the second floor. It was my first time upstairs. Off a small landing were two bedrooms and one small bathroom. She showed me her old room in the back of the house. An old trunk sat open on the floor. Personal effects spilled out of it. We didn't stay long. There was a lot here, she said, but probably nothing that would be of interest to me. She turned and urged me to come with her.

A vintage 1950s mahogany bedroom set dominated Emilia and Parigi's room. A peach and ivory bedspread was smoothed up to a rectangular headboard, above which hung a portrait of a Madonna and child. Two small nightstands flanked the bed. Across from the footboard an armoire rose like a night watchman. On the adjacent wall was the room's single window, which looked out on the laundry line, the valley, and the steep road to Artimino. The shutter opened against a high dresser. The daylight brightened the view into an oval mirror. It sat atop a wooden base with two drawers and a delicate shelf, which rested on an elegant white slab of marble. A number of objects were clustered there: in the middle was a decorative glass box shaped like a ball whose texture looked like rock candy, a fist-sized clock with a large face and black numbers, a purse-sized package of tissues, and, in the back, two small framed portraits, one of the widowed Ida Innocenti, who was Parigi's mother, and the other of Urbano Peruzzi, his brother. Atop the right drawer rested a bar of pink soap between the folds of a discolored doily. On the left drawer stood an elephant statuette with its tail pointing outward, away from three fancy boxes, one with a floral design and the words *Eucalyptus Oil*. To the far left was a miniature porcelain water well, complete with a tiny chain and bucket.

Decorative precious things also covered the low dresser across the room, next to the door. Prominent was a photograph of Emilia dressed for her first communion. She wore a fancy white gown with a mesh veil that extended three times the length of her dark shoulder-length hair and hung well beyond her back. There was also a postcard of her father, Emilio Raugei, in a fine light-colored suit at the spa in Bagni di Montecatini. An inscription on the back indicated he had sent it to Emilia's mother, Giovanna, around 1923.

Patrizia opened the dresser drawer in search of the letters, but there were none to be found. She showed me her grandmother's identity card: Giovanna Paolieri, born 19–10–1891, in Signa; resident of Carmignano; civil status, nubile; profession, housewife; height, 160 meters; hair, gray; eyes, clear; signature, incapable of signing, 24 July 1964. The status of "nubile" would suggest she and Patrizia's grandfather had never officially married. Patrizia seemed surprised but did not

Figure 11.   Still life, 2006. Photograph by Betsy Krause.

offer any explanation. Instead, she pointed out various treasures, which I admired and photographed. She offered some of them to me. I hesitated. She insisted. Most dear to me was a faded, thrice-folded quarter sheet of notebook paper with a handwritten documentation of military service between March 14, 1940, and November 9, 1945, at the Military Hospital of San Gallo in Florence.[1]

The scene would have been familiar to children who survive their parents; it was at once so ordinary and so strange, how things remain but the people do not. All we had were the memories that connected the place and the possessions with Emilia and Parigi. Time stopped as a stillness settled over the moment like the veil of a terracotta Madonna shrine.

Any hopes for letters dashed, my thoughts turned to contacting Carlo, the surviving brother. Rather than call him cold with a foreigner's accent, I sought help from Patrizia, but she declined, naming depression as her ally. I turned to Daniela, who was enthusiastic about doing me the favor. We found a listing in the phone book.

"I'll call him, then call you back," she offered. "But I'll wait until 2:30 in case he's napping."

A little while later she called back. Bad news. It was the wrong family. We double-checked the number. No error there. Daniela made a trip to the lane and chatted with some of the women. She called me back with news of where he lived plus some gossip, including a false rumor about me: that my husband and I had divorced. In another situation this might have bothered me. Instead, it tickled me, and I laughed. What a privilege to be part of the town talk, especially after not having lived there for nine years.

The next morning we set out for the neighborhood in the adjacent town where word had it we'd find Carlo. Daniela stopped into a hardware store and a flower shop to ask whether anyone knew where he lived. She even asked a woman on the street. Nobody knew him. Finally, someone in the pharmacy directed us to a nearby neighborhood.

We walked down a street passing iron gates and reading the names of the residents on the mailboxes.

"A Raugei!" I said.

Daniela rang the bell.

A small woman in a pastel floral housedress appeared from behind a doorway curtain. She had a distinctive oval-shaped face inscribed with deep wrinkles. Sure, she knew Carlo Raugei. He lived around the corner, next to her daughter. Look for a single house, then a row of houses.

We found a woman sitting on a second-floor terrace when we arrived. She glared down at us suspiciously, but Daniela warmed her up with her smile and promise that we were good people with no intention to be invasive.

Carlo wasn't at home.

"Will he be home soon?"

"At noon. You can come back then." We were hopeful. We joked about feeling like private investigators as we left.

We sat out the wait back at Daniela's house, a five-minute drive down the road. Just before noon we set out again. Excitement marked the mood as we drove. I labeled my audiotape, certain I would have the chance to use it. When we arrived, the couple was out on their terrace, waiting, and as Daniela gently pushed open the iron gate, down they came. Carlo was balding with an oversized nose. He walked ahead of his wife. I felt hopeful. Then they stopped midway down the staircase. He frowned.

"*Emilia non c'e' più,*" he said, grumpily. "*Da qualche anno.* Emilia's not around any more. Since a couple years."

"*Lo so,*" I said, acknowledging his loss and apologizing. "*Mi dispiace.*"

I explained my book, its focus on family changes, on Emilia and Parigi, and my interest in the fascist years, in his involvement as a partisan.

"No, no," he shook his head. "I don't remember anything." He choked on his words. His face was flushed.

"But what about the action at Nobel?"

"Ah, that's old stuff. No use talking about it now," he barked.

I grasped at straws, trying to establish my credibility, to charm him with my American smile.

"I lived in the house where Emilia was born, probably where you were born," I said, trying to sound persuasive and not desperate and careful to use the respectful *lei* form of address.

"Ah yes, the American, I heard about you," he said. His tone, like the words, was ambiguous. I sensed something hard and resentful in his voice. I directed myself to the woman with Parigi's last name.

"*Lei sarebbe un parente di Parigi Peruzzi?*"

"His sister," she said. "He was my brother."

"Ah," I said. "Emilia told me of the fire."

"Ah yes, the fire," she acknowledged. But it was a fleeting connection. My efforts soon dissolved. The couple stood above us on the steps. The cold body language did not change. It was not a good sign. Nothing going. We apologized for the interruption and left.

In the car Daniela's energy sank. I explained to her that I had set out on our mission with modest hopes. I knew the risks of approaching people cold, without some kind of intermediary contact. Not all people want to speak of the past, of the traumas they have lived through, of the hardship. Not everyone was inclined to reflection. Even my own Great-Uncle Otto, my father's only uncle who would have had any memories of the conditions under which my grandfather immigrated to the United States in the 1890s, refused to share with me and my parents anything about the life they had left as ethnic Germans in Lithuania. All I had was the image of my grandfather clad in a soldier's uniform and the story that he'd had enough after a year of service in the Prussian army.

As we drove the backroads of the industrial town of Seano, past sweater workshops, Daniela called Emilia's brother *scorbutico*, cantankerous. She said of the two of them, "*Non sono fatti della stessa pasta*—They aren't made from the same dough." She confided in me her sensation of feeling completely rejected. It hurt. She felt as if she had been cast out. I'd known the feeling many times, and I felt sorry to have put her through it. But I was also grateful. We had given it our best. At least I would not go home with regrets for not having tried to get one last angle on Emilia's story.

Across the ocean in my Amherst study, I rediscovered the manila envelope, on which I'd written in large letters across the center with a red Sharpie, "Materials from Emilia and Parigi's house, 7/06 Italy visit." Inside, the contents offered a reminder of the contradictions of postwar Italian society and the cultural roots of the tumultuous changes that had rocked the life of a generation. Upon Patrizia's insistence, I had ended up accepting a few mementos from the couple's dresser drawer. A purse-sized three-by-two-inch perfumed almanac held dainty booklets containing colored photographs of the *bellezze del cinema*, movie stars the likes of Anne Miller and Amélita Vargas, striking sexy poses. Below the year 1952 appeared a listing of saints for each day, and on another sheet civic holidays and the abbreviations for Italian license plates by province. To this juxtaposition of the old icons of Catholic reverence and the new idols of Hollywood sex symbols, of cars and stars, was added another influence: the rise of postwar working-class culture. Further evidence was tucked away in the form of an undated flyer for the Festival of l'Unità in the Parco della Rimembranza in Poggio a Caiano. This program, sponsored by the Italian Communist Party, the PCI, spanned four days in September and included the projection of a film called *The Life of Hitler*; a tournament of the popular Italian card game *briscola*; dancing with a jukebox as well as popular dance with an orchestra; and the election of a

Stellina de L'Unità, festival starlet, celebrating the leftist newspaper of the same name. Holding this yellowed flyer in my hand prompted memories from the 1980s, when I had been a wide-eyed, twenty-one-year-old undergraduate, of my first encounter with an Italian communist. I had been at a festival of the same name in a hilltown above Florence, beyond Fiesole. The man, an uncle of a close friend, had been wearing a Gucci suit, or so I recollect. In any case, it was a stunning piece of clothing, and my exposure to a stylish communist continued to confound me for years.

Emilia's story sorts out some of those contradictions. It reminds us that we can learn from the past. We can learn that perhaps the scientific discourses offer partial truth. Perhaps they erase a lot of it and generate new myths. Perhaps they are part of a conscious or unconscious strategy to create national coherence, a project that excludes as much as includes. The memories related to fertility decline reveal a history of hidden traumas that are all but forgotten. They testify to an embodied aspect of the history of global capitalism and demographic shift. Such aspects are absent in the surveys that document Europeans' overwhelming negative perception concerning so few of their own babies being born. Where do we read of the rural economies where giving birth could become a commodity and where a triangular trade among an underclass of women and children linked them in roles as wet nurses, weavers, and foundlings? How do we grasp the efforts to retain dignity in such arrangements? How do we comprehend the experiences of living through sharecropping, fascism, patriarchy, war, and then a booming economy with the seductions of a modern consumer society and the rebellions of youth, women, and the working class?

Emilia's story relates to the larger trend that women—and couples—stopped having numerous children because the cultural and economic contexts changed and because they could. Part I of this story ends with Emilia's experience of having only one child. She came to realize that having more children would not bring her more status or more respect in the family. In fact, there was strong pressure to have fewer children from the family as well as from medical experts. The Florentine doctor saw her as backward because she lived with a large, extended family. She walked away feeling stigmatized. By contrast, working as a straw weaver empowered her, even if her earnings were modest and respect was minimal. Emilia, like many other women of her day, found herself negotiating the capitalist market and the patriarchal household, whose head also had to contend with wealthy landowners. Such arrangements took their toll on individuals, who at a certain point sought to limit life's pain and traumas and, with time, to fulfill their own needs—not merely the primary ones but the secondary ones, personal desires and quality of life.

The wet nurse–weaver connection is hardly meant to explain fertility decline in its entirety, but the particular details are intended to expose family ruptures and the larger journey of becoming modern. The turn to small families became an outward sign of being current and up to date even before the feminist movement and the Pill. Everywhere, local experiences play out in profound ways with global processes. Throughout Italy today, reproductive trends reveal similarities and differences. In Naples, many women emphasize the importance of siblings and view two children as a necessity but frown upon having more than two. In Bologna, the focus is less on siblings and more on the serious and profound process of becoming a parent.[2] Regional contrasts lend different hues to dominant ideologies related to the family. These notions have histories. Memories infuse them. They shape desires and behaviors.

The juxtaposition of the two voices in this book was not mere folly. It served a purpose. Using a resonant voice atypical of social science in Part I gave me a chance to bring another world to life. Re-creating that world on its own terms meant tuning in to the vernacular. My hope is that I exposed the extraordinary in the ordinary. In Part II, the nonfiction voice aimed to show the process of making sense of a major social trend, to unravel an unexpected knot in the story that presented itself along the way, and to assert the value of allowing affection and relationships to be woven into the whole cloth. Fieldwork had prerequisites. Cultivating rapport anchored in mutual trust was fundamental. Tending to relationships with care required time, patience, and empathy. More often than not it meant balancing the role of objective participant-observer with that of a feeling human being.

Memories are similar to archival history: full of fragments. Why some are willing to speak of the past, to remember, and others are not, is a grand mystery; I was lucky to have found a great narrator in Emilia. Her memories were hardly an obligation. They were a gift. As the recipient of the gift, I felt a duty to reciprocate in the best way I could. The poet laureate Grace Paley once said, "When you write, what you do is you illuminate what's hidden, and that's a political act."[3] In recognition of the quiet revolution that Emilia Raugei lived, my crafting of this book stands as my effort to illuminate what is hidden in the most meaningful way possible, even if it has meant defying conventions of representing social life.

Notes

The epigraph is from Hunter Thompson (1971/1998:66–67).

1. Such processes of enumeration are what the French philosopher Michel Foucault (1978) elaborated in his ruminations on biopower—his influential insight that modern power is distinguished through its generative quality. In their quest to manage populations, for example, states generate all kinds of categories, numbers, and norms.

2. For the report on Italy and Spain, see Delgado Perez and Livi-Bacci (1992). Current fertility rates appear in Population Reference Bureau (2007). For a history of Italian population, see Livi-Bacci (1994); for a history of European population, see Livi-Bacci (2000).

3. See Golini, Mussino, and Savioli (2000) for the discussion of the trend as a "profound malaise"; for the "postponement syndrome," see Livi-Bacci (2001:147) and Sgritta (2003:65). Many other examples are discussed elsewhere in Krause (2001, 2005a, 2005b, 2005c) and Krause and Marchesi (2007).

4. The Federal Institute for Population Research and the Robert Bosch Foundation (2005:6) summarize the results of an international comparative research

project on the attitudes of the population toward demographic change and population-relevant policies. The report analyzes what respondents in fourteen European countries think about family, children, partnership, equity, and aging.

5. One interesting aspect of the *New York Times Magazine* piece was the observation that despite the so-called accepted demographic wisdom that "as women enter the job market, a society's fertility rate drops . . . in fact, something like the opposite has been the case" (Shorto 2008:39). European countries where women have higher official female labor force participation now have higher fertility levels, and vice versa, making for a north-south divide, with fertility rates lower in southern Europe and higher in northern Europe. Mills et al. (2008) shift the focus from labor participation to gender equity in their analysis. For scholarship on contemporary European birth trends and politics, see Balter (2006), Bialasiewicz (2006), Bongaarts (1998), Dalla Zuanna (2001, 2004), Douglass (2005), Eberstadt (2001), Golini (1991, 1994), Golini, De Simoni, and Citoni (1995), Joyce (2008), Krause and Marchesi (2007), Livi-Bacci (1994), Palomba (1991), and Sgritta (2001).

6. Abu-Lughod (1986, 2005), Geertz (1973), Hurston (1937/1991), Hecht (2006), Stoller (1999), Willis and Trondman (2000).

7. See Deresiewicz (2006:24, 26, 28) and Clifford (1986:6).

8. I define my academic work as a history of the present that grapples with the symbolic/ideational as well as material/economic drivers of history (see Wolf 1999). I originally set out to write a straightforward critical work about Italy's demographic changes that would contribute to two fields grounded in anthropology. For further reading related to *critical population studies,* see Anagnost (1995), Gal and Kligman (2000), Ginsburg and Rapp (1995), Greenhalgh (1995a, 1995b, 1996, 2003, 2008), Horn (1994), Kanaaneh (2002), Kertzer (1993, 1995), Kligman (1998), Martin (1987, 1991), Patriarca (1996), Paxson (2002), Rapp (1999), Rivkin-Fish (2003), Scheper-Hughes (1992), Schneider and Schneider (1996); for further reading related to *historical anthropology* and *social memory,* see Alonso (1988), Chatterjee (2001), Cohn (1980), Comaroff and Comaroff (1991), Hobsbawm (1983), Kertzer (1993), Passerini (1987), Popular Memory Group (1982), Rebel (1989), Roseberry (1989), Schneider and Rapp (1995), Seremetakis (1994), Stoler (1991), Striffler (2001), Terrio (2000), B. Williams (1989), and Wolf (1982). This book also results from thinking about the importance of memory work in researching a long revolutionary transformation whose histories, given the ideological stakes involved, are easily silenced and even forgotten. As for critical population studies, I try to push the limits of anthropological-demographic collaboration, as evidenced in this work and several other essays (Krause 2006, 2007).

9. The most accessible overview of the Princeton European Fertility Project can be found in Alter (1992). The scope of the project is described in Knodel and Van de Walle (1986:412) and Coale and Treadway (1986:31); see also Coale and Watkins (1986). The quote about cultural setting appears in Knodel and van de

Walle (1986:392). A recent review of the literature on demographic transition can be found in Johnson-Hanks (2008). An assessment of the cultural turn can be found in Kertzer and Hogan (1989:152) as well as Hammel (1990:456), who wrote, "The use of 'culture' in demography seems mired in structural-functional concepts that are about 40 years old, hardening rapidly, and showing every sign of fossilization." Demographers' use of the culture concept is also critiqued in Kertzer (1995:31–32, 43–48); see also Schneider and Schneider (1996) and Kertzer (1995:34) for explanations of differential, historic fertility decline. The Italian demographer Massimo Livi-Bacci (2001:146) argues that the current decline is due to social changes and a shared attitude among Italians of caring so deeply about providing for their children that they wait to attain a desirable personal, economic, and educational status first. My own work (Krause 2005a:184) has emphasized historical adjustments, at times traumatic, to the rigid pecking order of a patriarchal family. The breakdown of family hierarchy was deeply linked to economic shifts and necessitated a subsequent re-creation of modern, gendered subjects located in new socioeconomic consumption contexts that place an especially heavy responsibility for children's well-being on mothers (see Krause 2005c).

10.   A virtual tour of the famous Palazzo del Bò is available through a University of Padua Web site; see "Virtual Tour of the Palazzo Bo," n.d., www.unipd .it/esterni/visiteweb/, accessed March 2, 2007.

11.· Scholarly works on Mussolini's demographic campaign include de Grazia (1992), Ipsen (1996), Krause (1994), Passerini (1987), and Snowden (2006).

12.   The authors of the report, Mazzuco and Ongaro (2003:19), write: "As long as one is not talking about 'contraceptive error,' the conception of the first child is attributed to a moment of *sospensione della razionalità*, or suspended rationality, because if one were to truly evaluate the consequences of the decision to become a parent, nobody would ever have children" (my translation).

13.   An analysis by Castiglioni, Dalla Zuanna, and Loghi (2001:211) of data from the Fertility and Family Surveys found that 37 percent of conceptions in Italy during the 1990s were unplanned. Of births, some 26 percent of all children were unplanned. In the United States, the rates were higher as of 1988: 35 percent of births and 55 percent of conceptions fell in the unplanned category.

14.   E. P. Thompson's (1966) *Making of the English Working Class* opened readers' eyes to what conventional history was missing. Stuart Hall (1981) followed suit, bringing a British-Jamaican perspective to the project of writing popular history, and in cultural studies Raymond Williams (1977) drew on Antonio Gramsci's (1971) theories of hegemony to further the cause. Carlo Ginzburg's (1980) innovative *Cheese and the Worms* took the reader on a cosmological journey with a sixteenth-century miller. Sidney Mintz's (1960) *Worker in the Cane* aimed for objectivity in his life story of a Puerto Rican man named Taso. I took these works as my starting point and found courage in other writers' experiments with voice and genre. I went back

and read Truman Capote (1965), oft-cited inventor of creative nonfiction with *In Cold Blood*, and Hunter S. Thompson (1971/1998), who hallucinogenically blurs truth and fiction in *Fear and Loathing in Las Vegas*. Within anthropology, my muses included ethnographers such as Ruth Behar (1993, 1996, 1999), Lila Abu-Lughod (1986, 2005), Kirin Narayan (1999), Renato Rosaldo (1989), and Paul Stoller (1999) who have stretched the limits of objectivity and shown the power of subjectivity for arriving at cross-cultural understanding.

15.   The method is discussed in Foucault (1980:78–81, 85). Genealogy, as Foucault described it, involved "a painstaking rediscovery of struggles together with the rude memory of their conflicts" (1980:83). Foucault was not much for ethnography, but this prized anthropological method of participation and observation in its sundry forms surely qualifies as a "painstaking" method for accessing struggles that the common accounts of demographic transition elide.

16.   Clifford Geertz (1973) drew on William Dilthey and theories of hermeneutics to develop what he called interpretive anthropology. Interpretation here was understood as the process of developing an understanding of the practices and core symbols of another culture. This vein of anthropology remained very popular until the 1980s, when it drew harsh criticism from the emerging historical-minded anthropologists. William Roseberry's (1989) essay "The Balinese Cockfight and the Seduction of Anthropology" rates among the most influential critiques. Geertz, somewhat ironically, is the most popular and cited anthropologist among historians. Debates about representational politics reached a head in Clifford and Marcus's (1986) edited volume, *Writing Culture*. Polier and Roseberry (1989) offer a critique of that particular moment in postmodern ethnography from a political economy standpoint, as does di Leonardo (1989). Metcalf (2001) muses about slippage between truth and lying in the ethnographic project.

17.   Virginia Dominguez (2000) has advocated an anthropology that embraces a "politics of love."

CHAPTER 1: POSTCARDS

1.   A description of straw weavers' work appears in "Oggetto: Lavoro delle Donne nel Comune" [Subject: Report on Women's Work in the Commune], Comune di Carmignano, Archivio Storico del Comune di Carmignano, Categoria III, No. 93, Fascicolo No. 13, Filza 2, August 30, 1893.

2.   For details on Mussolini's cultural revolution and whether it was more fascist than nationalist, see Cannistraro (1972:119).

3.   Dates are inferred from estate ledgers in the Archivio Privato, Villa di Calavria, Carmignano. Changes in hands of tenant sharecroppers tending the

farm of Poggiola from 1897 to 1954 were listed as n.d., 1897, 1900, 1940, and 1954. Poggiola was one of the Michon Pecori family's twenty-one *podere*, or farms, split between the two hamlets of Comeana and Bacchereto in the Commune of Carmignano. This was considered a reasonable number of farms for one noble family to manage.

CHAPTER 2: ABANDONED

1.   In the local dialect of Carmignano, the saying goes like this: *Il padrone a i' contadino: Non fa sapere come gli'è buono il cacio co' le pere. Il contadino risponde: Padrone la 'un lo sa tutto come gli'è buono fichi co' i prosciutto.*

2.   For visual images of Italian peasants from 1919 to 1935, see the work of ethnologist Paul Scheuermeier (1980), who produced hundreds of photographs as part of a multiregional comparative study of peasant life and agrarian change. A selection of the photographs from Carmignano, including some of straw weavers that did not appear in the large collection, was published by the oral and visual historian Giovanni Contini (1993). A catalog from a Rome exhibit of Scheuermeier's work is also available in Miraglia (1981).

3.   See Contini (2004) for a discussion of the phenomenon of so-called aristocratic sharecropping families.

4.   A discussion of the investment of capital in the Tuscan countryside appears in Snowden (1989:20–32).

5.   Crehan (2002:16) provides an overview of the events in Turin, particularly as they related to the Italian revolutionary Antonio Gramsci. See also Forgacs (1986).

6.   Other structures were put into place for the day laborers: unions, minimum hourly wages, a weekly payday, and a commission to negotiate conflicts between the workers and the landowners. In fall 1920, the citizens of Carmignano were primed to elect their first socialist mayor, back before the Duce rid the country of democratic elements and nominated *podestas* to take the place of elected mayors of all municipalities. The local Carmignano historian Silvano Gelli (1998:53–55) documents the cooperative movement of the late nineteenth and early twentieth centuries. The movement for such worker rights had already begun some years earlier with a call for day laborers' increased salaries, regular work hours, decreased work for women, and norms for social assistance, as documented in Saba (1994:25).

7.   See Gelli (1998:58–60).

8.   The fascists' March on Rome, October 28, 1922, "was enshrined in fascist lore as the chief symbol of the revolution," according to Cannistraro (1972:117).

CHAPTER 3: TELLING TIME

1.   One political prisoner who wrote to Mussolini requesting release claimed that he had resigned from the Communist Party because it was no longer recognized "as part of the political organism of the country"; *New York Times*, May 29, 1927, 13.

2.   In her updated Carmignano dialect of the interwar period, Emilia said to him, "*Se vu mi dite 'che ore sono' io ve lo dico, se nò un vi dico più nulla.*" From my interview with Emilia and Parigi, January 28, 1997, transcription, 2.

3.   Antonio Gramsci distinguished between two types of intellectuals, traditional and organic, in his classic work *The Prison Notebooks*. "It can be observed that the 'organic' intellectuals which every new class creates alongside itself and elaborates in the course of its development, are for the most part 'specializations' of partial aspects of the primitive activity of the new social type which the new class has brought into prominence" (Gramsci 1971:6, 9). Gramsci's writings, subject to the gaze of a censor, require clarification here. His primary contribution on this topic was his insistence, against claims of traditional intellectuals who tended to ignore or deny class affiliations, that every social class "organically" produced thinkers from its own ranks and that it was therefore the job of those thinkers to put into words the feelings and experiences that the masses could not express on their own—at least not without first engaging in critical self-reflection and developing a sense of history. On that last point Gramsci (1971:324–25) wrote the following note: "The starting-point of critical elaboration is the consciousness of what one really is, and is 'knowing thyself' as a product of the historical processes to date, which has deposited in you an infinity of traces, without leaving an inventory." In her discussion of Gramsci's concept of intellectuals, Kate Crehan (2002:137) writes, "Organic intellectuals for Gramsci are those with fundamental, structural ties to particular classes." For an in-depth discussion of his concept of intellectuals, see Crehan (2002:128–61).

4.   The Anthony P. Campanella Collection of Giuseppe Garibaldi at the University of South Carolina, www.sc.edu/library/spcoll/hist/garib/garib.html, accessed May 6, 2008, offers an excellent resource on the life of Garibaldi.

5.   For a discussion of Italian history and the formation of the modern state, see Gramsci's *Prison Notebooks* (1971:55–90, esp. 61); his discussion of the relationship between the city and country spans pp. 90–102.

6.   Quoted in Crehan (2002:17).

CHAPTER 4: FASCIST FOLK

1. Antonio Gramsci, introduction to *The Prison Notebooks* (1971:xvii).

2. The full text of Mussolini's speech was printed in the *New York Times* (1927:1, 12–13).

3. From Mussolini's speech, *New York Times* (1927). The original *New York Times* version of the speech included audience reactions in brackets, but I have integrated them into the text for readability.

4. For more on Prato and the *biennio rosso*, the so-called two Red years of intense labor struggles between 1919 and 1920, see Pescarolo (1988:100–103).

5. The exchange rate in 1927 hovered around twenty lire to the dollar (in December 1926 it had been twenty-two lire to the dollar; by June 1927 it was eighteen lire to the dollar); see Fratianni and Spinelli (2001). At the time of Mussolini's speech, the dollar was worth eighteen lire.

6. Mussolini preceded his discussion of Italy's birthrate with statistics from other countries: "Let us probe even more deeply into this subject, which interests me highly. Some people hold that France is a country with the lowest birth rate in Europe. It is not true. The birth rate of France has stopped for the last fifteen years at about 18 per 1,000. Not only this, but in certain sections of France there is a reawakening of nativity. The nation which heads the list in this sad business is Sweden, whose birth rate is 17 per 1,000, while in Denmark it is 21, in Norway 19, and Germany is in full decadence in this respect. The birth rate in Germany has fallen from 35 per 1,000 to 20. . . . It is worth our while to see how Italy stands." Quoted from the *New York Times* (1927:12).

7. Mussolini contrasted his revolution with the French Revolution: "We have no idea of what terror is or what terror was under other revolutions, under the French Revolution from which were born those famous so-called 'immortal principles.'

"What terror was it that guillotined twenty heads on average every day in the Place de la Madeline? . . . Is it necessary for me to rehearse what that terror meant? No. . . . It is the history of 2,000 women who were guillotined, mothers often in the presence of their daughters, often whole families together, and often—this is most important—they were not aristocrats, but poor people found hugging a crucifix to their breast.

"You white sepulchers full of fetid elements, speak not of Fascist terror when the Fascist revolution is doing nothing but its duty when it defends itself." Quoted from the *New York Times* (1927:12).

8. Luisa Passerini (1987:80) discusses the transformation of political songs and the key role they played in the fascist cultural revolution. Passerini cites A. Gravelli, *I canti della rivoluzione* (Rome, 1926), 79, 86–88; A. V. Savona and M. L.

Straniero, *Canti dell'Italia fascista, 1919–1945* (Milan, 1979), 5; L. Mercuri and C. Tuzzi, *Canti politici italiani, 1793–1945* (Rome, 1962), 22; and D. Jalla, ed., *La musica: Storia di una banda e dei suoi musicanti. Piossasco, 1848–1980* (Bra, 1980), ch. 8.

CHAPTER 5: GIOTTO'S CIRCLE

1. Archivio Privato, Villa di Calavria, Carmignano; Foglio di Famiglia, 1931, Archivio del Comune di Carmignano.

2. Foglio di Famiglia, Frazione di Comeana, 1931, Archivio del Comune di Carmignano.

3. Interview with Emilia and Parigi, January 28, 1997, Commune of Carmignano, Italy, line 40.

4. Conversation elaborated from my fieldnotes, "97.06.25 giotto, memory." Giorgio Vasari (1957:6–9) in *Lives of the Artists* recounts a story similar to Emilia's. Vasari also tells of an incident of when Giotto was still a boy working in Cimabue's studio; he painted such a natural-looking fly on the nose of a face in one of Cimabue's drawings that "the master returning to his work tried more than once to drive it away with his hand, thinking it was real" (12).

CHAPTER 7: CHAINS

1. Fancelli (1871/1997) offers a flattering capitalist view of the straw industry. Pescarolo and Ravenni (1991) present a critical proletarian perspective. The Straw Museum of Signa offers a history of Domenico Michelacci and the importance of the straw industry to the otherwise largely agricultural, regional economy of the nineteenth and early twentieth centuries. See their Web site at www.museopaglia.it, accessed May 8, 2008.

2. Detailed descriptions of the strike appear in Pescarolo and Ravenni (1991:37–41).

3. See also Welcome Tuscany, "Santa Maria Novella Train Station," www.welcometuscany.it/transportations/railway/florence.htm, accessed May 8, 2008.

4. For an art historian's account, see White (1966/1993:27–30). An excellent online gallery for viewing the artworks mentioned in this chapter can be found at the Web Gallery of Art, www.wga.hu/index.html, accessed May 8, 2008. Frederick Hartt's (1966/2006) classic text offers an overview of Renaissance art.

5. The Commune of Florence provides a highly informative article, "Giotto's Crucifix: Restoration, Research Project, Discoveries," n.d., www.comune.fi.it/restauro/restaurocrocing.htm, accessed January 9, 2009.

6. Elaborated from interview, January 28, 1997, lines 275–333.

7. Luisa Passerini (1987:174–82), in her oral history of Turin workers, concluded that women often used abortion and birth control as antifascist measures. The official fascist line regarding the interference in the private lives of citizens, particularly regarding reproductive issues, was that it represented a step forward in terms of "overcoming 'so-called liberal democratic and individualistic rights,'" (1987:176). Passerini suggests that the abortion rates, reflected in part in oral histories as well as criminal records, serve as evidence that women not only were assuming responsibility for birth control but were rebelling against fascist demographic policy (1987:180–82). See her n. 46 for additional references related to abortion.

8. My fieldnotes, "99.06.15 emilia, parigi."

9. Elaborated from interview, January 28, 1997, lines 258–336. All youths were required to join a fascist group. From interview, January 28, 1997, line 319.

CHAPTER 8: RATIONS

1. A similar story is recounted in Pescarolo and Ravenni (1991:196–98).

2. My fieldnotes, "97.04.01 vecchiaia."

CHAPTER 9: WAR COUNTRY

1. For a discussion of diet in Italy during World War II, see Helstosky (2004:104–17).

2. The term *impannatore* describes the Prato-specific breed of entrepreneur who thrived on activities linked to the production of *lane povere*, cheap wool, such as the famous *cascinetto*, a fabric with a warp of cotton and a weft of wool, according to Pescarolo (1988:52). These textile manufacturers owned only part or even none of their equipment and, despite very limited capital, managed to find other small-scale artisans or entrepreneurs to do the work *per conto terzi*, or as subcontractors. The system, rooted in the Middle Ages, developed in Prato during the second half of the nineteenth century and according to Mannucci (1993:91) had become by the 1890s the predominant system of work organization. Many artisans worked as subcontractors for the incomplete-cycle woolen factories and above all for these go-between entrepreneurs, who, according to Dei Ottati (1998:125), were historically known for their "commercial and speculative talent," their capacity to invent new textiles, and their clever and, notes Pescarolo (1988:54), even exploitative use of short-term loans.

3. Dr. Joseph Goebbels, quoted in *The Gothic Line*, by the popular war historian Douglas Orgill (1967:3).

4.   For more details, see Orgill (1967:25).

5.   As Hitler embarked on the Gothic Line plan, his two commanders pulled him in opposing directions. Field-Marshal Erwin Rommel, who had fallen into a depression after guiding Germany's defeat in North Africa, was pessimistic about Hitler's idea. Field-Marshal Albert Kesselring, who had led a successful evacuation of the German forces from Sicily, was optimistic that an impenetrable defensive position could be constructed along the rugged mountainous terrain just north of Florence. If the Nazis could hold off the encroaching Allied forces for nine months, he reasoned, they could build defense fortifications along the mountains. Hitler hesitated for weeks. At last, he commanded that a telegram be sent to Rommel, the pessimist, giving him his orders. The message was in transmission when Hitler changed his mind. On November 6, he issued the command to Kesselring, the optimist. His senior officers read his flip-flopping as an ominous sign of the consequences of a bellicose strategy stretched beyond its limits. Hitler's cancellation of the telegram to Rommel, according to Orgill (1967:4), "changed the course of the war." Italy entered what Churchill called "the most tragic period of her history." Orgill writes: "Both sides were committed to an arduous and bloody campaign for 18 months over difficult terrain in appalling climatic conditions." In the end some 90,000 Allied and 110,000 German soldiers were buried on the Italian peninsula.

6.   Orgill (1967:42).

7.   Orgill (1967:28).

8.   By spring 1944, Hitler was displaying an obsessive unwillingness to yield ground to his enemies on all fronts, notes Orgill (1967:25). He was upping the ante. News of Mussolini's arrest on July 25, 1943, came as a relief for war-weary Italians, but it bruised Hitler's vanity and soured his optimism. His propaganda minister, Dr. Joseph Goebbels, wrote of Hitler's rage in his diary: "The Führer regards the whole Italian problem as a gigantic example of swinishness. . . . The Italians simply don't want to fight, they are happy when they can lay down their arms and even happier if they can sell them" (quoted in Orgill 1967:3). Hitler sensed that Italy's defection was near and feared that its betrayal would open southern Europe's "back door" to the Allied forces; he could not hold southern Italy without the Italian forces.

On September 8, 1943, Italy announced the armistice with the Allies. Resounding shouts of "*Viva la pace*—long live peace!" were short-lived in Rome as German soldiers occupied the city for a horrific nine months. The last of the Nazis there drove off in military trucks on June 4, 1944. They had managed to hold off the Allied troops, fighting numerous bloody battles, as their engineers oversaw feverish construction on the main German bastion some 155 miles north of Rome in the rugged and icy peaks of the Apennines, as described in Wallace (1978:36, 178–79).

9. Associazione Resistente, "Poggio alla Malva," in "La Resistenza nel pratese," n.d., www.associazioni.prato.it/resistente/pratese/, accessed May 12, 2008.

10. Dei Ottati (1998:126).

11. Other descriptions appear in Ginsborg (1990:54–59); my fieldnotes, "97.01.01 memory, via la volta."

12. My fieldnotes, "97.01.01 memory, via la volta."

CHAPTER 10: RESISTANCE

1. A local account of the youths' action, published by the Commune of Carmignano (sometime after 1977), laments the tragic death but celebrates their feat: "The factories of Prato were saved" (Comitato Unitario n.d.:11–12). The association describes the action in Carmignano as one of the most important partisan activities in Tuscany. More than seventy thousand Italians involved in resistance activities died between 1943 and 1945, with another forty thousand enduring severe injuries. The best-organized brigades were under communist leadership—a fact that would shape the political and social contours of postwar Italy (Mammarella 1966: 81). See an account of the action by Giovanni Baldini, "L'azione della stazione di Carmignano," 2004, www.resistenzatoscana.it/storie/l_azione_della_stazione_di_carmignano, accessed May 8, 2008. A contemporary though partial history of the dynamite factory of Nobel can be found at "Dynamite Factories," n.d., www.nobelcity.org/Pages/e_Itaprincipale.html, accessed May 8, 2008.

CHAPTER 11: AMERICAN CHOCOLATES

1. A detailed account of the events surrounding the war in central Italy can be found in Orgill (1967:11–25).

2. Newspapers reported the liberation of Bologna from fascist control on April 21, 1945, allowing what was left of the Allied armed forces to break through the Po Valley and the partisans to launch an insurrection of northern towns. On April 25, a disempowered Benito Mussolini met with representatives of the leading liberation committee in the north. The partisans demanded immediate and unconditional surrender. Fearing that his German allies might view admission of defeat as betrayal, the Duce refused, only to learn that the Germans had beaten him: his longtime supporters were already negotiating their surrender to the Allies. He got into his car with his mistress, Claretta Petacci, and a briefcase filled with documents and fled. His destination was

Como; the couple tried several times to cross the border into Switzerland but to no avail. They were caught on April 27 and executed on April 28, and their bodies were hung for public display the following day. A detailed account of Mussolini's demise is offered in Martin Clark's (2005:319–23) biography of Mussolini. A very abbreviated and different account of the disputed events appears in Mammarella (1966:83). The key partisan group was the Comitato di Liberazione Nazionale Alta Italia (Committee of National Liberation for Northern Italy).

CHAPTER 12: ONLY ONE

1. My fieldnotes, "04.01.24."
2. Archivio Privato, Villa di Calavria, Carmignano.
3. Details of the region can be found at Comuni del Montalbano, "Montalbano," www.montalbano.toscana.it, as well as Agenzia per il Turismo di Prato, "Carmignano," 2001, www.prato.turismo.toscana.it/comuni/ita/carmigna.htm, both accessed February 8, 2005. What is interesting about the historical discussions on these Web sites is that they extend back to the Etruscan period as well as the Medici period but omit the peasant cultural history and political turmoil of the twentieth century.
4. These details of the patron-client relationship established during the fascist years appear in Federazione Provinciale Sindacati Fascisti Agricoltori e Unione Provinciale Sindacati Fascisti Dell'Agricoltura di Firenze (1929:19).

CHAPTER 13: NEIGHBORS

1. A good introductory overview of European fertility decline appears in Gillis, Tilly, and Levine (1992).
2. Livi-Bacci (1977). An initial, international scientific report of Italy and Spain's low fertility appeared in *Family Planning Perspectives* (Delgado Pérez and Livi-Bacci 1992). As of 2007, the total fertility rate of Italian women rose slightly to 1.4 births, according to the Population Reference Bureau's 2007 World Population Data Sheet (2007:10). The bureau defines total fertility rate as "the average number of children a woman would have assuming that current age-specific birth rates remain constant throughout her childbearing years (usually considered to be ages 15 to 49)" (15). Italy's National Statistics Institute (Istat 2008:3) reported the average number of children per woman as 1.25 in 2001 and estimated the figure as 1.35 for 2006.
3. Elsewhere (Krause 2005b:594), I discuss several reasons why research related to memory allows social analysts to understand cultural struggles over

meaning and materiality. First, memories are socially situated. Second, they are symbolically loaded. Third, they are the ingredients that combine to create the stakes in ongoing struggles for hegemony. Alonso (1988:37) points out that the precise struggles in past-present relationships are not always evident. There is an extensive anthropological, sociological, and historical literature related to social memory. See, for example, Cavanaugh (2004), Comaroff and Comaroff (1992), Contini (1997), Halbwachs (1925/1992), Hartigan (2000), Olick and Robbins (1998), Passerini (1986), Popular Memory Group (1982), Stoler and Strassler (2000), Schwenkel (2006). On embodied, sensory aspects of memory, see Behar (1996), Bourdieu (1984), Cattell and Climo (2002:19–20), Comaroff and Comaroff (1991), Holtzman (2006), Leitch (2004), Mauss (1935/1979), Rosaldo (1989), Seremetakis (1994), Stoller (1994), and Terrio (2000).

4. The phrase *luxury mammal* appears in Gramsci (1971:218) in a note that offers a scathing critique of elite classes and their bankrupt morality, especially in relation to the embrace of consumer indulgence at the expense of civic participation: "But what is happening in America itself? The disjuncture in morality reveals that increasingly wider margins of social passivity are in the making. Women, it seems, have a prevalent role in this phenomenon. The male industrialist continues to work even if he is a millionaire, but his wife is turning more and more into a luxury mammal, and his daughters follow in their mother's footsteps. Beauty contests, the cinema, the stage, etc.; they select the feminine beauty of the world and put it up for auction. The women travel, continually crossing the ocean. They escape prohibition in their own country and contract marriages for a season."

5. A theoretical discussion of this point appears in Wolf, who observed that differences between classes in the capitalist world of consumer culture become transmuted "into distinctions of virtue and merit" (1982:389–90; see also Wolf 1999). The ability to consume therefore signals social victory. In a new moneyed context such as Prato the efforts of both parents were needed to ensure social victory, but the task of performing it seemed to fall especially to women.

6. My fieldnotes, "96.12.11 neighbors."

7. My fieldnotes, "96.10.29 mezzadria & sheep."

8. My fieldnotes, December 1996, Book #4, p. 50.

CHAPTER 14: A WEAVER'S TALE

1. The original Italian was as follows:

EMILIA: Ti dico ti do del tu. Io ti dico come—
BETSY: Sì. Sì dammi del tu.
PARIGI: Se no, la può—potrebbe andare anche pè berretti ultimamente—

EMILIA: Ma che! Se la vo sapere della paglia, la un vo sapè de—della lana.

PARIGI: Ma perchè ora faceano i berretti, gli facea i mi fratello.

EMILIA: No! Gli fanno ancora codesti.

PARIGI: Ma lei—

EMILIA: Ma lei la vo sapere i millesima. Lascia fare, lascia fare.

PARIGI: Sì, ma dei berretti non gli interessa?

BETSY: Lei—? La—?

PARIGI: Dei berretti per le donne?

BETSY: Ah. Berretti.

EMILIA: I berretti gli fanno ancora. Berretti di lana. Quelli li fanno ancora.

BETSY: Mi, mi interessa il lavoro—

EMILIA: della paglia!

BETSY: della—ma più delle donne e come ha cambiato—

PARIGI: Eh! Bah!

BETSY: insieme con come si fa famiglia. Perchè siccome ora c'è questa idea che prima le donne facevano la casalinga.

EMILIA: Sì. Casalinga. Sì. Ci mettevano un branco qui in questa casa qui ce n'era cinque, sei, sette, otto donne.

BETSY: Sì?

EMILIA: Sì.

BETSY: No, davvero?

EMILIA: Sì Sì. Bah! Oh! ma oh!

BETSY: Ma quando? In che epoca?

EMILIA: Eh, anche avanti la guerra, e più avanti la guerra.

PARIGI: Si ma a lei gli interessa anche i berretti—

BETSY: [laughter]

EMILIA: O stai zitto! i berretti!

PARIGI: E lei sta zitta!

EMILIA: Lei vo saper delle trecce ora. L'a un vole sapè dei berretti.

BETSY: Perchè quan—lei ha fatto anche berretti?

EMILIA: Io sì!

BETSY: Ah sì?

EMILIA: Ho fatto i turbanti.

BETSY: Ma perchè la paglia—

EMILIA: No! I berretti sono fatti di lana. Dopoguerra, la paglia dopoguerra è sparita. Quasi tutta sparita, c'è rimasto poco, poco. Poi si facea altri lavori. Che con la paglia si chiamava il rascello.

BETSY: Rascello?

(A changing market gave way to new materials, such as synthetic straw, and Emilia discussed the new challenges before changing the subject to women's artisan work.)

EMILIA: Gli era il lavoro delle donne. E si guadagnava. Io mi so fatta tutt'i corredo.

BETSY: Ah sì?

EMILIA: Sai i corredo per dì la biancheria lavorando avanti guerra. Dopoguerra questo lavoro è andat'a sparire—

BETSY: Ah, ho capito.

EMILIA: delle donne. È stato un po'—Gli era un'affare artigianale. Tutti artigiani.
          I su fratello, per esempio, la moglie di su' fratello, i su zio faceva pro-
          prio, e spediva in America.
BETSY: Ah si?
EMILIA: Sì, spediva in America. Perchè lei la c'aveva il babbo in America. Gli era
          scappato al tempo del fascismo.
BETSY: Ah sì? Perchè era—non—non andava bene con il fascismo?
EMILIA: Gli era comunista.
BETSY: Sì?
EMILIA: I su babbo. Tanto oh! Bisogna gli dica la verità. Un'era mica—
BETSY: Certo ma—
EMILIA: un' assassino. Non aveva l'idea del fascismo—
BETSY: Certo.
EMILIA: come c'era in Italia la dittatura.
BETSY: Ah sì.
EMILIA: E allora gli era perseguitata questa persona. Gli aveva *tre* figlioli.
BETSY: Ah.
EMILIA: Tre figlioli. Lui gli scappò in America, e imbarcò a v—a Genova.
BETSY: A che anno?
EMILIA: Ma proprio l'anno, l'a vedrà nel millenovecento ventidue, ventitre.
BETSY: Ah! presto, così presto.
EMILIA: *Eh!* Quand'è quando viense il fascismo in Italia. Il fascismo incominciò
          nel millenovecento ventuno. Io non me ne ricordo mica della data.
          Ero di già ero di già piccola italiana. A scuola bisogna esse piccoli
          italiani: magliettina bianca, sottanina nera, berrettino, cravattina
          nera, calzine bianche, e scarpine nere.
BETSY: Ah si?
EMILIA: Però ce le passavano. Ecco, s'eramo le piccole italiane di Mussolini.
          L'ha sentito rammenta' Mussolini?
BETSY: Sì, sì! Certo.
EMILIA: Allora i babbo della mia cognata scappò, in America, e fu spedito in
          una cassa di cappelli. Dice c'era i cappelli dentro mentre c'era lui.
BETSY: Ah, ho capito.
EMILIA: Perchè se dopo—lo potean prendere lo mandavan ai confine. Gli man
          davano ai confini, a—l'isole, ni mezzo ai mare ne mandonno tanti, ne
          mandonno i presidente, Pertini, d'Italia, ecco, allora. I fascismo. Poi
          dopo la guerra questa— un fo più queste treccie, un fo più. Le donne
          comincianno a andà a lavorar in fabbrica. Anch'io andai in fabbrica.

2. Part of this calling derives from a commitment to the importance of
working against trends in translation that reproduce homogenous, global
monoculture—particularly the selection for translation of tame stories that fit the
requirements of international publishers. In an issue of *Public Culture* devoted to
translation issues, anthropologist Elizabeth Povinelli (2001:x) notes that "the business of translation is booming, urged on by newly integrated global capital and
nation-states." But she emphasizes that despite the boom very few works receive
international visibility, particularly in the United States. Only a small number of

works end up being "palatable" to the tastes and political economies of the global market. In the same issue, Emily Apter (2001:3) identifies a trend toward the establishment of a "transnationally translatable monoculture" in which certain "linguistic superpowers—with English the clear victor—increasingly call the shots." The fact that these linguistic superpowers are also economic and cultural superpowers is hardly a coincidence. Some theorists have described this tendency to adapt translations, and the selection of works for translation, to the tastes and prejudices of readers as "domesticating" translations, in the sense of taming and homogenizing differences. Lawrence Venuti (1998) and others (e.g. Fox 2000; Tihanyi 2002) have maintained that the domestication of translations serves the interests of modernization at the expense of subaltern nations and peoples whose stories and voices are less translatable. Michael Herzfeld (2003:110) observes that choosing marginal communities and viewpoints can be a strategy to explore the forces that demarcate "marginal" from "central."

3. My fieldnotes, "97.02.16 generation, work." See also "96.09.30 marriage & motherhood."

4. See Patriarca (1998).

5. Foucault (1980:83).

6. See Gramsci's (1971) discussion of conformism.

7. The original Italian was as follows:

BETSY: Ma c'era uno che veniva a consegnare il lavoro?

EMILIA: Sì, c'era suo fratello. Gli sposò questa come gli ho detto. Lo zio suo faceva il cappellaio e le treccie che era il babbo quello che è andato via nel periodo del fascismo. A Genova montò in una nave e andò in America. Questa bambina— poi dopo la moglie, la madre di lei, la rimase quì, capito?

BETSY: Capito.

EMILIA: Poi lui volle che la fabbrica fosse in America, in Argentina. La mamma di lei, lui le volle che l'andasse in America, e le l'andò al tempo del fascismo, per mezzo di questi negozianti di cappelli, e la portò con sè le tre sorelle e laggiù la ne fece un'altro, un maschio e una femmina. E lui c'è stato da lei. Lui è ingegniere sa questi che fanno queste strade, e poi ha una tenuta che c'ha tanti capi di bestie ha fatto soldi, di preciso un lo sò, bisognerebbe farglielo dire a lei alla mi cognata, ma sa l'ha perso un pò. L'andette in America per via di lui. E i su—lo zio di lei, il fratello della su' mamma, gli disse, "Lasciami la—una bambina," gli disse, "almeno—" E gli lasciò questa Germena, che la sarebbe moglie del su' fratello, la mi cognata.

8. The narrator, who normally spoke with a storyteller's confidence, appeared to be glancing sideways. As Bakhtin (1940/1980:294) keenly observed, "Language is not a neutral medium that passes freely and easily into the private property of the speaker's intentions; it is populated—and overpopulated—with

the intentions of others." In a linguistic anthropology tour de force, Hill (1995) suggested that the dysfluency in Mexicano-speaking Don Gabriel's otherwise eloquent narrative indicated a peasant's struggle with two conflicting ideological systems: capitalist profit versus peasant reciprocity and solidarity.

CHAPTER 15: PROGRESS

1. This phrase was cited in a special circular on peasants available from Florence-area news stands in 2004 (De Simonis et al. 2004:12).
2. My fieldnotes, "97.02.06 spaventato."
3. My fieldnotes, "97.02.24 progresso, regresso." See also Povoledo (2008).

CHAPTER 16: SINGLES' SEXUALITY

1. Schneider and Schneider (1991, 1992:160, 1996).
2. Interview with Emilia and Parigi, January 28, 1997, tape #40.
3. Stuart Hall (1981:227) noted that this kind of moral education of the working classes commonly accompanied economic transformations to capitalism.
4. My fieldnotes, "97.01.01 new year's eve, single."
5. My fieldnotes, "96.12.26 zitelli, santo stefano."
6. See Livi-Bacci (2001:146).
7. Istat (2005:90; 2008:4).

CHAPTER 17: AMAZING GRACE

1. My fieldnotes, "97.01.01 dolce with neighbors."
2. I met a demographer-in-training under Massimo Livi-Bacci's tutelage who examined this trend in her thesis. See Mencarini (1994).
3. My fieldnotes, "97.03.03 benediction, casa."
4. My fieldnotes, "97.03.04, trust, fiducia."
5. My fieldnotes, "97.03.09 casa colonica."
6. My fieldnotes, "97.04.06 heart, neighbors."

CHAPTER 18: A BURNING QUESTION

1. Anthropologists have demonstrated that an approach involving not only intellect but also emotion can enhance cross-cultural understanding. The renowned anthropologist Renato Rosaldo (1989) came to a methodological innovation in his

book *Culture and Truth: The Remaking of Social Analysis* after a tragic personal loss. During his research on Ilongot headhunting in the Philippines he had been reluctant to accept local men's explanations that rage over a loved one's death drove them to hunt other men. He was convinced there was a rational explanation that involved hard calculation. One day his wife, the anthropologist Michelle Rosaldo, went to search for new housing for the couple and while hiking along a steep mountain path slipped and fell to her death. The widower was filled with rage. His grief led him to relate to the local men's reasoning about what motivated them to headhunt. With time and reflection, he brought his own life experiences to bear on analysis about cross-cultural practices and in doing so abandoned his former belief in the possibility of impartial analysis. Similarly, anthropologist Ruth Behar (1996) in her *Vulnerable Observer: Anthropology That Breaks Your Heart* draws on personal experience to tell moving stories that speak to large cultural issues, such as death and dying, or longing and belonging, and meanwhile exposes ways of knowing that are deeply subjective. That high standards of quality may be achieved through love and genuine affection for the people one studies, consults, or collaborates with is a position that anthropologist Virginia Dominguez (2000) has advocated in an essay on the politics of love in ethnographic research.

CHAPTER 19: GENERATION GAP

1.   See Contini (1993) for an interpretation of the photographs. Scheuermeier's work is also discussed in Miraglia (1981).

2.   The School of Salernum (Gherli n.d.:57) recommended *malva* for soothing the stomach and encouraging menstrual flow: *Che la Malva ammollisca il ventre, il dissero / Gli Antichi, le di lei rase radici / Sciolgon le fecci, e il mestrual flusso muovono.*

CHAPTER 20: "WET" AND HIDDEN ECONOMIES

1.   This quote appears in Pescarolo (1988:89). See Pescarolo and Bruno Ravenni (1991) for a full history, including oral accounts, of the industry.

2.   Kertzer (1999:589) explores the public health concerns related to the transfer of syphilis from infected infants to wet nurses and vice versa during the nineteenth century. In a recent work, Kertzer (2008) discusses artificial feeding (57, 148) and delves into the moral and legal issues that in the 1880s came to challenge foundling homes' practice of hiring rural wet nurses; his book focuses on the court case of a peasant woman and the attorney who sought justice for her. Prato's history of

public assistance for wet nurses as well as milk subsidies is outlined in Guarnieri (2002).

3. The qualifications for women to be employed as wet nurses are outlined in Kertzer (2008:15–16).

4. The translation here combines my own efforts and what appears in Piccini (1992:6).

5. See Kertzer (1993:82, 173); see also Barbagli and Kertzer (1990:376).

6. See Pirandello (1922/1985) and Bellocchio (1999).

7. Willson (2002). Dadà (1999b:26, 30, 1999a) documents the lives of migrant women who left their children to live in and work for wealthy households elsewhere.

8. Perry Willson (2002:19–20) writes of rural housewives, "Peasant women, particularly from Tuscany and Friuli, moved to the houses of the rich to breastfeed and care for a baby. This latter form of temporary migration could be very traumatic, uprooting women from their families and their own children, but it offered excellent wages." Kertzer (1993) elaborates on the institutional dimensions, including the church and state, related to this practice historically.

9. In this section, I draw on four types of documents related to wet nurse subsidies: (1) the Registro Generale dei Baliatici e Sussidi di Latte, a general register of wet nurse funds and milk subsidies spanning the years 1883 to 1902 and listing entries of requests made or denied; (2) deliberations of the Congregazione di Carità, a ledger listing the actions of the body that oversaw the requests; (3) reports of the Municipal Guard, describing the economic conditions of families; and (4) medical certificates documenting the condition of the woman whose case was under review. Together, these documents spell out criteria according to which the state deemed women as "moral." My thanks to Silvano Gelli for bringing these ledgers to my attention.

10. Archivio Postunitario del Comune di Prato, Fascicolo 14 (106), Miscellanea, Opere Pie, 1887–88, Casa Pia dei Ceppi di Prato, Risposte, March 16, 1887. A total of £5,490 was paid, with a minimum monthly subsidy of £2.52 and a maximim of £6.50. This amount represented about 18 percent of the sum paid out that year for charitable causes but only 10 percent of the recipients. Total births are from Bandettini (1966:118).

11. Meredith Small (1998:217–20) describes insufficient milk as a culturebound syndrome and offers an illuminating discussion of culture and biology related to breastfeeding. James McKenna's research on co-sleeping has implications for breastfeeding because sleeping side by side stimulates milk production due to increased skin contact. In addition, mothers who sleep safely with their infants get more sleep than those whose infants sleep in cribs, and the babies learn how to breathe regularly and suffer less frequently from sleep apnea as well as sudden infant death syndrome (McKenna and McDade 2005). A team of researchers

found that breastfeeding rates in Italy remain relatively low, with 42 percent of mothers nursing at three months, 19 percent at six months, and only 4 percent at 12 months (Riva et al. 1999).

12. Archivio Storico di Carmignano, Censimento Generale della Popolazione del Regno D'Italia, Provincia di Firenze, Comune di Carmignano, Frazione Poggio a Caiano, Elenco delle Famiglie e persone censite il 10 Febbraio 1901.

13. The report appears in "Oggetto: Lavoro delle Donne nel Comune" [Subject: Report on Women's Work in the Commune], Commune of Carmignano, Archivio Storico del Comune di Carmignano, Categoria III, No. 93, Fascicolo No. 13, Filza 2, August 30, 1893. The letter was located in Archivio del Comune di Carmignano, Congregazione di Carità del Comune di Carmignano, Protocollo delle deliberazioni, Fascicolo I 1, Scaffale F.

14. Archivio Storico del Comune di Carmignano, Atti di Nascita, Registro, Anno 1901, p. 253, No. 378, and pp. 311–13, No. 11, November 15, 1901, Ufficio di Anagrafe.

15. Archivio Storico del Comune di Carmignano, Fascicolo III 122, Affari Ordinari Anno 1901, Dalla Lettera A alla Lettera C. Filza No. 6, "Baliatici," Diversi documentazioni relativi ai sussidi di latte accordati o negati del Comune nel 1901.

16. See Gelli (1996, 1998).

17. Louise Tilly and Joan Scott propose two types of productive activity, one for household use and one for exchange. When women or men do housework or child care and do not get paid for their work, their activity is defined as a domestic activity; it is limited to its use value, i.e., the direct value the activity has to the people who benefit from it. When women or men engage in a productive activity that is market oriented, they earn wages, and hence their work also has exchange value; they exchange their work for a set value, or wage. Reproduction, according to this model, and the bearing and raising of children require time and effort but are not included in the term *work* (Tilly and Scott 1978:3). This scheme, though analytically useful in some cases, does not apply well to a situation in which women's productive activity is wage-earning work but is discounted or forgotten; nor is it very helpful for describing a situation in which women's reproductive activity has exchange value.

18. A view of folktales as social analysis by the peasant women who tell them is developed in Taylor and Rebel (1981). See Wolf (1982) for his classic anthropological contribution on articulating modes of production. Rebel (1989:131) suggests that those who live between articulating modes of production "are split internally by the double or triple lives they must lead." On contemporary gender relations in Italy, see Passerini (1996). On the undoing power of global capital, Wolf (1969:295) observed: "The spread of the market has torn men up by their roots, and shaken them loose from the social relationships into which they were born. Industrialization and expanded communication have given rise to new so-

cial clusters, as yet unsure of their own social positions and interests, but forced by the imbalance of their lives to seek a new adjustment."

19.   See Becattini (2001) on economic development in Prato. An earlier work of his (1998:83) addresses the role of family in regional industrial development, and another of his essays (1986:908) offers interpretations of the relevance of the peasant protest to economic transformation.

EPILOGUE

1.   The note read as follows: *chiamato alle armi 14 / marzo / 1940 / in sangedo 9 / Novembre 1945 / prestavo servizio all'ufficio Archivio / come Scritturale / dello Ospedale Militare di S. Gallo / Firenze.*

2.   See D'Aloisio (2007) and Gribaldo (2007).

3.   "Remembering Writer Grace Paley," National Public Radio, August 24, 2007, including interview with Terry Gross, *Fresh Air*, 1985, electronic audio resource, www.npr.org/templates/story/story.php?storyId=13924175, accessed November 8, 2007.

References

ARCHIVES

Archivio del Comune di Carmignano
Archivio Postunitario del Comune di Prato
Archivio Privato, Villa di Calavria, Carmignano
Archivio Storico del Comune di Carmignano

SECONDARY SOURCES

Abu-Lughod, Lila. 1986. *Veiled sentiments: Honor and poetry in a Bedouin society.* Berkeley: University of California Press.
———. 2005. *Dramas of nationhood: The politics of television in Egypt.* Chicago: University of Chicago Press.
Alonso, Ana María. 1988. The effects of truth: Re-presentations of the past and the imagining of community. *Journal of Historical Sociology* 1 (1): 33–57.
Alter, George. 1992. Theories of fertility decline: A nonspecialist's guide to the current debate. In *The European experience of declining fertility, 1850–1970: The*

quiet revolution, ed. John R. Gillis, Louise A. Tilly, and David Levine, 13–27. Cambridge: Blackwell.

Anagnost, Ann. 1995. A surfeit of bodies: Population and the rationality of the state in post-Mao China. In *Conceiving the new world order: The global politics of reproduction,* ed. Faye D. Ginsburg and Rayna Rapp, 22–41. Berkeley: University of California Press.

Apter, Emily. 2001. On translation in a global market. *Public Culture* 13 (1): 1–12.

Bakhtin, Mikhail. 1940/1980. *The dialogical imagination.* Austin: University of Texas Press.

Balter, Michael. 2006. The baby deficit. *Science* 312:1894–97.

Bandettini, Pierfrancesco, ed. 1961. *La popolazione della Toscana dal 1810 al 1959.* Florence: Camera di Commercio, Industria e Agricultura.

Barbagli, Marzio, and David Kertzer. 1990. An introduction to the history of Italian family life. *Journal of Family History* 15 (4): 369–84.

Becattini, Giacomo. 1986. Riflessioni sullo sviluppo socio-economico della Toscana in questa dopoguerra. In *Storia d'Italia: Le regioni dall' Unità ad Oggi, La Toscana,* 901–26. Turin: Einaudi.

———. 1998. The development of light industry in Tuscany: An interpretation. In *Regional development in a modern European economy: The case of Tuscany,* ed. Robert Leonardi and Raffaella Y. Nanetti, 77–94. London: Pinter.

———. 2001. *The caterpillar and the butterfly: An exemplary case of development in the Italy of the industrial districts.* Trans. Roger Absalom. Florence: Felice Le Monnier.

Behar, Ruth. 1993. *Translated woman: Crossing the border with Esperanza's story.* Boston: Beacon Press.

———. 1996. *The vulnerable observer: Anthropology that breaks your heart.* Boston: Beacon Press.

———. 1999. Ethnography: Cherishing our second-fiddle genre. *Journal of Contemporary Ethnography* 28 (5): 472–84.

Bellocchio, Marco, dir. 1999. *La balia* [The nanny]. Rome: Filmalbatros.

Bialasiewicz, L. 2006. "The death of the West": Samuel Huntington, Oriana Fallaci and a new "moral" geopolitics of births and bodies. *Geopolitics* 11:701–24.

Bongaarts, John. 1998. Demographic consequences of declining fertility. *Science* 282:19–20.

Bourdieu, Pierre. 1984. *Distinction: A social critique of the judgement of taste.* Cambridge, MA: Harvard University Press.

Cannistraro, Philip V. 1972. Mussolini's cultural revolution: Fascist or nationalist? *Journal of Contemporary History* 7 (3/4): 115–39.

Capote, Truman. 1965. *In cold blood.* New York: Random House.

Castiglioni, Maria, Gianpiero dalla Zuanna, and Marzia Loghi. 2001. Planned and unplanned births and conceptions in Italy, 1970–1995. *European Journal of Population* 17:207–33.

Cattell, Maria G., and Jacob J. Climo. 2002. Introduction: Meaning in social memory and history: Anthropological perspectives. In *Social memory and history: Anthropological perspectives*, ed. Jacob J. Climo and Maria G. Cattell, 1–36. Walnut Creek, CA: Altamira Press.

Cavanaugh, Jillian. 2004. Remembering and forgetting: Ideologies of language loss in a northern Italian town. *Journal of Linguistic Anthropology* 14 (1): 24–38.

Chatterjee, Piya. 2001. *A time for tea: Women, labor, and post/colonial politics on an Indian plantation*. Durham: Duke University Press.

Clark, Martin. 2005. *Mussolini*. Harlow: Pearson/Longman.

Clifford, James. 1986. Introduction: Partial truths. In *Writing culture: The poetics and politics of ethnography*, ed. James Clifford and George E. Marcus, 1–26. Berkeley: University of California Press.

Clifford, James, and George E. Marcus, eds. 1986. *Writing culture: The poetics and politics of ethnography*. Berkeley: University of California Press

Coale, Ansley J., and Roy Treadway. 1986. A summary of the changing distribution of overall fertility, marital fertility and the proportion married in the provinces of Europe. In *The decline of fertility in Europe*, ed. Ansley J. Coale and Susan Cotts Watkins, 31–181. Princeton: Princeton University Press.

Coale, Ansley J., and Susan C. Watkins, eds. 1986. *The decline of fertility in Europe*. Princeton: Princeton University Press.

Cohn, Bernard. 1980. Anthropology and history: The state of play. *Comparative Study of Society and History* 22 (2): 198–221.

Comaroff, Jean, and John Comaroff. 1991. *Of revelation and revolution*. Vol. 1. Chicago: University of Chicago Press.

Comaroff, John, and Jean Comaroff. 1992. *Ethnography and the historical imagination*. Boulder, CO: Westview Press.

Comitato Unitario per l'Ordine Democratico. n.d. *11 Giugno 1944: Contributo di sangue per la libertà*. Comune di Carmignano. Prato: La Tipografica Pratese.

Contini, Giovanni. 1993. Le fotografie di Scheuermeier a Carmignano. *AFT, Rivista di Storia e Fotografia* 9 (18): 11–20.

———. 1997. *La memoria divisa*. Milan: Rizzoli.

———. 2004. *Aristocrazia contadina. Sulla complessità della società mezzadrile: Fattoria, famiglie, individui*. Siena: Protagon.

Crehan, Kate. 2002. *Gramsci, culture and anthropology*. Berkeley: University of California Press.

Dadà, Adriana. 1999a. Partire per un figlio altrui. In *Altrove: Viaggi di donne dall'antichità al Novecento*, ed. Dinora Corsi. Rome: Viella.

————. 1999b. Storia e memoria dell'emigrazione femminile da Ponte Buggianese nel '900. In *Il lavoro di balia: Memoria e storia dell'emigrazione femminile da Ponte Buggianese nel '900*, ed. Adriana Dadà, 15–34. Ospedaletto, Pisa: Pacini Editore.

Dalla Zuanna, Gianpiero. 2001. The banquet of Aeolus: A familistic interpretation of Italy's lowest low fertility. *Demographic Research* 4 (5): 133–61.

————. 2004. Few children in strong families: Values and low fertility in Italy. *Genus* 60 (1): 39–70.

D'Aloisio, Fulvia. 2007. Non oltre due figli, ma due figli almeno: Centralità e valore dei fratelli a Napoli. In *Non son tempi per fare figli: Orientamenti e comportamenti riproduttivi nella bassa fecondità italiana*, ed. Fulvia D'Aloisio, 69–93. Milan: Guerini Scientifica.

de Grazia, Victoria. 1992. *How fascism ruled women, Italy, 1922–1945.* Berkeley: University of California Press.

De Simonis, Paolo, Alessandro Falassi, Alessandro Fornari, Silvano Guerini, Italo Moretti, and Renato Stopani. 2004. *Cultura contadina in Toscana*. Vol. 1. *Il lavoro dell'uomo*. Florence: Casa Editrice Bonechi.

Dei Ottati, Gabi. 1998. Case study I: Prato and its evolution in a European context. In *Regional development in a modern European economy: The case of Tuscany*, ed. Robert Leonardi and Raffaella Y. Nanetti, 124–52. London: Pinter.

Delgado Pérez, Margarita, and Massimo Livi-Bacci. 1992. Fertility in Italy and Spain: The lowest in the world. *Family Planning Perspectives* 24 (July–August): 162–73.

Deresiewicz, William. 2006. Review of *The novel*, ed. Franco Moretti. *Nation*, December 4.

di Leonardo, Micaela. 1989. Malinowski's nephews. *Nation*, March 13, 350–52.

Dominguez, Virginia. 2000. For a politics of love and rescue. *Cultural Anthropology* 15 (3): 361–93.

Douglass, Carrie B., ed. 2005. *Barren states: The population implosion in southern and eastern Europe*. London: Berg.

Eberstadt, Nicholas. 2001. The population implosion. *Foreign Policy* 123:42–53.

Fancelli, Carlo. 1871/1997. *Sul fondatore dell'industria della paglia in Toscana*. Comune di Signa, Museo della Paglia e Dell'Intreccio "Domenico Michelacci." Signa: Tipografia NOVA.

Federal Institute for Population Research and Robert Bosch Foundation. 2005. *The demographic future of Europe: Facts, figures, policies. Results of the Population Policy Acceptance Study (PPAS)*. Stuttgart: Robert Bosch Foundation. www .bosch-stiftung.de/content/language2/html/4460.asp.

Federazione Provinciale Sindacati Fascisti Agricoltori e Unione Provinciale Sindacati Fascisti Dell'Agricoltura di Firenze. 1929. *Contratto collettivo di lavoro per la conduzione dei fondi rustici a mezzadria nella regione Toscana*. Florence: G. Ramella.

Forgacs, David, ed. 1986. *Rethinking Italian fascism: Capitalism, populism and culture.* London: Lawrence and Wisehart.

Foucault, Michel. 1978. *The history of sexuality.* Vol. 1. *An introduction.* New York: Vintage Books.

————. 1980. Two lectures. In *Power/knowledge: Selected interviews and other writings, 1972–1977,* ed. and trans. Colin Gordon, 78–108. New York: Pantheon Books.

Fox, Richard G. 2000. Hearing where we're coming from—ethically and professionally. In *Ethics and anthropology: Facing future issues in human biology, globalism, and cultural property,* ed. Anne-Marie Cantwell, Eva Friedlander, and Madeleine L. Tramm, 1–8. New York: New York Academy of Sciences.

Fratianni, Michele, and Franco Spinelli. 2001. Italian deflation in the gold-exchange standard. Paper prepared for the Claremont Conference on Deflation, Claremont, CA, April 26–28.

Gal, Susan, and Gail Kligman. 2000. *The politics of gender under socialism.* Princeton: University of Princeton Press.

García Márquez, Gabriel. 2003. *Living to tell the tale.* New York: Vintage International.

Geertz, Clifford. 1973. *The interpretation of cultures.* New York: Basic Books.

Gelli, Silvano. 1996. *Q.M.P. Le epigrafi nel cimitero di Poggio a Caiano: Testimonianze di storia poggese (1884–1954).* Signa: Tipografia Nova.

————. 1998. *Movimento cooperativo e lotte sociali nel territorio orientale del Montalbano (1872–1922).* Quaderni di Ricerche Storiche 5. Signa: Tipografia Nova.

Gherli, Fulvio. n.d. *Regimen Sanitatis Salernitanum. Regola Sanitaria Salernitana (The School of Salernum).* English version. Ed. and trans. Sir John Harington. RAI Radiotelevisione Italiana. Rome: Christangraf.

Gillis, John R., Louise A. Tilly, and David Levine, ed. 1992. *The European experience of declining fertility, 1850–1970: The quiet revolution.* Cambridge, MA: Blackwell.

Ginsborg, Paul. 1990. *A history of contemporary Italy: Society and politics, 1943–1988.* London: Penguin Books.

Ginsburg, Faye D., and Rayna Rapp. 1995. Introduction to *Conceiving the new world order: Global politics of reproduction,* ed. Faye D. Ginsburg and Rayna Rapp, 1–17. Berkeley: University of California Press.

Ginzburg, Carlo. 1980. *The cheese and the worms: The cosmos of a sixteenth-century miller.* Trans. John and Anne Tedeschi. Baltimore: Johns Hopkins University Press.

Golini, Antonio. 1991. Introduction to *Crescita zero,* ed. Rossella Palomba, vii–xv. Scandicci, Florence: La Nuova Italy.

————. 1994. Preface to *Tendenze demografiche e politiche per la popolazione: Terzo rapporto IRP sulla situazione demografica italiana,* ed. Antonio Golini, 7–12. Milan: Il Mulino.

Golini, Antonio, A. De Simoni, and F. Citoni, eds. 1995. *Tre scenari per il possibile sviluppo della popolazione delle regioni italiane al 2044.* Rome: Consiglio Nazionale delle Ricerche / Istituto di Ricerche sulla Popolazione.

Golini, Antonio, Antonio Mussino, and Miria Savioli. 2000. *Il malessere demografico in Italia.* Bologna: Il Mulino.

Gramsci, Antonio. 1971. *The prison notebooks.* New York: International Publishers.

Greenhalgh, Susan. 1995a. Anthropology theorizes reproduction: Integrating practice, political economic, and feminist perspectives. In *Situating fertility,* ed. Susan Greenhalgh, 3–28. Cambridge: Cambridge University Press.

———. 1995b. The power in/of population. *Current Anthropology* 36 (5): 875–78.

———. 1996. The social construction of population science: An intellectual, institutional, and political history of twentieth-century demography. *Comparative Study of Society and History* 38 (1): 26–66.

———. 2003. Planned births, unplanned persons: "Population" in the making of Chinese modernity. *American Ethnologist* 30 (2): 196–215.

———. 2008. *Just one child: Science and policy in Deng's China.* Berkeley: University of California Press.

Gribaldo, Alessandra. 2007. La "produzione" del genitore: Vincoli culturali alla fecondità a Bologna. In *Non son tempi per fare figli: Orientamenti e comportamenti riproduttivi nella bassa fecondità italiana,* ed. Fulvia D'Aloisio, 115–30. Milan: Guerini Scientifica.

Guarnieri, Patrizia. 2002. L'assistenza baliatica e il dispensario per lattanti di Prato all'inizio dell '900. *AFT, Rivista di Storia e Fotografia* 35:43–56.

Halbwachs, Maurice. 1925/1992. *On collective memory.* Ed. and trans. Lewis A. Coser. Chicago: University of Chicago Press.

Hall, Stuart. 1981. Notes on deconstructing the popular. In *People's history and socialist theory,* ed. Raphael Samuel, 227–40. London: Routledge and Kegan Paul.

Hammel, E. A. 1990. A theory of culture for demography. *Population and Development Review* 16 (3): 455–85.

Hartigan, John, Jr. 2000. Remembering white Detroit: Whiteness in the mix of history and memory. *City and Society* 12 (2): 11–34.

Hartt, Frederick. 1966/2006. *History of Italian Renaissance art: Painting, sculpture, architecture.* 6th ed. Upper Saddle River, NJ: Pearson Prentice Hall.

Hecht, Tobias. 2006. *After life: An ethnographic novel.* Durham: Duke University Press.

Helstosky, Carol. 2004. *Garlic and oil: Food and politics in Italy.* Oxford: Berg.

Herzfeld, Michael. 2003. The unspeakable in pursuit of the ineffable: Representations of untranslatability in ethnographic discourse. In *Translating cultures,* ed. Paula G. Rubel and Abraham Rosman, 109–34. Oxford: Berg.

Hill, Jane H. 1995. The voices of Don Gabriel: Responsibility and self in a modern Mexicano narrative. In *The dialogic emergence of culture*, ed. Dennis Tedlock and Bruce Mannheim, 97–147. Urbana: University of Illinois Press.

Hobsbawm, Eric. 1983. Introduction: Inventing traditions. In *The invention of tradition*, ed. Eric Hobsbawm and Terence Ranger, 1–14. Cambridge: Cambridge University Press.

Holtzman, Jon D. 2006. Food and memory. *Annual Review of Anthropology* 35:361–78.

Horn, David. 1994. *Social bodies: Science, reproduction and Italian modernity.* Princeton: Princeton University Press.

Hurston, Zora Neale. 1937/1991. *Their eyes were watching God.* Champaign: University of Illinois Press.

Ipsen, Carl. 1996. *Dictating demography: The problem of population in fascist Italy.* Cambridge: Cambridge University Press.

Istat (Istituto Nazionale di Statistica). 2005. *Diventare padri in Italia: Fecondità e figli secondo un approccio di genere. A cura di Alessandro Rosina e Linda Laura Sabbadini.* Rome: Istat. www.istat.it/dati/catalogo/20051020_00/.

———. 2008. *Italy in figures.* Rome: National Institute of Statistics.

Johnson-Hanks, Jennifer. 2008. Demographic transitions and modernity. *Annual Review of Anthropology* 37:301–15.

Joyce, Kathryn. 2008. Missing the "right" babies: U.S. Christian conservatives warn of a looming demographic winter in Europe. *Nation*, March 3, 11–18.

Kanaaneh, Rhoda Ann. 2002. *Birthing the nation: Strategies of Palestinian women in Israel.* Berkeley: University of California Press.

Kertzer, David I. 1993. *Sacrificed for honor: Italian infant abandonment and the politics of reproductive control.* Boston: Beacon Press.

———. 1995. Political-economic and cultural explanations of demographic behavior. In *Situating fertility: Anthropology and demographic inquiry*, ed. Susan Greenhalgh, 29–52. Cambridge: Cambridge University Press.

———. 1999. Syphilis, foundlings, and wetnurses in nineteenth-century Italy. *Journal of Social History* 32 (3): 589–602.

———. 2008. *Amalia's tale: A poor peasant, an ambitious attorney, and a fight for justice.* Boston: Houghton Mifflin.

Kertzer, David I., and Dennis P. Hogan. 1989. *Family, political economy, and demographic change: The transformation of life in Casalecchio, Italy, 1861–1921.* Madison: University of Wisconsin Press.

Kligman, Gail. 1998. *The politics of duplicity: Controlling reproduction in Ceausescu's Romania.* Berkeley: University of California Press.

Knodel, John, and Etienne van de Walle. 1986. Lessons from the past: Policy implications of historical fertility studies. In *The decline of fertility in Europe*, ed.

Ansley J. Coale and Susan C. Watkins, 390–419. Princeton: Princeton University Press.

Krause, Elizabeth L. 1994. Forward vs. reverse gear: The politics of proliferation and resistance in the Italian fascist state. *Journal of Historical Sociology* 7 (3): 261–88.

———. 2001. "Empty cradles" and the quiet revolution: Demographic discourse and cultural struggles of gender, race, and class in Italy. *Cultural Anthropology* 16 (4): 576–611.

———. 2005a. *A crisis of births: Population politics and family-making in Italy.* Belmont, CA: Wadsworth/Thomson Learning.

———. 2005b. Encounters with "the peasant": Memory work, masculinity, and low fertility in Italy. *American Ethnologist* 32 (4): 593–617.

———. 2005c. Toys and perfumes: Imploding Italy's population paradox and motherly myths. In *Barren states: The population implosion in southern and eastern Europe,* ed. Carrie B. Douglass, 159–82. London: Berg.

———. 2006. Dangerous demographies and the scientific manufacture of fear. Corner House, Briefing Paper No. 36. www.thecornerhouse.org.uk/.

———. 2007. Memory and meaning: Genealogy of a fertile protest. *Journal of Modern Italian Studies* 12 (4): 406–16.

Krause, Elizabeth L., and Milena Marchesi. 2007. Fertility politics as "social Viagra": Reproducing boundaries, social cohesion and modernity in Italy. *American Anthropologist* 109 (2): 350–62.

Leitch, Alison. 2004. Slow Food and the politics of pork fat: Italian food and European identity. *Ethnos* 68 (4): 437–62.

Livi-Bacci, Massimo. 1977. *A history of Italian fertility during the last two centuries.* Princeton: Princeton University Press.

———. 1994. Introduction to *Tendenze demografiche e politiche per la popolazione: Terzo rapporto IRP sulla situazione demografica italiana,* ed. Antonio Golini, 13–16. Milan: Il Mulino.

———. 2000. *The population of Europe.* Oxford: Blackwell.

———. 2001. Too few children and too much family. *Daedalus* 130 (3): 139–55.

Mammarella, Giuseppe. 1966. *Italy after fascism: A political history, 1943–1965.* Notre Dame: University of Notre Dame Press.

Mannucci, Umberto. 1993. *Parole in fabbrica: Vocaboli ed espressioni dell'industria tessile pratese (1940–90).* Prato: Edizioni del Palazzo.

Martin, Emily. 1987. *The woman in the body: A cultural analysis of reproduction.* Boston: Beacon Press.

———. 1991. The egg and the sperm: How science has constructed a romance based on stereotypical male-female roles. *Signs* 16:485–501.

Mauss, Marcel. 1935/1979. Body techniques. In *Sociology and psychology: Essays,* 97–123, trans. Ben Brewster. London: Routledge and Kegan Paul.

Mazzuco, Stefano, and Fausta Ongaro. 2003. La bassa fecondità italiana tra costrizioni economiche e cambio di valori: Uno studio con focus groups. Paper presented at the workshop, Il contributo degli studi qualititativi per la comprensione dei comportamenti familiari e riproduttivi, Padua, Italy.

McKenna, James, and Thomas McDade. 2005. Why babies should never sleep alone: A review of the co-sleeping controversy in relation to SIDS, bedsharing and breast feeding. *Paediatric Respiratory Reviews* 6:134–52.

Mencarini, Letizia. 1994. Aspettative e intenzioni su famiglia e figli: Un'indagine campionaria sulle studentesse fiorentine. PhD diss., Università degli Studi di Firenze, Facoltà di Scienze Politiche.

Metcalf, Peter. 2001. *They lie, we lie: Getting on with anthropology.* New York: Routledge.

Mills, Melina, Letizia Mencarini, Maria Letizia Tanturri, and Katia Begall. 2008. Gender equity and fertility intentions in Italy and the Netherlands. *Demographic Research* 18 (1): 1–26.

Mintz, Sidney. 1960. *Worker in the cane: A Puerto Rican life story.* New Haven: Yale University Press.

Miraglia, Marina, ed. 1981. *Paul Scheuermeier, fotografie e ricerca sul lavoro contadino in Italia, 1919–1935.* Milan: Longanesi.

Narayan, Kirin. 1999. Ethnography and fiction: Where is the border? *Anthropology and Humanism* 24 (2): 134–47.

New York Times. 1927. Army of 5,000,000 is Mussolini's aim; full text of Mussolini's speech outlining his plans for a greater Italy. May 29, 1, 12–13.

Olick, Jeffrey K., and Joyce Robbins. 1998. Social memory studies: From collective memory to historical sociology. *Annual Review of Sociology* 24:105–40.

Orgill, Douglas. 1967. *The Gothic Line: The Italian campaign, autumn, 1944.* New York: W. W. Norton.

Palomba, Rossella. 1991. *Crescita zero.* Scandicci, Florence: La Nuova Italia.

Passerini, Luisa. 1986. Oral memory of fascism. In *Rethinking Italian fascism: Capitalism, populism, and culture,* ed. David Forgacs, 185–96. London: Lawrence and Wishart.

———. 1987. *Fascism in popular memory: The cultural experience of the Turin working class.* Cambridge: Cambridge University Press.

———. 1996. Gender relations. In *Italian cultural studies,* ed. David Forgacs and Robert Lumley, 144–59. Oxford: Oxford University Press.

Patriarca, Silvana. 1996. *Numbers and nationhood: Writing statistics in nineteenth-century Italy.* Cambridge: Cambridge University Press.

———. 1998. Gender trouble: Women and the making of Italy's "active population," 1861–1936. *Jounral of Modern Italian Studies* 3 (2): 144–63.

Paxson, Heather. 2002. Rationalizing sex: Family planning and the making of modern lovers in urban Greece. *American Ethnologist* 29 (2): 307–34.

Pescarolo, Alessandra. 1988. Modelli di industrializzazione, ruoli sociali, immagini del lavoro (1895–1943). In *Prato storia di una città,* vol. 3, *Il tempo dell'industria (1815–1943),* ed. Giorgio Mori, 51–114. Comune di Prato, Florence: Le Monnier.

Pescarolo, Alessandra, and Gian Bruno Ravenni. 1991. *Il proletariato invisibile: La manifattura della paglia nella Toscana mezzadrile (1820–1950).* Milan: Franco Angeli.

Piccini, Attilio. 1992. The Innocenti: Art and history. In *Spedale degli Innocenti: The foundling hospital and its museum,* ed. Becocci Editore, 5–16. Siena: Centrooffset.

Pirandello, Luigi. 1922/1985. La balia. In *Novelle per un anno,* ed. Mario Costanzo, 112–42. Milan: Arnoldo Mondadori Editore.

Polier, Nicole, and William Roseberry. 1989. Tristes tropes: Post-modern anthropologists encounter the other and discover themselves. *Economy and Society* 18:245–64.

Popular Memory Group. 1982. Popular memory: Theory, politics, method. In *Making histories: Studies in history writing and politics,* ed. Richard Johnson et al., 205–52. Minneapolis: University of Minnesota Press.

Population Reference Bureau. 2007. World population data sheet. Washington, DC. www.prb.org/Publications/Datasheets/2007/2007WorldPopulationDataSheet.aspx.

Povelodo, Elisabetta. 2008. Italy struggles with immigration and aging. *International Herald Tribune,* June 22. www.iht.com/articles/2008/06/22/europe/migrants.php.

Povinelli, Elizabeth. 2001. Translation in a global market, editor's note. *Public Culture* 13 (1): ix–xi.

Rapp, Rayna. 1999. *Testing women, testing the fetus: The social impact of amniocentesis in America.* New York: Routledge.

Rebel, Hermann. 1989. Cultural hegemony and class experience: A critical reading of recent ethnological-historical approaches (part 1). *American Ethnologist* 16 (1): 117–36.

Riva, E., G. Banderali, C. Agostoni, M. Silano, G. Radaelli, and M. Giovannini. 1999. Factors associated with initiation and duration of breastfeeding in Italy. *Acta Paediatrica* 88 (4): 411–15.

Rivkin-Fish, Michele. 2003. Anthropology, demography, and the search for a critical analysis of fertility: Insights from Russia. *American Anthropologist* 105 (2): 289–301.

Rosaldo, Renato. 1989. *Culture and truth: The remaking of social analysis.* Boston: Beacon Press.

Roseberry, William. 1989. *Anthropologies and histories: Essays in culture, history and political economy.* New Brunswick: Rutgers University Press.

Saba, Vincenzo. 1994. L'evoluzione del sistema contrattuale. In *Studi sull'agricoltura italiana: Società rurale e modernizzazione*, ed. Pier Paolo D'Attorre and Alberto De Bernardi, 17–35. Milan: Fondazione Giangiacomo Feltrinelli.

Scheper-Hughes, Nancy. 1992. *Death without weeping: The violence of everyday life in Brazil*. Berkeley: University of California Press.

Scheuermeier, Paul. 1980. *Il lavoro dei contadini*. Milan: Longanesi.

Schneider, Jane C., and Rayna Rapp, eds. 1995. *Articulating hidden histories: Exploring the influence of Eric R. Wolf*. Berkeley: University of California Press.

Schneider, Jane, and Peter Schneider. 1991. Sex and respectability in an age of fertility decline: A Sicilian case study. *Social Science Medicine* 33 (8): 885–95.

———. 1992. Going forward in reverse gear: Culture, economy, and political economy in the demographic transitions of a rural Sicilian town. In *The European experience of declining fertility, 1850–1970: The quiet revolution*, ed. John R. Gillis, Louise A. Tilly, and David Levine, 146–74. Cambridge, MA: Blackwell.

———. 1996. *Festival of the Poor: Fertility decline and the ideology of class in Sicily: 1860–1980*. Tucson: University of Arizona Press.

Schwenkel, Christina. 2006. Recombinant history: Transnational practices of memory and knowledge production in contemporary Vietnam. *Cultural Anthropology* 21 (1): 3–30.

Seremetakis, C. Nadia, ed. 1994. *The senses still: Perception and memory as material culture in modernity*. Chicago: University of Chicago Press.

Sgritta, Giovanni B. 2001. The situation of families in Italy in 2001: European Observatory on the Social Situation, Demography, and Family. www.oif.ac.at/archiv/pdf/gm_01_italy_sgritta_en129.pdf.

———. 2003. Family welfare systems and the transition to adulthood: An emblematic case study. In *Family forms and the young generation in Europe: Report on the Annual Seminar 2001*, ed. Lynne Chisholm, Antonio de Lillo, Carmen Leccardi, and Rudolf Richter, 59–86. http://europa.eu.int/comm/employment_social/eoss/milan_docs_en.html.

Shorto, Russell. 2008. Childless Europe: What happens to a continent when it stops making babies? *New York Times Magazine*, June 29, 34–41, 68–71.

Small, Meredith F. 1998. *Our babies, ourselves: How biology and culture shape the way we parent*. New York: Anchor Books.

Snowden, Frank M. 1989. *The fascist revolution in Tuscany, 1919–1922*. Cambridge: Cambridge University Press.

———. 2006. *The conquest of malaria: Italy, 1900–1962*. New Haven: Yale University Press.

Stoler, Ann Laura. 1991. Carnal knowledge and imperial power: Gender, race, and morality in colonial Asia. In *Gender at the crossroads of knowedge*, ed. Micaela di Leonardo, 51–101. Berkeley: University of California Press.

Stoler, Ann Laura, and Karen Strassler. 2000. Castings for the colonial: Memory work in "New Order" Java. *Comparative Studies in Society and History* 42 (1): 4–48.

Stoller, Paul. 1994. Embodying colonial memories. *American Anthropologist* 96 (3): 634–48.

———. 1999. *Jaguar: A story of Africans in America.* Chicago: University of Chicago Press.

Striffler, Steve. 2001. *In the shadows of state and capital.* Durham: Duke University Press.

Taylor, Peter, and Hermann Rebel. 1981. Hessian peasant women, their families, and the draft: A socio-historical interpretation of four tales from the Grimm Collection. *Journal of Family History* 6:347–78.

Terrio, Susan J. 2000. *Crafting the culture and history of French chocolate.* Berkeley: University of California Press.

Thompson, E. P. 1966. *The making of the English working class.* New York: Vintage Books.

Thompson, Hunter. 1971/1998. *Fear and loathing in Las Vegas.* New York: Vintage Books.

Tihanyi, Catherine. 2002. Ethnographic and translation practices. *Anthropology News* 43 (6): 5–6.

Tilly, Louise A., and Joan W. Scott. 1978. *Women, work and family.* New York: Holt, Rinehart and Winston.

Vasari, Giorgio. 1957. *Lives of the artists.* New York: Noonday Press.

Venuti, Lawrence. 1998. *The scandals of translation: Towards an ethics of difference.* London: Routledge.

Wallace, Robert. 1978. *The Italian campaign.* Alexandria, VA: Time-Life Books.

White, John. 1966/1993. *Art and architecture in Italy, 1200–1400.* New Haven: Yale University Press.

Williams, Brackette F. 1989. A class act: Anthropology and the race to nation across ethnic terrain. *Annual Review of Anthropology* 18:401–44.

Williams, Raymond. 1977. *Marxism and literature.* New York: Oxford University Press.

Willis, Paul, and Mats Trondman. 2000. Manifesto for ethnography. *Ethnography* 1 (1): 5–16.

Willson, Perry. 2002. *Peasant women and politics in fascist Italy: The Massaie rurali.* London: Routledge.

Wolf, Eric R. 1969. *Peasant wars of the twentieth century.* New York: Harper Colophon Books.

———. 1982. *Europe and the people without history.* Berkeley: University of California Press.

———. 1999. *Envisioning power: Ideologies of dominance and crisis.* Berkeley: University of California Press.

Index

Page numbers in italics indicate illustrations.